REAL TALK ABOUT CLASSROOMS BUILT ON DIGNITY, AUTHENTICITY, AND CONNECTION

ANGIE FREESE

Solution Tree | Press

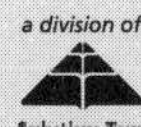

555 North Morton Street
Bloomington, IN 47404
800.733.6786 (toll free) / 812.336.7700
FAX: 812.336.7790

email: info@SolutionTree.com
SolutionTree.com

Printed in the United States of America

Library of Congress Cataloging-in-Publication Data

Names: Freese, Angela, author.
Title: Meant for more : real talk about classrooms built on dignity, authenticity, and connection / Angie Freese.
Description: Bloomington, IN : Solution Tree Press, [2023] | Includes bibliographical references and index.
Identifiers: LCCN 2023019934 (print) | LCCN 2023019935 (ebook) | ISBN 9781951075712 (paperback) | ISBN 9781951075729 (ebook)
Subjects: LCSH: Educational change--United States. | Classroom environment--United States--Evaluation. | Reflective teaching--United States. | Teacher-student relationships--United States. | Teaching teams--United States. | Discrimination in education--United States.
Classification: LCC LA217.2 .F74 2023 (print) | LCC LA217.2 (ebook) | DDC 370.973--dc23/eng/20230802
LC record available at https://lccn.loc.gov/2023019934
LC ebook record available at https://lccn.loc.gov/2023019935

Solution Tree
Jeffrey C. Jones, CEO
Edmund M. Ackerman, President

Solution Tree Press
President and Publisher: Douglas M. Rife
Associate Publishers: Todd Brakke and Kendra Slayton
Editorial Director: Laurel Hecker
Art Director: Rian Anderson
Copy Chief: Jessi Finn
Senior Production Editor: Tonya Maddox Cupp
Text and Cover Designer: Fabiana Cochran
Acquisitions Editor: Hilary Goff
Assistant Acquisitions Editor: Elijah Oates
Content Development Specialist: Amy Rubenstein
Associate Editor: Sarah Ludwig
Editorial Assistant: Anne Marie Watkins

Acknowledgments

First and foremost, I would like to acknowledge the educators for whom this book is written. Some of you I know, and others I have yet to earn the privilege of meeting; the pages of this book hold thousands of strong, capable, and humble teacher, principal, and administrator voices. It has been an honor to work alongside such fierce educators, relentless in their pursuit of excellence in spite of all the noise and worry and disheartening moments over the years prior to publication of this manuscript. You have courageously faced the individuals who want to talk about things they have no experience with and no desire to understand; people who point the finger, are quick to lay blame, and would just as soon drive you into a permanent state of shame and despair than recognize how inclusion and belonging provide the gateway to our future. I know this because I have seen it and heard it while in partnership with you and, at times, it frightened me. And so, I was tenacious in my attempt to rewrite that narrative into one of hope and possibility, capturing your stories of courage and dignifying your efforts. I hope that you feel seen, heard, and valued through my efforts to pen them into something meaningful and supportive for others on their journey, too. Whether you intend to be or not, each of you—regardless of role—serves as a beacon of hope for another. It's why you continue to carry the torch in pursuit of excellence for your students, your peers, and yourself. You just can't help it. You were meant to do this *life-giving work*. And you know that you're not done just yet. There is still one more kid, one more colleague, one more school that absolutely *needs you*. You are rejuvenating, reconnecting, and rehumanizing our profession. For your efforts, I offer my gratitude.

I would also like to thank the amazing staff at Solution Tree, first to my friend and mentor, Claudia Wheatley. She was the first person within the organization who saw me—at six months pregnant, no less—as having potential to become something more than I currently was. I appreciate the chief executive officer, Jeff Jones, and president and publisher of Solution Tree Press, Douglas Rife, for believing in and lifting these words into print. Each of you mean more to me than you know.

To a few of my closest partners on the Solution Tree Press team: Amy Rubenstein, who balanced her thoughtful words of encouragement with mindful, gentle reminders that I could save a *few* words for the next book; Kelly Rockhill and Shik Love, who graciously dove into my brain to mastermind the essence of this text—at one point, in fewer than twenty words!; Rian Anderson, who fully authenticated my vision for the cover and honored my color choices as representations for the elements of bravery, truth, dignity, and loyalty woven throughout this book; and Tonya Maddox Cupp, who was a relentless cheerleader, showing me grace when I missed deadlines and dignifying my overzealous drive to keep improving how the words landed on the page and in the hearts of the reader. To each of you, I believe this newest collaborative endeavor will be our best yet.

To my grandmother: you forged a path for women to become leaders throughout this amazing profession and left your legacy for those that follow. You taught me the value of knowing myself and being comfortable in who I was and what I had to offer in my time on this earth. The attributes presented on the pages to come represent much of what you nurtured in me. I hope that I continue to make you proud. I know you're watching.

To my forever person: there are no words to articulate what you mean to me. You were my first reader, my first reviewer, and my first admirer. You sat right beside me throughout this endeavor, celebrating every milestone and lifting me through every setback. You took care of me in ways I didn't know I needed. I am so fortunate we get to spend our days together. You are truly a maximizer in every way.

And finally, to my daughter. Becoming a mother instantly gave me a whole new perspective on the magnitude of this incredible profession that others so simply refer to as *teaching*. In so many ways, this book is dedicated to you—as a reminder of what you are worth and what you should demand from your educational experiences. You, like every other kid today, are indeed *meant for more*.

Solution Tree Press would like to thank the following reviewers:

Taylor Bronowicz
Mathematics Teacher
Sparkman Middle School
Toney, Alabama

John D. Ewald
Educator, Consultant, Presenter, Coach
Retired Superintendent, Principal, Teacher
Frederick, Maryland

Amber Gareri
Instructional Specialist, Innovation and Development
Pasadena ISD
Pasadena, Texas

Kelly Hilliard
Math Teacher
McQueen High School
Reno, Nevada

Louis Lim
Vice Principal
Richmond Green Secondary School
Richmond Hill, Ontario, Canada

Lauren Smith
Assistant Director of Elementary Learning
Noblesville Schools
Noblesville, Indiana

Nyles Varughese
Curriculum Coordinator
Edmonton Public Schools
Edmonton, Alberta, Canada

Visit **go.SolutionTree.com/schoolimprovement** to download the free reproducibles in this book.

Table of Contents

Reproducibles appear in italics.

About The Author

Angie Freese is the founder of the Meant for More Collaborative, an organizational network committed to rejuvenating school systems by igniting creativity, inspiring hope, and investing in the power of human connection. As a former classroom teacher, school administrator, and district-level leader, Angie now spends her time working alongside educators across all levels of the organization—from classroom to boardroom—as a facilitator, coach, practitioner, and mentor. She empowers educators' efforts to interrupt antiquated and ineffective practices by revitalizing collaborative teams with the competencies, skills, and tools required for sustainable growth and performance for *all.*

Angie is also a certified Gallup Global Strengths Coach, teaching people how to identify, understand, and appreciate their own unique talents. She reconnects individuals and teams to what they already do well and actively coaches them on how to maximize those innate talents into strengths for their own personal and professional excellence.

To learn more about Angie's work, connect to @meantformorementum on social media.

To book Angie Freese for professional development, contact pd@SolutionTree.com.

Introduction

It is a Saturday morning in June 2020. I wake to a bright yet brisk summer morning in Minnesota—the kind of morning where the sun is just starting to welcome the world but still requires a sweatshirt and a cup of coffee to keep warm. I am sitting on my front porch, laptop in hand, breathing in the quiet grace and peace of this new day. I am struck by the irony of this sense of calm that surrounds me as I prepare for the fervor of my intended purpose. I sharpen my focus and re-engage, now poised and ready.

I am ready to unleash my thoughts and emotions, grounding them in research, evidence, and experience; hungry to craft those thoughts into meaningful words and mindful actions in order to gracefully reveal our courage and tenacity as educators; positioned to share my truth about what actions are necessary to disrupt the systems *and structures that make a mockery of our public school system. Committed to disrupting the normalized marginalization of vulnerable student populations—particularly naming the disparities for students of color and students facing gender discrimination. Poised to maintain a steadiness and a resolve to collectively transform our current teaching and learning models by creating spaces in which every single student is seen, heard, and valued.*

In the pages to come, the magnitude of our next steps as educators is revealed, made accessible and embraced with commitment and conviction. We mindfully explore the attributes and core tendencies that evolve within *Meant for More* classrooms, and learn how these cultivated classrooms include, but are not limited to, assets such as authenticity, connection, curiosity, voice, resilience, and learning to give grace to oneself and others. Let us begin.

Why I Wrote This Book

I have had this book in my heart for a while. Starting my career as a teacher in a high-poverty, high-mobility school, I was conscious of the achievement gap before anyone named it as such. The disparities were clear from the first glance at our school's data; you didn't need to spend much time analyzing our students' performance to notice that instruction in our building was working better for some students than others. Our mission statement included the customary language of *high levels of learning* for every student, but our data were not even close to honoring our declaration of purpose. And when students did make gains, we had difficulty sustaining them due to the high incidence of relocation among families. Challenges with steady employment and the compacted locations of affordable housing in our community promoted a constant shuffling of students between two or three schools each year. At the school where I first taught, only one-quarter of the fifth-grade students in our building had started kindergarten with us. Despite collaboration among teachers and leaders across the various schools in the district, we were chasing a version of success that seemed impossibly out of reach. I am troubled to share that I had similar experiences as a curriculum specialist, a building leader, and a district administrator. We tried to bring about change, yet ultimately kept bumping up against the inequitable ceilings of policy, organizational history, and past traditions.

During my tenure as a director of research, assessment, and accountability for a large district in Minnesota, I was keenly aware of the power of quantitative data and its use in our field. One aspect of my district-level position was data analysis and interpretation. I would pore over spreadsheets, elbow to elbow with teachers and principals, analyzing and discussing patterns and trends while trying to make valid inferences about what the data were telling us about student performance. We would then surmise why the data might look the way it did. We asked direct and difficult questions.

- Did we know *why* our school was working for some of our students but not all?
- Did we know how to identify and then sustain those practices that were working in order to ensure we did not mistakenly allocate resources *away* from those practices in our efforts to improve?
- Did we know *how* to take action to improve our effectiveness?
- Did our students have enough access and enough time to *learn* what was expected?
- To what degree was *formative feedback* part of the learning environments that yielded these results?
- Were students involved as *equal partners* in the learning process, working collaboratively with their teachers, in their shared quest for growth and achievement?

We sought answers that would support our attempts to generate solutions. Structural mandates, policy requirements, or inadequate planning efforts often created dissonance between the work we knew we needed to do and the time in which we had to do it.

All of these professional conversations served as a powerful reminder that the voice of the most important stakeholder—the *student*—was missing from the dialogue. School systems have historically utilized precise, systematic ways in which they attempt to draw a line from point A to point B when it comes to how to "fix" students. Our students don't need to be fixed. Rather, they need to be *understood.* Their unique assets as well as their unique needs must become visible in our classrooms if we expect to elevate the value of each learner and truly create sustainable, transformational change in our schools.

Let's consider another part of my position, which was overseeing state testing; our department trained teachers and coaches to administer state or benchmark testing with fidelity. I was witness to the anxiety these practices and processes caused the people who were with students each day. These educators experienced firsthand how data could be used to punish and threaten their credibility as practitioners rather than be used as a catalyst to review how current policies, protocols, and processes resulted in certain groups of students being under*served*, under*appreciated*, under-*valued*, under-*fill-in-the-blank*. So many students have felt *under*-ed by their teachers and peers on such a regular basis that too many among us have come to see the teasing, casting of doubt, and minimization of spirit as an unspoken rite of passage through the schooling experience. Instead, let us speak. Let's use the pages to come as fuel for further dialogue. I am eager to share how my experiences suggest that students rarely under*perform*—rarely *under*- anything—when conditions are set up for their academic, cultural, and emotional success.

I am in a fortunate position in this regard, as my career now affords me the opportunity to work with hundreds of educators across the country each week. I am equally inspired and humbled by the blood, sweat, and tears that emerge from our teachers and leaders who work tirelessly each day on behalf of students to navigate the gross inequities of the system in which they work. The fatigue is rooted in a fundamental framework that does not provide teachers and principals with the necessary tools, training, and resources to implement the fundamental reforms needed. Such reforms would bring about the systemic change required to interrupt the unauthorized versions of success we—consciously or subconsciously—assign to each student upon their arrival in our schools and classrooms. We are simply exhausted as our will is continually muted by the levels of tolerance that confine our profession within the status quo.

And still, we must remain a bold, fierce, driven, compassionate, and humble cohort. Quiet and graceful at times, tenacious and steadfast in others. We engage in the daily grind because we deeply understand that the enormity of our potential for impact is striking. Yet, sometimes, we find ourselves getting in our own way. One of our most daunting challenges is that—despite the courage and heart we display as a *group* of people—too few *teams* in education are encouraged to create spaces where students feel free to communicate their thoughts, ask questions, and be seen for who they are as *people* before we see them as students, numbers, or data. To be seen before they are categorized with labels like *gifted*, *poor*, *bubble kids*, *meets proficiency*, or *special education*; labels that inherently do not get us any closer to ensuring they have the necessary skills and dispositions to know what to do when they take that first step off the graduation stage and enter their next chapter as independent adults. To be seen for how they first join our learning spaces, innately full of passion, inquiry, and perseverance. To be recognized by their faces and personalities instead of just numbers or names on a roster. But for some, as they cycle through the system, their light of possibility has all but diminished completely. How can our students be brave, assured, and confident in their learning pathway amidst such darkness?

Despite the constant wave of aftershocks we feel as educators, whether from policies, procedures, or pandemics, I believe that our profession is not intended to be consumed by bureaucracy. It's not supposed to feel rigid, isolating, or scary. We can no longer accept what we have been told or conditioned to tolerate. We can make it better because we deserve better, and so do our students. We are meant for more.

What This Book Offers

This book provides the opportunity to consider conditions for learning that could legitimately flip the switch for many students and promote an even brighter experience for each one. We will draw out how to mindfully reshape each of our classrooms to be places that value, inspire, and lift each student to capitalize on their assets and—most importantly—to allow them feel safe while doing so. We want our classrooms to function with respect and grace for our learners. We must provide the same consideration to our adults, and this book both equips teachers with realistic, can-do approaches to creating these conditions in their classrooms and also supports them as individuals *and* as members of a team in their efforts.

In addition, the book offers a collection of practical processes, strategies, and tools that teachers, site administrators, and district leaders can use to authentically evaluate the cohesion between equity and agency for students and the current infrastructure within our classrooms. The purpose of such reflection is to acknowledge how established spaces at school where student and staff voices, perspectives, experiences, cultures, and identities are not just honored but intentionally lifted. At its core, the book is intended to serve as a framework to recognize and celebrate your individual strengths and assets—as well as boldly explore places of vulnerability—regarding the conditional barriers that are contributing to the current achievement and engagement trends in your classroom, school, or district. Our schools can no longer continue to be places where intentional design prevents some students or staff from being able to succeed. This change can start right now.

To move from awareness to action, there is an underlying problem of practice that this book fervently confronts: *we still have adults in positions of influence over our students who do not believe all students can learn at high levels, nor do they believe that each learner carries intrinsic value.* These mental models result in some adults continuing to predetermine opportunity and access for each student based on judgments or perceptions rather than acknowledgments and evidence of who students are and what they really need. These mental models can appear as *microaggressions*, which are "everyday verbal, nonverbal, and environmental slights, snubs, or insults, whether intentional or unintentional, which communicate hostile, derogatory, or negative messages to target persons based solely upon their marginalized group membership" (University of North Carolina, n.d.).

These mental models can be found throughout the system, from the hallways to the main office, from the bus stop to the cafeteria, and from the classroom to the boardroom. Students continue to enter our schools with varying skills and experiences—academically, socially, and emotionally—and they also struggle to find relevance and meaning in the content and delivery of our teaching. Our students' struggles are often perpetuated and amplified by the deeply rooted, adult-determined norms for how classrooms should look, feel, and sound. The concurrence of these limitations in our education systems enable the achievement and opportunity gaps to not only continue but to exponentially intensify.

As a start, we can collectively take notice of whether students are prepared to demonstrate attributes such as, but not limited to, the following.

- Listen to one another.
- Talk to others and meaningfully contribute to the conversation.
- Stay true to themselves by belonging, rather than fitting in.
- Engage in dialogue with others who have different opinions or views and still maintain healthy relationships with those people.
- Be comfortable in their own skin.
- Admit when they are wrong.
- Learn to repair or recover relationships.
- Innovate, create, and problem solve.
- Anticipate, recognize, and consider other people's feelings in various situations.
- Stand up for themselves and others.
- Advocate their needs with confidence.

Creating emotionally safe environments in which students and adults are seen, heard, and valued can nurture deep levels of student engagement and investment, since:

> Reflecting on and "sitting with" the perspective of those who are excluded, dehumanized, or devalued for each of these reasons is worthwhile to feel

> the urgency of the work in cultivating welcoming, safe, and inclusive classrooms for students across the full range of variability. (Jung, 2023, p. 24)

One way emotional safety can actualize itself in our classrooms is through lifting the dignity of each learner, and then creating authentic connections whereby all learners feel comfortable to use their voice, learn, take risks, and display vulnerability. Emotionally safe environments don't just allow students to develop their strengths but actively encourage the display of those strengths. Our adult learning communities could be places that do the following.

- Focus on student self-efficacy and integrity of self.
- Shift from tightly controlled curricular and instructional delivery models to inquiry-focused, personalized, modern learning spaces.
- Heighten the relevance of content for our students by inviting them to be curious and centering it in their lives.
- Respect each learner's gifts, talents, and virtuosities in a call for truly equitable learning environments.
- Interrupt the paralysis experienced by adults attempting to be agents of change for authentic, inclusive learning spaces.

This process of reshaping seeks to increase students' sense of self and purpose in the classroom, enabling their unique identities, passions, and creativities to emerge. The renewal of learning environments in this manner fosters the skills and dispositions our students need for their futures. These types of learning spaces can develop our recognition of how we are meant for more.

As you study this work, either on your own or with your team, the book will create small, actionable principles of practice to consider.

- How do I get myself ready?
- How do I get my team ready?
- How do I get my students ready?
- What infrastructure do I need to make it happen?

It is in the infrastructure—and the need to protect what's working and disrupt and eliminate what isn't—that we learn about and develop strategies for fixing the system, instead of further dehumanizing and debilitating our classrooms and schools by simply trying to "fix" the people inside. These questions—and the genuine responses they generate—will guide you through the intentional design of classrooms that are meant for more.

The overarching premise of this manuscript is grounded in three key principles: (1) dignity, (2) authenticity, and (3) connection. Our journey honors dignity by focusing on inclusive strategies such as being open and listening to our own stories and perspectives as well as those of others, and understanding and accepting the qualities that make each of us unique. It is difficult to display dignity without displaying respect for both ourselves and others. Our journey honors how authenticity happens when our words, actions, and behaviors consistently match our core identity. It is difficult to be authentic if you don't believe in yourself and your ability to shape your life the way you want it. Our journey honors connection by acknowledging our human need to be in relation with one another. It is difficult to connect with others if you struggle to connect with (and appreciate) what makes you, *you*.

We also explore how inclusivity in schools happens by design, not by chance. In *Meant for More* classrooms, staff and students reveal their individualized strengths and focus on intentionally creating spaces (and policies, instructional design, and feedback loops) that empower the needs of the collective. The belief that all students are capable learners may be in school mission and vision statements, but the behaviors required to bring the belief into reality are inconsistent, as evidenced by global achievement and growth data that reveal we still have cohorts of students for whom school is not working (Brassard, 2022; Global Partnership for Education, n.d.; Henebery, 2021; Mahboubi & Higazy, 2022; Malala Fund, 2023; National Center for Education Statistics, 2022).

The Poorvu Center for Teaching and Learning (n.d.a) at Yale University states that inclusive teaching "builds upon an instructor's basic instinct to ensure all voices are heard and that all students have a chance to participate fully in the learning process, by digging a little deeper into why participation imbalances exist." Inclusive learning environments are crafted to honor the independent, ability, cultural, religious, linguistic, and social distinctions that acknowledge each learner as a unique contributor to the classroom environment.

How to Use This Book

This book's organization lends itself to individual study, group study, or even a year-long deeper dive by focusing on reading, having discussions based on real talk, and applying the content from each chapter. Chapter 1 establishes background for the content and why it matters. I highlight research around two specific classifications for inequity—race and gender—because they are the most egregious examples of the dehumanization of our educational system and the people in it. The book also explores how inadequate and misaligned professional learning for teachers and having a limited workforce may be perpetuating our results. This chapter opens the door to the *Why this; why now?* discussion, and uses both story and research to introduce answers to the questions, "How can I, as an individual, implement the changes necessary?" "How do I support others to do the same?" and finally, "How will I prepare the students in my classroom or school?" In chapter 1, the student section is purposefully omitted because our students are less responsible for activating our capacity to rehumanize and reinvigorate the legitimacy of our work as educators. I also identify strategies and tools for navigating conflict and managing change around this shift in practice.

Chapters 2 to 7 guide you through each of the identified attributes of *Meant for More* classrooms: authenticity, connection, curiosity, voice, resilience, and grace. Each chapter begins with a sample problem of practice and further describes how I define each of these attributes within the context and purpose of this book. In addition, a three-part framework (you, team, and students) helps you consider each of the attributes and how they might present in your personal learning spaces. The first part walks *you* through some introspection, asking you to consider how you will prepare to make meaning of the attribute yourself. The second part provides suggestions and considerations to prepare your *team* for this work, and the final part offers recommendations for *student* readiness. Although we must advocate for urgency in this process, we must also anticipate the need to be patient with people in order to accommodate shifts in thinking, shifts in practices, and ultimately, shifts in outcomes.

Each chapter includes a section describing the infrastructure needed to elevate each attribute in your learning environment. Visit **go.SolutionTree.com/schoolimprovement** for a free reproducible "Chapter Summarization Tool to Inspire Action" and use it to keep track of your thoughts, feelings, ideas, and potential actions before starting the next chapter. The chapters close with a Meant for MoreMENTUM story from an educator currently practicing each attribute, as well as a continuum to monitor your comfort level with the element discussed in that chapter. Brief descriptions of each *Meant for More* attribute follow.

- Chapter 2, Embracing Authenticity, describes an exploration of creating genuine, inclusive learning spaces for adults and students, and provides strategies and language to develop this type of environment that celebrates the unique gifts and talents of each individual.

- Chapter 3, Fostering Connection, reminds us that we are meant to be in relation with others. Learning from and with each other helps us make meaning and develop understanding, and also promotes a climate and culture of belonging.
- Chapter 4, Cultivating Curiosity, calls us to activate student interests, desires, and strengths in order to increase relevance in the classroom, value student inquiry, and co-create meaningful learning experiences that are centered in the lives and futures of our students.
- Chapter 5, Empowering Voice, is an anthem for each of us to develop the language and tone of advocacy and agency in our learning environments, fostering trust, letting students speak, and investing in a culture of belonging.
- Chapter 6, Nurturing Resilience, teaches the power of determination and provides practical strategies for the development of perseverance, grit, and self-love.
- Chapter 7, Giving Grace, invites us to practice patience and forgiveness with ourselves and toward others, promote affirmation and gratitude, and intentionally consider how to use our words and energy. We explore how to accept the same grace for ourselves that we so readily extend to others.

Note that this resource is not intended to be a prescriptive how-to playbook, nor is it intended to provide explicit directions for addressing the systemic inequities we've already discussed here in the introduction and will continue to explore in chapter 1. However, I offer plenty of tools, strategies, and language for you to make sense of and meaningfully apply these attributes in your own learning environments, among your colleagues and students. I cannot wait to share these ideas with you and have you personalize the competencies for yourself and the students you are so blessed to serve.

The book, as such, is intended for all practitioners in our field. There are many lenses through which this book can be read and reread; table I.1 is an example of my thinking for how some roles in our incredible profession could access this resource.

TABLE I.1: How to Use This Resource

If You Are a . . .	Use This Resource as . . .
Teacher	An introspection on current practices and how your efforts are impacted by the realities of your organization, environment, or community.
Team leader	A launching pad for discussion to explore inclusive mindsets, strategies, tools, and practices among the adults providing service to students and families.
Principal or site administrator	An exploration into current policies, programs, and mindsets on campus and their correlation to student and family perception data as well as academic achievement and growth for each cohort of learners.
Instructional coach	A tool for supporting teacher teams to create authentic, inclusive learning environments as they navigate the unique academic and social needs of their students.
District administrator	An overarching framework to aid in the clarification of who we are, why we exist, and what we promote as a district learning community.

As you engage in this journey, I have one request: be patient with yourself. My hope is that this book is balanced with affirmations of your practice as well as opportunities for mindful reflection. This work is not hard to understand, but the successful application of the work is incredibly complex. Please utilize the frames of reference and spaces for reflection throughout the text. Fill up the margins and use **#mfmrealtalk** on social media to join forces with others on their journey. Talk to each other, but most importantly, find some time to talk with *students*. Ask questions and be open to their insights and potentially constructive feedback.

"Although we must advocate for urgency in this process, we must also anticipate the need to be patient with people in order to accommodate shifts in thinking, shifts in practices, and ultimately, shifts in outcomes."

You are meant for more.

Your teammates are meant for more.

Your students are meant for more.

Now turn the page, my friend. We have incredible work to do.

Chapter 1

Building Awareness to Rehumanize Our Profession

Jason, Margaret, Susanna, and Omar are members of the seventh-grade science team at the local middle school. They are engaging in a data review of their current list of students with Ds and Fs at the end of the first trimester. The team notices that, overall, their percentage of failing grades is lower than in previous years. They celebrate this data point and attribute much of their recent success to revising their retake and homework policies. However, on a closer look at the data, they notice 60 percent of their failing grades come from students who receive special education services. Although this cohort represents less than 10 percent of the student body as a whole, they account for the majority of Ds and Fs in this course.

The principal has asked the team to complete a data review protocol that would acknowledge their points of pride regarding student performance as well as recognize any areas for improvement, along with creating an action plan for addressing those identified needs. Susanna notices, during deeper examination of the data, a distinction between Ds and Fs. A majority of students who received an F (80 percent of the group) also received supplemental special education services, compared to 80 percent of the Ds, which came from students who did not receive those same services.

Margaret states, "Well, that makes sense; those students have alternative learning plans, and we cannot expect them to make the amount of growth required to pass this course in one year's time. Speaking of, I have an IEP meeting for a student in ten minutes, so let's whip through this protocol thing so I can be up to the conference room on time."

Omar counters, "Wait, we are supposed to move *all* students to proficiency. Shouldn't we at least talk about why such a disproportionate number of our failing grades are coming from students who have an identified academic, behavioral, or social need for additional time and support?"

Jason chimes in, sharing, "I understand where you're coming from, Omar, and in a perfect world, we'd actually have time, resources, and training to be able to help those students. My vote is that we just create an action plan to focus on our general education students, since we can actually address their learning issues."

Just then, the team hears a noise in the hallway. Jason walks to the door and sees the father of Margaret's student, Jovan. The man apologizes for interrupting and says he thought the IEP meeting was in the classroom. Jason, visibly flushed, turns to Margaret for help. It is clear that Jovan's father heard Jason's comments, which implied that students in special education have needs that general education teachers simply can't or shouldn't meet. Margaret grabs her things, rushes over, and walks Jovan's father to the conference room. As they walk away, Jason turns to his teammates and asks, "Do you think he heard me?" Susanna and Omar try to comfort Jason, but they know the damage has been done.

Margaret and Jovan's father arrive in the conference room and are greeted by four other adults who provide service to Jovan: the social worker, the case manager, the school counselor, and the principal. As the meeting begins, Jovan's father hears from the school team how his son is a "nice kid, well-mannered, and quiet." When reviewing his son's current progress, he hears phrases like, "Given his goals, this is good work for Jovan," and "Jovan is currently on track to master basic mathematics skills." Jovan's father tries to understand why his son's goals are so far below grade level and so easily attainable; they don't seem to stretch Jovan, and at this rate, his son wouldn't have enough instructional time to close the gap between himself and many of his classmates. The case manager says, "Well, he tries really hard, and we praise him for his effort, but he really needs a lot of help. We just don't have the resources to provide him with the level of support he needs. So, we've created goals that are actually attainable and that represent his current abilities as a learner."

Jovan's father is stunned. He *knows* his son and what he is capable of. He just needs specific, targeted instruction to accelerate his progress and help him meet his goals. He is afraid to speak, worried if he opens his mouth that either the tears will begin to flow beyond his control or the anger and frustration will spew from his lips in an unbecoming manner. He smiles, nods, and thanks them. The principal chimes in with, "We're doing the best we can. Before you go, can you sign the IEP so we can continue with services? Also, here is an application for modified lunch costs, in case you need it."

As you reflect on the story, take a moment to reflect or jot down your thinking in figure 1.1.

What is your reaction to this story?
Do you know if there are students in your school with similar stories? To what degree does your school community seek student voices regarding their well-being and safety as important decisions about their learning are made?
If you were the family in this story, how would you have responded?
As you review your thoughts, what privileges or rights do you have or not have that enable you to respond in such a manner?

FIGURE 1.1: Story reflection.

It seems inconceivable that we continue to have school systems—places intended to foster community and learning—struggling with their efforts to interrupt the inequities and injustices felt across our student populations. You just read the experience of one family within one system, but we know there are hundreds of thousands more who carry similar degrees of pain, anger, shame, and humiliation. All these stories, despite their intricate themes around the limitations of students promoting positive self-efficacy or masking the pervasive undercurrent of racial or gender inequities, collectively represent a hard truth: *our system is not yet designed to equally and equitably honor each learner who comes into our classroom.*

This is not what we intend. It is not what we desire. We have pockets of excellence throughout our system; in fact, your classroom may be one of them! But as we read these words, and as we start to see the faces of students in our school, perhaps we squirm a bit in *our* chair. We know the pervasiveness of this inequity at its core, but we hesitate to acknowledge its existence. Because acknowledging it means we have to be responsible for it. And that's where things can *really* get uncomfortable.

It's a much safer mental space to think this might be someone else's reality. That it's not at *our* school. We are the well-meaning, hard-working, never-take-a-day-off kind of people. We would literally do anything for our students. We would never knowingly be part of a system that would harm them.

Right?

The real talk here is that the sooner we garner the courage to build awareness of these realities for our students, the sooner we can acknowledge and address them. As we peer inside the intricacies of our system, we may start to notice that students are not the only recipients of these inequities. Our colleagues may be as well.

Although such narratives of race-, ability-, or gender-based injustices may not be indicative of the direct experience of every student within our school, let us take care to recognize that they *indirectly* affect each and every one. Unaddressed words and behaviors not only contribute to the belief systems held by affected students but also the attitudes and perceptions that students then learn to hold toward *each other.*

What Do We Mean by *Building Awareness*?

Let's first take a step back to explore a chronicled view of how we may have gotten here. There are several strategies, tools, and resources in the pages to come that will help you navigate *how* to create *Meant for More* classrooms. An important aspect to productively interrupting the current narrative is to thoughtfully examine the polices, practices, and systems that have brought us to this moment.

It may feel jarring to dive into these weighty and challenging topics right from the start. I have chosen to move forward this way because you may be determined to craft a renewed direction for student advocacy and belonging in your schools—not only for students and families but for colleagues (and perhaps, even yourself). As such, you recognize that this requires digging into hard truths about many commonly held, yet inappropriate, education systems and practices. We dig deep, not only to chart the best course for interrupting the systems that have blocked us from what we desire but to also redefine how our classrooms can look, sound, and feel for our students and for each other.

The following sections address three key barriers that ignite a sense of urgency toward building awareness as well as the advocacy for rehumanizing our profession: (1) insufficient knowledge of systemic racism and how it manifests in schools, (2) misunderstandings regarding student and staff gender expression, and (3) inadequate levels of teacher preparedness and fragmented professional learning opportunities. Each of these areas has impacted—and will continue to impact—the development of authentic, inclusive learning environments in your school or district.

Barrier One: Insufficient Knowledge of Systemic Racism and How It Manifests in Schools

Each of us has either experienced directly or bore witness to the paramount impacts of systemic racism. For those among us who have not felt directly affected, horrific and avoidable happenings such as the murder of George Floyd in Minneapolis, Minnesota in May 2020 demand that we re-examine embedded mindsets about our society that may not hold up to scrutiny (Arango et al., 2022). These tragic and infuriating events challenge us to acknowledge and confront the universal dissonance perpetuated by laws, rules, and policies that sideline and dehumanize particular groups and cultures, especially those who are not White.

Robin DiAngelo (2020), author of *White Fragility: Why It's So Hard for White People to Talk About Racism*, surfaces a perspective that the survival of racism in our institutions is actually independent from our beliefs about it. For example, you may agree that no person should be treated differently based on their race. You may even be exhausted by the pervasiveness of these conversations within our school communities. Yet, the continuance of conversation exists because we are still plagued by the gross repetition of these blatant inequities within our schools, such as an overrepresentation of Black boys in special education, as well as higher numbers of disciplinary referrals for so-called disruptive behavior from students of color as compared to white students (Delahunty & Chiu, 2020; McNair, 2021; National Center for Learning Disabilities, 2020).

For example, professors Kate Wegmann and Brittanni Smith (2019) researched disparities in discipline based on racial and ethnic identities of students. Their findings reveal that not only are Black students less likely than White students to be warned about misbehavior but also that Black students experience "escalated consequences" for their misbehavior. Additional findings (National Institute of Mental Health, 2022; Owens, 2023) reveal the intersectionality of race and socioeconomic status on teachers' acknowledgment of student behavior. One preschool study (Sabol et al., 2021) notes, "regardless of race, children in the lower socioeconomic status group received more childcare provider behavioral complaints than children in the Black nonpoor and the White/Hispanic nonpoor groups, even though researchers saw no objective differences in behavior between the groups." Such data confirm how schools can be microcosms of the outside world:

> By maintaining differential consequences for behavior infractions committed by African American students vs. White students, schools can mirror racialized differences in policing and the criminal justice system, and through their role as agents of socialization, normalize such unequal systems for youth. (Wegmann & Smith, 2019)

In an interview with Robin DiAngelo, a consultant, educator, and facilitator on issues of racial and social justice, Ari Shapiro (2020) explores the systematic preservation of racial inequality with DiAngelo, citing her assertion that "if we don't interrupt the systems we live within, then we're complicit in them." As educators, most of us lack the influence to grapple with systemic racial injustice on a state, provincial, or national scale. But we *can* interrupt the school and classroom environments that prevent some students from telling us about the injustices they see and experience. Later in this chapter (page 22), we further explore the identification of these systems within our current environments and organizations. For the moment, jot down some of your initial thinking and observations on this topic here.

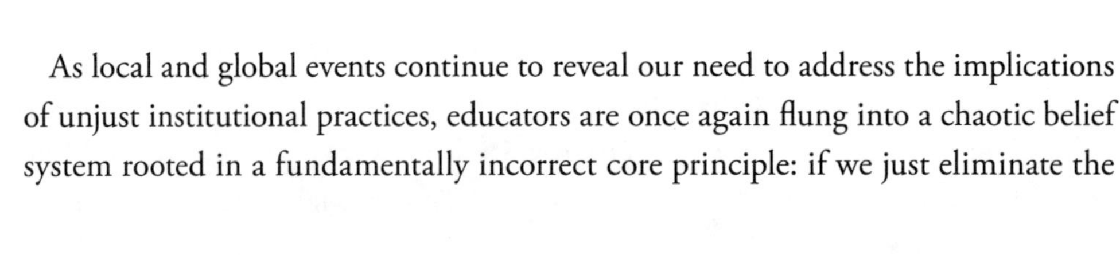

As local and global events continue to reveal our need to address the implications of unjust institutional practices, educators are once again flung into a chaotic belief system rooted in a fundamentally incorrect core principle: if we just eliminate the "achievement gap," and "fix" the students who comprise it, equity can be achieved. This mindset harms generations of students and adults in the process. An example of such faulty logic follows:

If most students who come from low-income homes do poorly in school, and

+

If most low-income homes house families of color, then

=

Most students of color must also be from low-incomes homes and, as such, will perform poorly in school.

Although easy to understand, this type of reasoning is far from simple to correct and overcome. And to be extra clear, *this mindset is also not accurate.*

The Pedagogy of Confidence: Inspiring High Intellectual Performance in Urban Schools author Yvette Jackson (2011, as cited in the National Urban Alliance, n.d.) asserts:

> This [*achievement gap*] label exacerbates the cultural myth that the only way to close the gap is by focusing on weaknesses. As a result, we have been obsessively misdirected to turn our backs on the vast intellectual capacity of these students and to regard minimum proficiency as the ceiling. In so doing, we dismiss two inherent truths about learning:
>
> 1. All people have an intrinsic desire to learn and to be self-actualized. (Maslow, 1943).
> 2. All brains are the same color. Learning does not happen differently from one culture to another.

One of the most detrimental mindsets to exist in classrooms is one in which adults project a belief that not all students are worthy of accessing high-quality, engaging, and rigorous instruction; the one in which we deprive students who are receiving intervention from the fun, relevant experiences and opportunities had by the rest of the students; the one in which our students continue to be dependent on their teachers, leading them to be woefully unprepared for the cognitive demands required to navigate in the world around them.

This reliance turns problematic when we ignore the infrastructure our students need in order to become independent learners, and instead push them through their schooling experiences without ensuring they learn how to engage in the process of learning itself (Hammond, 2015). The combination of this mindset and these actions produces data that poignantly display how students of color are, by design, being "pushed *out* of school because they cannot keep up academically because of poor reading skills and a lack of social-emotional support to deal with their frustration" (Hammond, 2015, p. 13, italics added). Such data might indeed be born from some educators' inherent blind spots of which they may or may not be aware.

One reason that building awareness of how our mindsets—conscious or unconscious—directly connect to our data is that continued ignorance by the educational system at large means it will produce learners who are inconsistently equipped to contribute to the betterment of our communities and society as a whole. Educator, blogger, and founder of the Cult of Pedagogy Jennifer Gonzalez (2021) underscores the urgency around this awareness here:

> Without the tools to recognize, address, and dismantle racism, [these marginalized students'] world becomes more full of hate, fear, and violence. They will be less likely to see themselves as people who can influence how their world operates. Without an accurate and complete understanding of history, they are less likely to recognize harmful practices, policies, and leadership. They are less likely to spot problems before they grow out of control. Without a curriculum that includes and celebrates all identities, they are less likely to grow into fully actualized human beings who can pursue their passions and contribute to the world with their unique gifts and talents.

We explore the interplay of adult mindset and action (and inaction) with student independence later in this chapter and throughout the text as well.

As part of a special report on the big ideas for confronting racism in our public schools, the EdWeek Research Center (2020) gathered evidence on how educators felt in regards to equity and anti-racist teaching in their schools.

- In response to the statement, *Schools are effective at bridging equity gaps*, 66 percent of White educators believed that schools had been successful in addressing equity, as compared to 49 percent of educators who are not White.
- Eighty-one percent of educators identify themselves as anti-racist educators; however, only 14 percent of educators say they have the resources and the professional learning to teach in an anti-racist manner effectively.
- A mere 18 percent of educators state they have received anti-racist training in their educator preparation programs, and only 33 percent of educators say they received this type of training in their schools or districts.
- While 84 percent of educators claimed a relative willingness to teach or support the implementation of an anti-racist curriculum,

> 8 percent of respondents said they were "somewhat unwilling" and another 8 percent said they were "very unwilling" to support or implement such a curriculum.

Consider this final data point. These data suggest that *16 percent of teachers are unwilling to support a shift in practice that mobilizes all students to find value in themselves and in each other.* That's approximately one in six.

One in six.

Although we can and should celebrate the likelihood that the majority of teachers on our campus would openly acknowledge the need to transform current practices, consider the impact on students that one in six of their teachers would *not* do this. To which students will we assign those teachers who have openly proclaimed, "That's not for me"? What rationale will we use when talking to students and their families about such classroom placements?

Pause here for a moment to consider the following questions: How do the data listed in this section manifest in your school or district? How would a conversation about the presence of systemic racism in your school or district unfold and develop? Figure 1.2 offers an example template that enables you to jot down questions, concerns, or observations that are meaningful to you. The purpose of this reflection template, available as the reproducible "Current Reality Reflection" (page 46), is simply to activate your own awareness of how data reflecting systemic racism are represented (or are not represented) in your own setting.

<table>
<tr><th colspan="2">Data to discuss: High school graduation rates, disaggregated by student group</th></tr>
<tr><td>How do these data represent in our school?

We know that 78 percent of our students who identify as White graduate from high school as compared by 55 percent of students who identify as Hispanic, 37 percent who identify as Black, and 45 percent of students who identify as multiracial. We do not collect graduation rates for students who identify within other racial groups due to smaller populations (and a violation of data privacy as such).</td><td>How do these data represent in our district?

Although we have higher graduation rates on our campus as compared to the district, we are not satisfied with our student performance in any cohort.</td></tr>
<tr><td colspan="2">How do these data manifest with regard to student achievement?

Although students are graduating, 68 percent of students received at least one D or F each grade during their high school career. Of those students, 85 percent received more than one failing grade during their freshman year. We also know that nearly one-quarter of our students who graduate and pursue college need tutoring or remedial coursework during their first semester.

For students who do not graduate, 9 percent dropped out of school by the end of their junior year, 15 percent were truant, 17 percent have been arrested for drug or weapon possession, and 3 percent have gone to prison.</td></tr>
</table>

FIGURE 1.2: Example current reality reflection.

Racism is an insidious cancer. It manifests in the forms of physical and visible harm (slavery and physical abuse), denied access and opportunities (segregation, both state-sanctioned and unspoken), or punitive measures (mass incarceration, deportation, or internment), and in a horrific pinnacle that uses all three of the aforementioned measures to ever subtly (or not) send the message that not all humans are worthy of being equally seen, heard, and valued. Few educators would ever openly acknowledge they share such beliefs. Few parents would openly declare these as reasons for not sending their children to certain neighborhood schools. Yet, by upholding systems and structures designed to benefit some students, but not all, we contribute to the terrifying cycle of injustices that do not provide all students with access to the same pathways for success.

Barrier Two: Misunderstandings About Student and Staff Gender Expression

Given that schools are natural influencers of social norms, diversified thinking and perspectives, and preparedness for citizenship and contribution to community, it stands to reason that schools will also be environments where gender identity is more authentically understood and represented. In order to support the heightened awareness and reality of our students and staff, all educators need to be equipped to acknowledge the multiple gender identities that staff and students might express. The stigmatization of gender expression results in false information sharing and the perpetuation of stereotypes and misunderstandings, which further isolate and alienate individuals and groups (King, Hughto, & Operario, 2021; Parliamentarians for Global Action, n.d.; Williams, 2022b).

Educators require specific, accurate levels of support to build awareness regarding the language, tools, and strategies appropriate for ensuring equitable and protective environments for each student. An example of such support could include working with your colleagues to define *gender stereotyping*. Identify evidence of its presence in your school community, examine sample news articles or current events to notice examples of gender stereotyping, or make a T-chart (*men* on one side and *women* on the other) to name behaviors, communication styles, or professions that have traditionally been associated to members who identify with each gender binary. Then, read an article that provides research on the detriments of these stereotypes as related to each child's development.

We want to be cautious here about neutralizing gender expression by avoiding learning opportunities that may make us uncomfortable. People with varying gender identities are coming to our classrooms and schools every day, whether we are ready or not. Pause to acknowledge how each individual who walks into our schools is a human being first; someone who simply wants (and needs) to be seen, accepted, and validated. Lee Ann Jung (2023), clinical professor at San Diego State University, advocates:

> Normalizing variation in sexual orientation and gender identity through our words, actions, and representation in classroom content, show that we value all students and all variations of sexual orientation and gender identity. Because so often the default is *no* representation or an ignoring of these topics, students who don't fit the majority categories are essentially invalidated. And their perspectives are never heard. People are not heard. Thus, *an intentional validation can have an enormous protective effect for the student who feels alone.* (p. 31, italics added)

The United Nations Human Rights Office of the High Commissioner (2020), the foremost United Nations entity in the field of human rights, with a "unique mandate to promote and protect all human rights for all people," defines a *gender stereotype* as a generalization about characteristics and roles men or women "should" have or perform. They further assert that gender stereotyping refers to "the practice of ascribing to an individual woman or man specific attributes, characteristics, or roles by reason only of her or his membership in the social group of women or men" (United Nations Human Rights Office of the High Commissioner, 2020).

Pause for a moment and use figure 1.3 to reflect on your own experiences in the K–12 system.

What did you notice about how the teachers or administrators spoke to students of a different gender identity than you?	
How did adults respond when you showed interest in an activity that seemed counter to the assumed behavior of your gender assigned at birth?	
Did your teachers or other school staff encourage certain career pathways that might now be viewed as identifying with the norms and assumed roles aligned with your birth-assigned gender?	
Additional reflections:	

FIGURE 1.3: Current reality—Gender expression.

*Visit **go.SolutionTree.com/schoolimprovement** for a free reproducible version of this figure.*

When students perceive pressure from trusted adults to engage in gender-conforming behaviors, emotions, or professions (or disengage from perceived non-conformity), they demonstrate decision making that mirrors these messages, even into adulthood (Masters & Barth, 2022). The American Association of University Women (2020) highlights some conventional gender-based categorizations that perpetually limit students in relation to their academic performance and emotional engagement within our schools, as shown in table 1.1, as well as their post-school aspirations or occupational pursuits (Masters & Barth, 2022; Widlund, Tuominen, Tapola, & Korhonen, 2019).

TABLE 1.1: Conventional Gender-Based Categorizations

Traditionally, Girls Are . . .	Traditionally, Boys Are . . .
Expected to be well behaved, compliant, and polite, and pressured to conform to feminized behavior, appearance, tradition, and norms	Expected to be tough, physical, and athletic, and exposed to damaging "boys will be boys" messaging around misbehavior and violence
More likely to believe that only boys can be "really, really smart"	More likely to believe that doing well in school is "for girls"
More often discouraged from mathematics—despite no evidence of innate performance differences	More often discouraged from reading and writing—despite no evidence of innate performance differences
Exposed to same-gender role models like elementary school teachers, most of whom are women	Exposed to same-gender role models like scientists and mathematicians, most of whom are men

Source: American Association of University Women, 2020.

Joseph Cimpian (2018), associate professor of economics and education policy at New York University, writes about the cultural changes needed in the education system to prevent assumptions regarding gender identity:

> Exploring deeper, we found that the beliefs that teachers have about student ability might contribute significantly to the gap. When faced with a boy and a girl of the same race and socio-economic status who performed equally well on math tests and whom the teacher rated equally well in behaving and engaging with school, the teacher rated the boy as more mathematically able—an alarming pattern that replicated in a separate data set collected over a decade later.
>
> Another way of thinking of this is that in order for a girl to be rated as mathematically capable as her male classmate, she not only needed to perform as well as him on a psychometrically rigorous external test, but

> also be seen as working harder than him. Subsequent matching and instrumental variables analyses suggested that teachers' underrating of girls from kindergarten through third grade accounts for about half of the gender achievement gap growth in math. In other words, if teachers didn't think their female students were less capable, the gender gap in math might be substantially smaller. (Cimpian, 2018)

A 2022 study from the United Nations Women and the Unstereotype Alliance, an organization developed to eliminate harmful stereotypes in advertising and media, surveyed twenty countries in their ongoing research to track attitudes on gender. Although 91 percent of respondents agreed that gender equality is critical to the success and sustainability of their nation, these additional findings from the same study provide an important alternate view (UN Women, 2022).

- Sixty-three percent of respondents agreed that it is easy for men to run for elected office as compared to 38 percent agreement toward women (UN Women, 2022).
- One quarter of respondents agreed with the statement, "In times of food shortages, priority should be given to men," and just over one-third agreed that "when jobs are scarce, men should have more right to a job than women" (UN Women, 2022).
- Although 90 percent of respondents agreed that equal pay for equal work was important to their nation's future and success, "52% of men aged 16–19 and 54% of men aged 20–34, agree that 'women should work less and devote more time to caring for their family'" (UN Women, 2022).

These glorified gender stereotypes—and the subconscious manner in which we preserve them—dampen students' courage to navigate a new course to overcome such established boundaries. It can guide them into a pattern of thought that then transforms into a belief system. Further complexities emerge as we consider our transgender and non-binary students, as many schools are not yet equipped to accommodate—let alone recognize—gender identities beyond the binary of female and male. Such constraints can mute students' desire to even explore new pathways that would unleash their unique assets and talents for personalized success.

Visit www.aclu.org/report/schools-transition to access a guide for supporting transgendered and gender-nonconforming students to thrive socially and academically in schools; the guide was created through the pioneering research and collaborative advocacy of the American Civil Liberties Union (ACLU), Gender Spectrum, Human Rights Campaign Foundation (HRCF), National Center for Lesbian

Rights (NCLR), and the National Education Association (NEA). This tool offers a key foundation for the development of truly inclusive learning environments, including talking points, sample transition plans, and tips for teaching about gender identities and expressions. This collective research defends:

> School is the place where our children should be exploring ideas and discovering new skills. No child should be prevented from pursuing their passions simply based on others' perceptions of their gender. By sending a message that certain pursuits are off limits simply because of a person's gender, we lose access to an incredible source of human potential. (Orr et al., 2023, pp. 11–12)

From sports teams to field trips to bathroom and locker room use, school environments that have not consistently developed procedures to honor and affirm the various expressions of gender can create disruption and invalidation for *all* students. The GLSEN (formerly the Gay, Lesbian & Straight Education Network; www.glsen.org/policy-maps), an education organization committed to ending discrimination, harassment, and bullying based on sexual orientation, gender identity, and gender expression, communicates state legislation proposals or laws that maintain either a disinterested ("we're not going to address it at all") or undesirable ("we will address it by openly declaring against it") stance toward students' gender expression and the responsibilities and roles of school systems to protect individuals' human rights in this way.

To put this challenge into context, consider that Pew Research Center (2019) reports that 81 percent of Australians, 85 percent of Canadians, and 72 percent of people living in the United States believe that homosexuality should be accepted by the general public. Contrast this information with the following examples of laws enacted in the United States.

- One law claimed "homosexuality is not a lifestyle acceptable to the general public" (Alabama State Code § 16–40A-2(c)(8)).
- Health education "may not include a discussion of alternate sexual lifestyles from heterosexual relationships including, but not limited to, homosexual relationships except in the context of instruction concerning sexually transmitted diseases" (S. C. Stat. § 59–32–30(5)).

These are not underlying assumptions; these are statements of law. In light of this, consider the following questions: What are the laws in your district, state, province, or country, and how do they impact what you can and cannot say or do in the classroom? What is the incentive for students to determine their own identity and truth in who they are, especially when it may be counter to their assigned gender? What have you been taught about gender expression and how to respond to students and families who are transitioning?

Let's explore more deeply to name some of the questions that we or others may be thinking but are hesitant to ask out loud.

- Will LGBTQ+ students plant ideas in the minds of cisgender students that will make cisgender students question their own gender identity? (*Cisgender* is an "adjective that describes a person whose gender identity aligns with the sex they were assigned at birth" [Wamsley, 2021].)
- If a cisgender student is in a class or an activity with an LGBTQ+ student, will the cisgender student become gay or transgender from knowing or interacting with someone who identifies as such?
- Do I associate with people who believe the preceding statements to be true?
- Do I wonder about these things too?

Please understand that these questions are unavoidable. You don't need to respond yet, whether it be with support or hesitation about the questions; letting these thoughts marinate for a while is important. With a group of trusted colleagues, a faith community, or your closest friends and family, or with the kinds of people you don't normally associate with but who are open to civil dialogue, you can use these questions as you explore the current truths in how you *and* your school, district, or community are proactively poised to acknowledge, validate, and defend students' expression of gender. Questions for consideration include, but are not limited to, those in figure 1.4.

What gender identities are recognized in your school or district?
What questions do you have about gender expressions other than male and female?
How has the implementation of conventional gender roles affected student and staff success in your classroom or school?

FIGURE 1.4: Questions for gender expression reflection.

As you may recognize, these are complex questions that do not often yield simple solutions. You can use figure 1.5 to reflect on your own tendencies. Use a pencil to mark the column that appropriately reflects your current personal level of comfort with each of the statements listed. You may also consider inserting the date, rather than a checkmark, so that you could revisit these self-reflections over time to honor your own development through the work. Then, jot down your reactions to the questions posed at the end of the self-reflection tool.

Statement	**I can or already do this.**	**I commit to learning more about this.**	**I am not ready to commit at this time.**
I believe every student has the right to feel safe, welcomed, and valued in our school.			
I am willing to actively seek, learn, and use strategies, language, and tools that will best support the gender expressions of my students.			
I am willing to express gender neutrality when discussing course, career pathways, or extracurricular activities with my students.			
I am willing to unpack my own fears and uncertainties about the things I do not know or understand before making decisions that will directly impact the future of students in my school.			
I will advocate for all adults who interact with students to have the appropriate training, skills, and mindset to support the gender expressions of our student body.			
I understand that gender identification and expression can be dynamic and evolving, and will create (or uphold) systems, structures, policies, and processes that are adaptable to any emerging needs.			
I commit to both protecting and advocating for a safe learning environment for each of my students, regardless of their gender expression.			
I will respect and affirm the gender identities expressed by my students, and I commit to communicating with my colleagues or my administrators if I have questions, concerns, or tensions about my ability or role in treating each student with dignity.			

Which of the preceding statements made sense to you?
Which statements were the most difficult to answer?
How would your thoughts and responses benefit students?
Other thoughts or reflections:

FIGURE 1.5: Personal comfort regarding my students' gender expression.

Visit ***go.SolutionTree.com/schoolimprovement*** *for a free reproducible version of this figure.*

OK. Take a deep breath. Thank you for walking through some *fierce* reflection with me. I am grateful for your bold step forward.

So are your students and colleagues.

Let's continue.

Barrier Three: Inadequate Levels of Teacher Preparedness and Fragmented Professional Learning Opportunities

My grandmother, who was a schoolteacher and principal herself, used to remind me that if you try to throw all the spaghetti at the wall at once, only a few pieces are actually going to stick (D. Freese, personal communication, n.d.). And such is the case for the manner in which both teacher preparedness programs and ongoing professional learning have existed in our school systems. The system saturates teachers

with disconnected learning experiences or, worse, can hinder their abilities to implement and then sustain new learning by changing the learning objectives from year to year. As an example, mathematics teacher educator Natalie Odom Pough (2021) reflects on the absence of pedagogical training on classroom management strategies in many teacher preparation programs, let alone culturally responsive teaching strategies, in her own experience. She expresses that, too often, teachers are prepared for textbook scenarios where each student in class has the same needs on the same day, operates with the same background knowledge, and comes to class with all the physical, mental, and social tools needed to succeed. Teacher Cornelius Blanding advocates instead that educators need teacher preparation programs and professional learning opportunities in *real-world* scenarios, along with the skills, tools, and strategies required to navigate them (as cited in Pough, 2021).

Pause for a moment: our schools could be more effective (and efficient) if we simply gave clear guidance, regularly monitored progress, and provided feedback and support along the way, both in teacher preparation programs and through targeted professional learning once teachers are hired.

TEACHER PREPARATION PROGRAMS

The Center for American Progress (2019) alerts us that, since 2010, enrollment in teacher preparation programs nationwide has declined by more than one-third. Nine states have seen enrollment decreases of 50 percent in their undergraduate education programs. In addition, when teacher preparatory enrollment was disaggregated by race, the study found a decrease of 25 percent in enrollment for Black and Latino candidates. Given that 80 percent of the existing teacher workforce identifies as White, this data presents great concern. Research shows that for Black children, having even one Black teacher in elementary school (especially before third grade) increases the likelihood of college enrollment (Camera, 2018). Yet, teacher preparation programs enrolled almost 15,000 fewer Black candidates in 2018 than in 2010. More alarming is that, even before the impact of COVID-19, 54 percent of adults said they wouldn't want their children to become teachers (Phi Delta Kappan, 2018). A 2022 poll showed responses to this same question increased to 62 percent (PDK International, 2022). For those adults who are currently in the profession, *over half* stated they had seriously considered leaving teaching altogether.

Education is a demanding profession, both mentally and emotionally, and the effects of such demands are further compounded when teachers are placed in situations for which they have not been adequately prepared. The National Council on Teacher Quality (n.d.), in its review of over 1,200 undergraduate and graduate teacher preparation programs, finds the following startling data.

- Only 7 percent of teacher preparation programs enroll students of color at or above the rate of their institution, suggesting that it is not just geography which may have an impact on a program's ability to be diverse but also factors related to the teaching major or teaching as a career.
- Only 22 percent of teacher preparation programs successfully enroll teacher candidates that are at least as diverse as the community in which they reside.
- Praising students for positive behavior is a powerful tool, yet only about a quarter of teacher preparation programs require it to be modeled.
- Three-quarters of teacher preparation programs do not require applicants to hold a B average. In fact, 12 percent of programs do not even consider applicants' academic records for admission into the program.
- Of all institutions, 84 percent address most science and social studies content that elementary teachers need in current course options, but only 3 percent of these institutions require candidates to take the *right* courses in most topics. For example, 95 percent of institutions or programs currently have a course within existing requirements covering forces, waves, and energy, but only 41 percent of institutions or programs explicitly require candidates take a course covering the topic, despite all fifty states and the District of Columbia requiring elementary teachers to teach this topic.

Given that many teacher preparation programs are not actually preparing teachers to *teach*, coupled with the limited number of teacher mentorship programs or opportunities offered by school districts, we can understand how the lack of preparation has resulted in many teachers—traditionally trained or not—feeling overwhelmed, unappreciated, and undervalued.

In *Inside Higher Ed*, Christianne Warren (2020) connects back to the first two barriers addressed in this chapter—(1) insufficient knowledge of systemic racism and (2) misunderstandings about gender expression—asserting that we cannot piecemeal undergraduate coursework to address and prepare students for the complex issues emerging in our classrooms, especially regarding social justice issues. For this, she states:

> We need to design programs to include mandatory courses that discuss the various intersections of oppression in different societies rather than leave them as electives. As long as diversity-related courses largely remain as add-ons or electives that are plugged into existing curricula in order to meet the diversity requirement for accreditation purposes, we are only completing a small percentage of the required work. Mandatory courses, especially those usually taken in the first two years in college, as well as many liberal arts requirements, have to be fully intellectually representative, including diverse experiences into standard courses beyond the handful of notable representatives and events. We also have to address more strategically how academic programs are designed and what courses are required, and vastly limit the remaining electives.

This perspective also reinforces how the current infrastructures are inappropriately designed by placing the newest teachers in classrooms where the most effective instruction is required.

PROFESSIONAL DEVELOPMENT OPPORTUNITIES

In the same spirit, school districts should be explicit about their expectations regarding the intention, implementation, and resulting impact of the professional learning provided for teachers and staff. If your district has a mission or vision statement that articulates "all students can learn" or "all students will be prepared to contribute to their community," it can no longer be acceptable to offer professional learning pathways that do not require teachers to learn, nurture, and grow strategies that promote *all* students being able to achieve that mission. Normalizing diversity of thought, while learning through multiple perspectives and modalities, can be at the heart of ongoing, job-embedded learning.

Professional learning has long been a topic of conversation among educators that can bring joy, misery, or anything in between. We've all been victim to professional learning experiences where we find ourselves exasperated, looking at the clock, checking our phone, and sitting through content that is not at all relevant to our experiences or the timely needs of our students. Conversely, we have also experienced those moments when we think, "Yes! This is finally something I can make actionable in my classroom!" In these latter moments, we find ourselves hungry to learn even more.

In 2017, the Bill and Melinda Gates Foundation partnered with the Boston Consulting Group to interview roughly 1,300 teachers on this topic. Their research revealed that while teachers want professional learning in order to best help their students succeed, the implementation and impact of said learning opportunities left much to be desired. And with over $18 billion a year being spent on professional learning opportunities across the United States (Gates Foundation, 2017), our education system literally can no longer afford the continued fragmentation of focus nor the overwhelming disconnect between what district leaders and teachers believe is most essential learning for the moment.

The Gates Foundation (2017) study reveals that only 29 percent of teachers are highly satisfied with how professional learning is currently offered and executed in their schools. In addition, most teachers do not believe in the efficacy of the professional learning experience. Part of this may be due to autonomy. The majority of educators "have little influence over such basic decisions as curriculum, instructional materials, the content of professional learning opportunities, discipline policies, and educator hiring practices and evaluation" (National Education Association, n.d.). Given how educational practices and reforms are dynamic and evolving, teachers consistently crave opportunities to support their growing practical and pedagogical needs. This also requires teacher leaders, advocates, and administrators to relieve teachers of certain expectations or responsibilities, in order for there to even be *space* for the learning to occur.

Post-pandemic needs have made the topics of technology, accelerated learning, student mental health support, and educator self-care urgent (National Math and Science Initiative, 2021).

Look at your school's or district's professional learning plan and consider the following.

1. Notice how much time is dedicated for you to grow your learning as related to the mission of your district.
2. Review *when* it is happening—is it all at the beginning of the year during pre-school workshop, or is it thoughtfully embedded throughout the year?
3. Next, consider the following.
   + How is that time being spent?
   + What is the follow-through to the learning?
   + How is professional learning measured and assessed in terms of its benefit to students?

Use figure 1.6 to help you think through and identify the impact of your current systems of professional learning.

Questions	Responses
What are the intended learning outcomes of your school's or district's professional learning plan?	
Does the plan articulate learning for all stakeholders in the organization (for example, teachers, principals, district administrators, clerical staff, and so on), or just for the instructional staff?	
When will the learning happen throughout the school year? Is it one-time or ongoing?	
How are staff spending that time? (*For example, are you listening without time for application, or do you have time to reflect and collaborate with your colleagues? Are you being given time to implement and operationalize the learning into practice, or are you expected to do that by yourself, on your own time?*)	
What is the follow-through to the learning? (*For example, are you able to receive additional coaching and support as necessary to actualize this new learning in a manner that enables you to achieve your goals? Is your building or district leader guiding, advising, and monitoring progress of implementation during the course of the school year?*)	
How is the professional learning being measured and assessed in terms of its benefit to students? Are the trainings offered directly aligned with creating safe, inclusive spaces where every student is able to learn at high levels?	

FIGURE 1.6: Current reality—Status check on the impact of professional learning.

Visit ***go.SolutionTree.com/schoolimprovement*** *for a free reproducible version of this figure.*

Simply put, we cannot change the trajectory of what happens in our schools and classrooms until we address the perceptions and experiences of the students benefiting from (or being hindered by) systemic inequalities each day. Adults need professional learning to both hear and respond to the information that is shared by students.

How Do I Get Myself Ready?

At this point, I imagine that your brain is firing on all cylinders. You have been exposed to some information that has both affirmed and challenged what you have known to be true. You have walked through some fierce self-reflection while also becoming more deeply engaged in reviewing current school and district language regarding inclusivity and belonging for each of your students. At this point, you might be asking, "Now what?" In this section and those that follow in this chapter, I provide a few ideas to explore, connect, and experience your own *Meant for More* moments. Here is some of the reflective language that you'll hear throughout the duration of this book: *notice*, *normalize*, and *nurture*. Read more about these elements in the sections to come, and jot your thinking or any connections as you go.

Notice How Your Heart and Mind Interact With the Content

I have been intentional in designing this book to ensure that you, the reader, feel safe to interact with and react to the ideas and recommendations presented here. While some technical, practical components are revealed throughout the text, there is also highly adaptive content that might feel personal to you. The mind and heart will definitely tag team this experience, creating both logical and emotional responses. Kendra Cherry (2022), a psychology educator and author, cites three components of an emotion worth drawing your attention to:

- **Subjective:** How you experience the emotion
- **Physiological:** How your body reacts to the emotion
- **Expressive:** How you behave in response to the emotion

We know how emotions can help you make decisions, avoid danger, and motivate action but they can also help you connect to others, help other people connect with you, and, most importantly, help you connect with yourself (Cherry, 2022; Elmer, 2022; Mamorsky, n.d.). You can think of emotional regulation this way:

> a practice of cultivating a sacred buffer of time between feeling the emotion and your reaction to that emotion. [Emotional regulation] is the

> ability to take in information, maintain your composure in proportion to the experience, and effectively communicate your needs to others. For example, pausing to collect your thoughts before you respond. (Lebow & Casabianca, 2022)

In addition, licensed therapist Chelsea Vinas (as cited in Elmer, 2022) recommends both writing down your emotions and experiences and then unpacking how or why they affected you. With this research-based advocacy in mind, use the prompts in figure 1.7 to refresh your ideas and reflections from what you have read in this chapter so far. This tool enables you to recap where we have been and refresh your thinking about the ideas. Moving forward, visit **go.SolutionTree.com/schoolimprovement** to access the reproducible "Chapter Summarization Tool to Inspire Action" after reading each chapter to monitor your thinking and establish any productive calls to action.

Part I: Affirmations
Go back and flip through the pages in this chapter. Remind yourself of the moments that affirmed your current set of beliefs. *What section stood out to you the most?* *Why does this section mean so much to you?*
Part II: Wonderings
Flip through the pages of this chapter again. This time, identify a moment that gave you pause; a place that left you questioning or where you noticed your mind starting to wonder how this made sense. *Write down the sentence or page number where this pause happened.* *What parts of this section challenged you most?*

Are you open to seeking more information to learn more and possibly even resolve this challenge? Why or why not?
Part III: Inspired Action *Which parts of this chapter are you inspired to talk about with a colleague?* *What do you hope will emerge from that conversation?* *When will you act on your inspiration, and schedule this conversation with your colleague?* *During the next month? The next week? The next twenty-four hours?*

FIGURE 1.7: Chapter summarization tool to inspire action.

Visit ***go.SolutionTree.com/schoolimprovement*** *for a free reproducible version of this figure.*

Normalize the Ebb and Flow of Your Emotional Response to the Content

We have only completed the first chapter in our *Meant for More* journey, yet I imagine you already have some raw, authentic emotions emerging. Cherry (2022) cites how emotions can "motivate us to act in particular ways and give us the tools and resources we need to interact meaningfully in our social worlds." Use the continuum shown in figure 1.8) to monitor your level of comfort of interaction with this content as we take our next step forward. Our work might be easy to name, but it is certainly complex to understand.

Acclimating	Acknowledging	Addressing	Advancing
I am ready to privately examine my own mental models.	I am ready to examine my own mental models with a group of trusted friends.	I am ready to publicly examine my mental models with my colleagues.	I am ready to publicly examine my mental models with my students and families.

FIGURE 1.8: Level-of-comfort continuum—My readiness for rehumanizing our profession.

Nurture Your Confidence to Take a Next Step

Remember: you have permission to be exactly where you are. My ask is that you just not be complacent in staying there. We can use strategies and tools to develop a level of emotional regulation that enables us to interact with others in a collaborative, resourceful, and productive manner, whether faced with moments that are rewarding or contentious or anything in between. What we feel is "valid and natural" (Lebow & Casabianca, 2022). I promise that you have what you need inside you already. Let's boost our confidence in those skills as they connect to the creation of *Meant for More* classrooms because this work requires that you give yourself both patience and grace as you engage in the journey. As you heighten your self-awareness, then you can become more successful in championing the efforts along with your colleagues and other stakeholders.

How Do I Get My Team Ready?

After you have completed the chapter summarization tool to reveal your own points of awareness and comfort, you may now feel more knowledgeable and more equipped to bring your thoughts forward to discuss and dialogue with someone else. Stepping into conversations to acknowledge and address the systems, structures, or policies that inhibit each student in your learning environment from feeling seen, heard, and valued might cause some trepidation among the stakeholders who are collectively preparing to take action. In fact, you may have already experienced those feelings of uncertainty or hesitation as you were reading. But fear not, friends.

The following tools for processing and preparing could further aid the discussion.

- Evidence that inspires action (figure 1.9) is a reflection tool to identify how we know there is a concern to be systematically addressed.
- Determining our desired state (figure 1.10) is a tool to support clarifying the desired mental models, systems, structures, and adult actions that will be necessary for *Meant for More* classrooms. (You can use this tool in parts or all at once.)

The tool at https://buildingcontentknowledge.nctq.org can help your team identify gaps as well. Visit **go.SolutionTree.com/schoolimprovement** for links to the websites mentioned in this book.

What is the key concern we are trying to resolve?	
Where do we currently find success?	Where do we currently find struggle?
What evidence of success exists?	What evidence of struggle is there?
What is our statement of purpose that can now help us move forward?	

FIGURE 1.9: Evidence that inspires action.

Visit ***go.SolutionTree.com/schoolimprovement*** *for a free reproducible version of this figure.*

When our successes are realized, what will they look like, sound like, and feel like for the staff, students, and community of our district?	
Desired Mental Models	
Desired Systems and Structures	
Desired Adult Actions	

FIGURE 1.10: Determining our desired state.

Visit ***go.SolutionTree.com/schoolimprovement*** *for a free reproducible version of this figure.*

What Infrastructure Do I Need to Make It Happen?

Many tools and strategies are presented in this chapter. As we lay the foundation for our work, the deep reflection required *before* we take action can feel laborious or even burdensome at times because we are so inspired to begin. However, you know from experience that taking action without first seeking information inevitably results in a reconstruction of the work or limits the chances for successful sustainability.

While we may feel that our students don't have time to wait for us to learn and grow, the sentiment behind that statement is more purposefully directed at feeling like we have to wait for the *organization* or *system* to respond before we, as individuals or teams, can take action. The truth is, we can't put a bandage on a wound that is hemorrhaging. As such, be mindful of the time you and others may need to move forward. My friend and colleague Tom Schimmer talks about being urgent with the process but patient with the people (personal communication, June 29, 2019). Let us heed similar advice today. We owe it to ourselves, our students, and our communities to engage in the opportunities that emerge from *introspection* rather than the obligations and reparations revealed during retrospection. Read the Meant for MoreMENTUM story for an example of how such introspection positively impacted a school community.

Meant for MoreMENTUM: Stories To Ignite Us

Arthur F. Corey School is a public elementary school located in Buena Park, California, a large suburban area east of Los Angeles. The student population is roughly 450 students, and the school serves students in grades K–6. The school's enrollment for students of color is 87 percent, with 56 percent of students identified as economically disadvantaged. The student-teacher ratio is 20:1, boasting twenty-two classroom teachers and one full-time school counselor.

In the spirit of continuous improvement, the staff at the Corey School took on the task of studying their current inclusion program to improve access to general education services for all students, as well as determine how to reshape the current special education service model to meet the evolving needs of their community. What started as an arduous task resulted in a unifying opportunity to transform into a learning environment where all stakeholders could thrive in a *Meant for More* classroom.

Principal LaRonda Ortega sought a cross-section of staff to collaboratively lead this self-examination of their current practices. She was able to create an initial task force with representation from staff who taught either general education, full inclusion, special education, or engaged in co-teaching, as well as ensure staff on the task force had a range of knowledge of and access to the inclusion services being provided on campus. This cohort gathered staff feedback through various surveys and self-assessments that revealed the staff had differing ideas on how to define inclusion and the role and work of inclusion teachers, as well as opinions on how different teachers were or were not equitably addressing the needs of students across the school community. Common themes emerged for areas of improvement or additional learning, including training, mindset, collaboration, parent partnership and advocacy, and compassion. As such, their next step was dreaming up what could be; the team thought, "what legacy could we have that would benefit generations of students to come?"

From there, four goals emerged.

1. One-hundred percent of staff will participate in three professional learning events related to inclusive learning environments by the end of this school year.
2. One-hundred percent of staff will participate in a book or podcast study about inclusive culture during this school year.
3. Eighty percent of parents will become aware of full inclusion at Corey School as measured by beginning of year and end of year survey data.
4. Ninety percent of students with disabilities will feel that they have supportive peer relationships at Corey School as measured by fall, winter, and spring Panorama Student Survey (www.panoramaed.com/panorama-student-survey) results.

With this inspiration, the task force was primed with an additional question: What adult actions are necessary to create an inclusive community?

First, the team agreed on what they wanted their community to be and established the following statement of practice:

> Corey School has an inclusive and collaborative whole-systems approach to education where all learners have equal access to deliberately designed, student-centered curricula intended to challenge, support, and respect students' inherent dignity and autonomy. The school community has a problem-solving mindset devoted to optimizing learning opportunities, ensuring every student achieves at the highest level—socially, emotionally, academically, and physically.

The team also learned that providing appropriate language for recognizing a student's disability was important as well. Some staff and students would overlook or dismiss a student's needs, and the team understood that if we negate a student's disability, we negate who they are and what they need. The task force provided specific instruction to students and staff to help them learn about varying abilities. The behavior team worked with staff to determine the best ways to teach students how to acknowledge students with disabilities, including a schoolwide book chat using *Just Ask! Be Different, Be Brave, Be You* by Justice Sonia Sotomayor (2019). The team agreed to share their book chat with parents as well, providing sample questions that would support parents with inclusive language.

LaRonda beams, "The beauty is that something that emerged from compliance became something we could *own* as a staff. We learned the benefit of cross-collaboration and the impact our collective work could have on the students, the staff, and the community, and we are better now than we've ever been" (L. Ortega, personal communication, January 24, 2023).

Figure 1.11 is a protocol to support your reflection, discussion, and action orientation with regard to creating your *Meant for More* classroom or school. I reference this protocol throughout the remainder of the book, and pieces of it may feel helpful at certain times during our journey. This protocol is intended to encourage collective awareness and promote a systems-thinking approach for you and whatever other levels of the organization you desire. The whole protocol is here so you can see where we are heading by the end of this book. However, at this time, the most useful pieces are the shaded parts—A-1: Affirm your school or district mission and A-2: Become aware. Take this tool in stride, and please know that it is *not* intended to be something you complete and check off the list. The protocol was intentionally designed to stoke essential conversations and allow teams to engage in discovery and purposeful response moving forward.

<table>
<tr><td colspan="2">Use this protocol when discussing inequitable and systemic challenges within your school or organization. The protocol supports you to outline a reason for change as well as how students will benefit from the success of that change.
Affirm—Aware—Acknowledge—Address—Amend—Activate—Advance</td></tr>
<tr><td colspan="2">A-1: Affirm your school or district mission. Write your mission statement. Circle any words or phrases in that statement that inspire your purpose and commitment. How do you align your behaviors with those phrases, on behalf of the students that you serve?</td></tr>
<tr><td>Adult Actions Needed</td><td>Benefit to Students</td></tr>
<tr><td colspan="2">A-2. Become aware. What are we hearing or observing that alerts us to a disruption of student belonging, confidence, and efficacy within our school community?</td></tr>
<tr><td>Adult Actions Needed</td><td>Benefit to Students</td></tr>
<tr><td colspan="2">A-3. Acknowledge the disruption or inequity. What do we believe are the marginalizing or debilitating conditions for our students, and what are the contributing factors to the disruption or inequity?</td></tr>
<tr><td>Adult Actions Needed</td><td>Benefit to Students</td></tr>
<tr><td colspan="2">A-4. Address the barriers or challenges that are reinforcing the inequity. What sources (practices, structures, policies, or mindsets) are interfering with students' sense of belonging, confidence, and efficacy within our school community? How did that weaken the alignment to our mission?</td></tr>
<tr><td>Adult Actions Needed</td><td>Benefit to Students</td></tr>
<tr><td colspan="2">A-5. Amend the systems to interrupt the inequity. How will we acknowledge and address mindsets that are disconnected from our mission for all? How will the wording, intention, or implementation of certain practices, structures, or policies be revised in order to rectify the inequity?</td></tr>
<tr><td>Adult Actions Needed</td><td>Benefit to Students</td></tr>
<tr><td colspan="2">A-6. Activate the pathways for change with cross-stakeholder collaboration. How will all members in our school community work collaboratively to seek common ground, establish a renewed vision, and consistently implement the conditions for attaining that vision?</td></tr>
<tr><td>Adult Actions Needed</td><td>Benefit to Students</td></tr>
<tr><td colspan="2">A-7. Advance the organization to achieve its mission and ensure each student is equally equipped and equitably empowered for success. How will we actively engage all stakeholders to hold the system accountable for its actions and ensure each student feels seen, heard, and valued as a resulting impact?</td></tr>
<tr><td>Adult Actions Needed</td><td>Benefit to Students</td></tr>
</table>

FIGURE 1.11: Seven As protocol for interrupting inequities and systemic barriers.

Visit ***go.SolutionTree.com/schoolimprovement*** *for a free reproducible version of this figure.*

Use the sample scenario in figure 1.12 to support your initial entry into this type of reflective protocol. I proposed a scenario in A-1 and A-2 that addresses dehumanizing behavior toward students in the form of assaults and aggressions, but feel free to choose a local scenario of your own.

<table>
<tr><td colspan="2">Use this protocol when discussing inequitable or systemic challenges within your school or organization. The protocol supports you to outline a reason for change as well as how students will benefit from the success of that change.

Affirm—Aware—Acknowledge—Address—Amend—Activate—Advance</td></tr>
<tr><td colspan="2">A-1: Affirm your school or district mission. Write your mission statement in this space. Circle any words or phrases in that statement that inspire your purpose and commitment. How do you align your behaviors with those phrases on behalf of the students you serve?

We are committed to the mission of "igniting a passion for lifelong learning" through collaboration, continuous improvement, equity, integrity, and relationships.</td></tr>
<tr><td colspan="2">A-2. Become aware. What are we hearing or observing that alerts us to a disruption of student belonging, confidence, and efficacy within our school community?

Students are reporting an increase of aggressive words and behaviors in places on campus that inherently have less active supervision, such as playgrounds, cafeterias, and bus stops. Students are anxious coming to school, requesting to move seats in the classroom, and asking to eat with their teachers or other adults in the cafeteria.</td></tr>
<tr><td>Adult Actions Needed
• Validate the student's experience and affirm how the student is/was feeling about the disruption.
• Talk with additional students who were directly and indirectly involved to better understand the what, when, and where of the disruption.
• Review video footage (or ensure cameras are installed) to reveal any pre-disruption events.
• Ask students (and their families) what the school could do to reduce their anxiety and/or what would be helpful to eliminate the disruption and ensure opportunities to all.</td><td>Benefit to Students
• Reduces anxiety about coming to school
• Reclaims their sense of safety and security at school
• Sets a boundary to preserve the dignity and integrity of students
• Reminds students that they are seen members of their school community and have equal value</td></tr>
</table>

FIGURE 1.12: Example scenario—Seven As protocol.

Visit ***go.SolutionTree.com/schoolimprovement*** *for a free reproducible version of this figure.*

All through the book, we will affirm beliefs, thoughts, and action steps in order to create sustainability. You will continue to self-reflect and self-assess to promote your own definition of *meant for more* as you determine how you will grow it in your own space.

You are the only person who can make sense of what *you* need most. You've got this.

Tool to Inspire Action

After reading each chapter, complete the reproducible "Chapter Summarization Tool to Inspire Action"; you completed this in figure 1.7 (page 36; visit **go.SolutionTree.com/schoolimprovement**). It appeared earlier in this chapter to model the practices of introspection and reflection, which are pivotal to creating *Meant for More* classrooms. Now, use the continuum in figure 1.13 to monitor your level of comfort as we take our next step forward. As previously mentioned, our work might be easy to name, but it is certainly complex to understand.

Acclimating	Acknowledging	Addressing	Advancing
I am ready to privately examine my own mental models.	I am ready to examine my own mental models with a group of trusted friends.	I am ready to publicly examine my mental models with my colleagues.	I am ready to publicly examine my mental models with my students and families.

FIGURE 1.13: Level-of-comfort continuum—My readiness for building awareness.

"Remember: you have permission to be exactly where you are. My ask is that you just not be complacent in staying there."

Current Reality Reflection

Data to discuss:	
How do these data represent in our school?	How do these data represent in our district?

How do these data manifest with regard to student achievement?

Chapter 2

Embracing Authenticity

It was early in my career as a teacher and I was relentless in my pursuit of taking care of my students. I worked tirelessly to plan the perfect bulletin board, the most engaging lesson plan, the most innovative seating arrangements, the most—well, you get the picture. I wanted to make sure that the students in my classroom were getting the benefit of everything I had to offer. Being so new to the profession, I was determined to make up for my lack of knowledge and experience with my energy, determination, and commitment to "getting it right" for my students.

I was a workhorse, and soon both my colleagues and my students' parents took notice. Although I wasn't trying to attract attention, the fact is that I was reliable, followed through on my work, and was driven to achieve at high levels. I was fun and energetic, and I loved my students as if they were my own. Nothing in my professional life was done halfway—or half speed, for that matter.

Unfortunately, I didn't realize anything was going awry until it was far too late. I was leading a book study, facilitating our site leadership team, and running our after-school program in addition to being the grade-level collaborative team leader and—most importantly—trying to plan my daily lessons. I was not clear in my boundaries; I let people take advantage of my work ethic and, from my perspective, the fact that I didn't yet have a family of my own. People had grown to see me as someone who held herself to a high standard and could get things done. But the truth was, I was drowning. Drowning in the work, yes, but also drowning in my own ambition while chasing someone else's version of what success meant or looked like for me. My peers only saw the part of me that was helping them with their specific project, rather than the sum of all those parts. I was so busy doing and contributing for others that I didn't have time to let people get to know the truest version of me—the one who was indeed driven to succeed but who also craved belonging and deep connection with other people. I was near burnout due to a nonexistent work-life balance. When I did eat, I was not eating well, and I was not prioritizing my other physical health needs or interests. My life train was already moving way too fast, and yet somehow I was still gaining speed. I was about to run out of metaphorical track and catapult off the edge of that cliff.

Fortunately, I was able to course correct. I finally broke my silence and told others how I was feeling. And, to my surprise, people were startled that I hadn't asked for help sooner! Because I had chosen to compartmentalize each project or task I was working on, people didn't realize how much I was trying to carry as a whole. My colleagues empathized with my situation, yet also offered firm guidance and reminders about setting boundaries, saying no, and, most importantly, being more transparent and communicative about my needs. Through the support of my family and the conscientiousness of my colleagues, my world regained balance. As I pen this manuscript, I can say that I practice intentionally scheduled self-care (it's noted as a daily appointment in my calendar; more on that in chapter 7, page 229). I model the standards of dignity and self-respect that I want my daughter to learn and hold true for herself. I have nothing but gratitude for the people who saved me from myself.

As you reflect on the story, take a moment to reflect or jot down your thinking in figure 2.1.

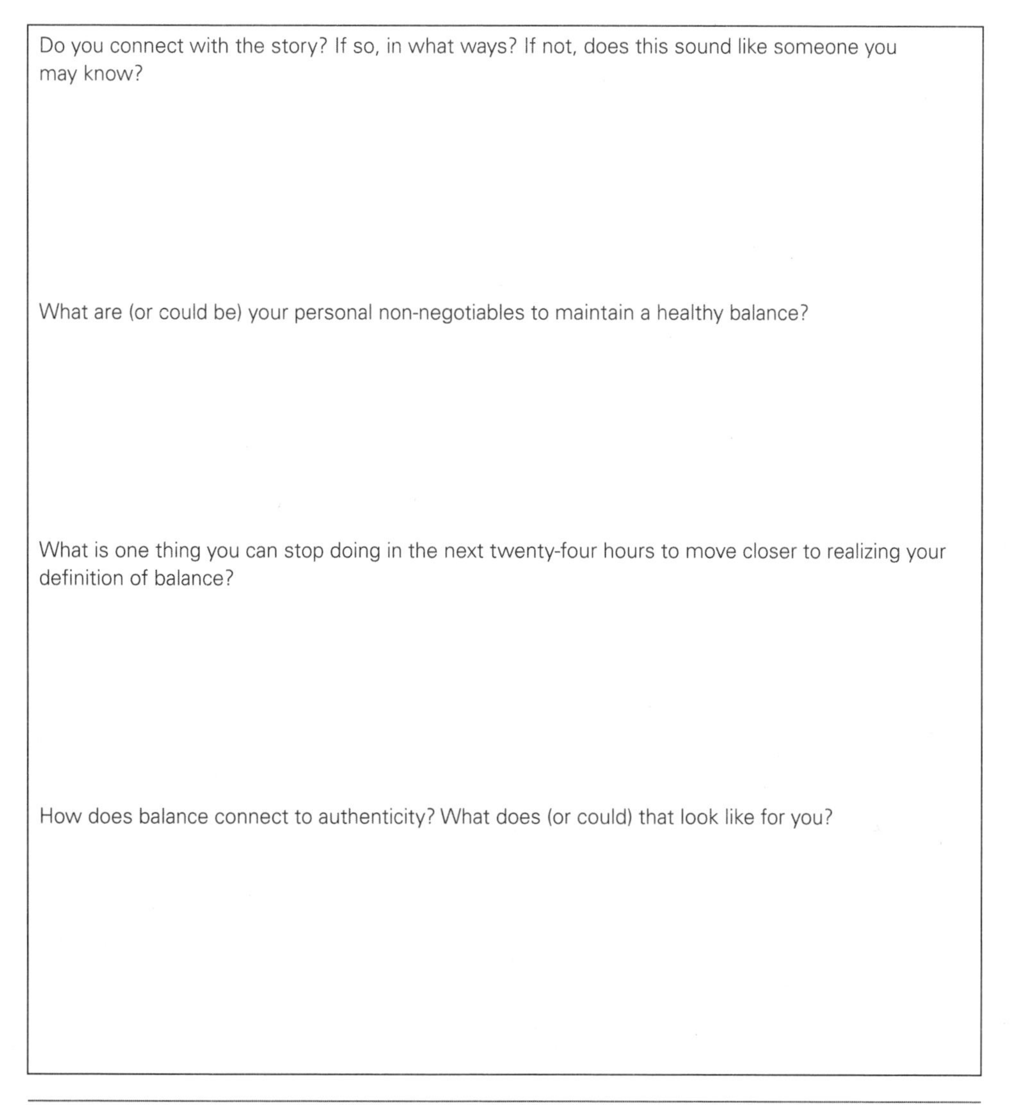
Do you connect with the story? If so, in what ways? If not, does this sound like someone you may know?

What are (or could be) your personal non-negotiables to maintain a healthy balance?

What is one thing you can stop doing in the next twenty-four hours to move closer to realizing your definition of balance?

How does balance connect to authenticity? What does (or could) that look like for you?

FIGURE 2.1: Story reflection.

I didn't place value on being myself with my colleagues during my early years of teaching. Of course, I *loved* who I was with my students—authentic, caring, eager, focused, and kind. But I lost my authenticity somehow as I developed partnerships with my peers. Maybe I got mired in a culture that continued in accordance with the way things had always been done. Maybe my grit, perseverance, and hunger to learn took over as I tried to prove my worth and establish my career. Maybe I didn't have enough confidence in who I was and what I offered. Madeline Miles (2022) states that "authenticity in the workplace goes hand-in-hand with a deep sense of belonging." As we define what embracing authenticity looks like in the *Meant for More* classroom, notice the presence of belonging woven throughout the additional research and stories as well.

What Do We Mean by *Embracing Authenticity*?

Many people might define authenticity as "being yourself" but if so, then what is authenticity in the *classroom*? Jenny Foristall (2019), founder of the Umbrella Project, an organization focused on social-emotional wellness for children, parents, and educators, defines *authenticity* as, "our ability to be our genuine selves, staying true to our values and beliefs, while still adapting to the world around us."

Vulnerability researcher Brené Brown (2010) defines *authenticity* this way:

> The daily practice of letting go of who we think we're supposed to be and embracing who we are. Choosing authenticity means:
>
> - cultivating the courage to be imperfect, to set boundaries, and to allow ourselves to be vulnerable;
> - exercising the compassion that comes from knowing that we are all made of strength and struggle; and
> - nurturing the connection and sense of belonging that can only happen when we believe we are enough. (p. 50)

How can we nurture authenticity when not all students have been equally prepared to accept themselves for who they are, rather than who someone else wants them to be, behave, or become? Why can't we let students do their own thing, and even more so, why would we have to talk about any of this in schools? Isn't it a family's job to equip them with the self-acceptance they require to be successful and authentically engage in their life?

Let's pause for a moment here to clarify what we mean by *self-acceptance* as compared to *self-esteem*. As cited in Ackerman (2018), psychologist and author Leon Seltzer (2008) explains the difference this way:

> Whereas self-esteem refers specifically to how valuable, or worthwhile, we see ourselves, self-acceptance alludes to a far more global affirmation of self. When we're self-accepting, we're able to embrace *all* facets of ourselves—not just the positive, more "esteem-able" parts. As such, self-acceptance is unconditional, free of any qualification. We can recognize our weaknesses or limitations, but this awareness in no way interferes with our ability to fully accept ourselves.

This explanation got me thinking: when we stop judging ourselves or inappropriately aligning our behaviors with our identity, we can move closer to a position of unconditional self-acceptance. Wow. *Unconditional. Self. Acceptance.* That sounds like a nice place. Let's go there!

Self-acceptance is a primary ingredient of valuing and embracing our authentic, unfiltered selves (Ginsburg & Jablow, 2020). Noted psychologist and author Albert Ellis (1977) states that unconditional self-acceptance means that "the individual fully and unconditionally accepts himself whether or not he behaves intelligently, correctly, or competently and whether or not other people approve, respect, or love him" (p. 101). Read that quote again, especially that last part, and consider the questions in figure 2.2.

To what degree do you unconditionally accept yourself, regardless of whether other people approve of, respect, or love you?
Why should this practice of personal self-acceptance even be a consideration for how you approach your work with students?

FIGURE 2.2: Self-acceptance reflection.

Visit ***go.SolutionTree.com/schoolimprovement*** *for a free reproducible version of this figure.*

Meant for More classrooms can embrace authenticity through intentional efforts to express your authentic self, be intentionally inclusive, and practice and model humility.

Express Your Unique Self

Authenticity at work can be defined as "when employees feel safe, secure, and comfortable showing up as their whole selves. To fully show up authentically, employees need a deep sense of belonging and psychological safety" (Miles, 2022). However, authentic expression of our whole selves *doesn't* mean we have to share our whole life story, try to befriend everyone, or compromise our beliefs or boundaries just to fit in.

However, some practical ways to warm up to the idea of authentically expressing yourself follow.

- Wearing clothes or accessories or doing your hair or makeup in a manner that represents your own style
- Personalizing your workspace with photos, posters, or images that are meaningful to you

- Establishing boundaries and expectations for your engagement and participation in staff meetings, social activities, or conversations in the teacher's lounge

In addition to these visible expressions of self that may be more indicative of your personality, consider how you might also convey your professional beliefs and expectations about your colleagues and your students in the classroom. For example, when looking at student work with your teammates, does the way you talk about students align with your beliefs about what they are capable of? When you overhear a colleague using language that marginalizes, such as *babies*, *low kids*, or *the SPED students*, do you walk away and let it be or do you respectfully remind your colleagues how such language continues the cycle of inequity for some student populations?

From a social-emotional lens, educational psychologist Michelle Borba (2021) highlights concerning research that reveals 25 percent of children between ages nine and sixteen consider their appearance to be one of their primary concerns. She frames the student perspective for us, stating, "Focusing on 'what I look like, wear, or weigh' eclipses 'who I am' and contributes to fragile, inaccurate self-hoods by sending a superficial message: 'Your identity is what you have, not who you are'" (Borba, 2021, pp. 34–35). Expressing your true self, professionally and perhaps personally as well, may begin the process of becoming more comfortable at work while also modeling the bold, confident expressions of authenticity that our students need to see most.

Be Intentionally Inclusive

Despite renewed commitments from organizations to revitalize their diversity, equity, and inclusion (DEI) efforts, one in four employees say they do not feel a sense of belonging within their organization, and a mere 30 percent believe their leader models inclusive practices (Wood, 2021). Reframing organizations to become more authentic and inclusive places requires strategic, futuristic thinking. This type of thinking considers both the magnitude of using multiple people, with multifaceted approaches, as well as the sustainability of time, energy, and resources.

Perhaps these logistical and operational complexities prohibit many DEI efforts from barely getting off the ground before they are paused indefinitely. Perhaps the value assigned to time spent in individual and collective restoration is misaligned with the urgency of deadlines, deliverables, and productivity. Even more, since we are still learning how to best measure the impact of our DEI efforts for advancing mindsets, enhancing practices, and improving outcomes, the lack of data and metrics further contributes to initiative fatigue and, sometimes, abandonment.

Professor and special education expert Lee Ann Jung (2023) reminds us that "to create equitable, inclusive classrooms where everyone is embraced, we can't wait until we need to react to an obvious conflict or expressed stress. We have to assume this probability and plan proactively" (p. 24). As such, it is important to consider the concept of being *intentionally inviting*. This concept is grounded in four critical components—(1) trust, (2) respect, (3) optimism, and (4) caring—and when these components are included in our learning space design, we can create an environment that is safe, warm, and welcoming for every student (Jung, 2023).

However, there are attributes that can compromise this concept's integrity. If one can be intentionally inviting, then one could also be intentionally *un*inviting, as well as unintentionally inviting and unintentionally uninviting:

> **Intentionally Inviting** means I acted in a way on purpose to enhance the positive outcomes or potential of a person.
>
> **Unintentionally Inviting** means I didn't plan to, but I acted in a way that enhanced the positive outcomes or potential of a person.
>
> **Intentionally Disinviting** means I behaved with the intent to disrupt the positive outcomes or potential of a person.
>
> **Unintentionally Disinviting** means I accidentally did something that disrupted the positive outcomes or potential of a person. (Jung, 2023, p. 27) [Bold added]

Invitation connects to inclusivity in the most fundamental, human-centric manner; when we believe each individual has inherent intrinsic value, we demonstrate an understanding that all people are worthy of respect and dignity, can achieve their goals, and deserve to belong in the school community.

Practice and Model Humility

The practice of humility enables an individual to be fully present with, and equally accepting of, both their unique talents and their flaws (Birt, 2023; Blain, 2022; Stroman, 2019). While being humble can be perceived as a sign of weakness, we should boldly accept humility, rather, as an asset. Humility can strength our connection with others, broaden our self-perception, and improve our well-being and connection to the world around us (Blain, 2022).

When we deliberately seek the perspective of others and listen to the people around us, we understand that it's more important to learn from them than it is that they learn from us. There are four potential benefits to practicing humility in the workplace, and honoring the following increases humility in one's personal practice:

> **Persuasive:** Influence increases with humility. Because they feel safe around you, people want to learn and grow from your experience.
>
> **Productive:** By recognizing the strengths of others, you will bring out the best in them and build a stronger team, increasing productivity.
>
> **Peaceful:** When you have a clear picture of your strengths and weaknesses, you can feel comfortable with yourself and not feel the need to prove anything.
>
> **Potential:** Humble people invite instruction and correction, which helps you recognize the areas you need to change and make the necessary corrections. (Stroman, 2019)

We can model humility with our students and colleagues by asking for help, asking questions, acknowledging mistakes or when we don't know something, and accepting feedback to continue to improve our relationships and effectiveness (Johnson, 2019; Stroman, 2019; Stuart, 2015). In the school environment, this could look like the following.

- Reviewing the content of next week's lesson with a colleague, if you're feeling a bit confused and overwhelmed with how to best present it to students
- Observing your colleague teach a particular learning target because his class achieved better scores on the common formative assessment
- Asking the school counselor and social worker for some new strategies to work with a particular student, because although you thought you could handle it (and dismissed their offer to help last week), you are still not connecting with this student and need some support and guidance
- Apologizing to a colleague for dismissing an idea she brought to the team's attention; you were tired and reacted poorly, and are hoping she will extend you some grace

Humility defers to others in some cases, since it "means you recognize that others may have a better way of doing things or an idea that's stronger than the original, and that you welcome these differences, celebrate them and actively try to incorporate them into the workplace" (Birt, 2023). There is the potential for humility to model respect as well, since, "Instead of focusing on reaching our own potential solely, we understand that we can help propel others along the way" (Johnson, 2019). As such, both individuals and teams can expect higher levels of productivity, better ideas from improved innovation, stronger professional relationships, and, as a culminating impact, increased happiness that generates improved retention through the intentional ways we practice and model humility (Birt, 2023).

How Do I Get Myself Ready?

Embracing one's authentic self involves treating yourself with compassion and care. But what does that actually look and feel like? How will you know when you're there? Positive psychology researcher Courtney E. Ackerman (2018) offers that you have achieved self-acceptance when you can "accept every last bit of what makes you who you are, and when you no longer try to mitigate, ignore, or explain away any perceived faults or flaws—physical or otherwise."

Make Friends With Your Flaws

In the Madeleine L'Engle (1962) book *A Wrinkle in Time*, there is a scene when the lead protagonist, Meg, along with her brother, Charles Wallace, and her friend, Calvin, are on a journey to find her father. The children are about to be abandoned by the three fantastic beings (Mrs. Whatsit, Mrs. Who, and Mrs. Which) who have been their guides thus far, but not first without sharing a few important gifts. Charles Wallace and Calvin are each bestowed gifts that enhance their existing character strengths—resilience and communication, respectively. However, when it is Meg's turn to receive, Mrs. Whatsit turns to Meg and says:

> "Meg, I give you your faults."
>
> "My faults!" Meg cried.
>
> "Your faults."
>
> "But I'm always trying to get rid of my faults!"
>
> "Yes," Mrs. Whatsit said. "However, I think you'll find they'll come in very handy on Camazotz." (L'Engle, 1962, p. 112)

Meg is perplexed. She doesn't understand how her faults—namely, her stubbornness—would be an asset in their quest to find her father.

Haven't many of us, like Meg, been conditioned to assume that faults are a sign of weakness? If we are not good at something, or cannot make something work correctly, then that generally isn't an area of our lives that we choose to promote. In fact, most of us protect ourselves by keeping our faults hidden from the rest of the world. We may rationalize this protection, in that if we choose to let only the brightest and proudest parts of our being shine for others to see, our hearts can be protected from any unwanted judgment, gossip, or shame.

Take a few moments to engage in the reproducible "Self-Assessment—Embracing Authenticity" (page 74) self-assessment, or visit **go.SolutionTree.com/school improvement** to download a free copy. You may need to read it and then let the questions marinate a bit before responding. The only person who needs to see any of this is you, although you may choose to let others benefit from your thoughtful reflections and awareness as well. Your reflection about your step forward could be the impetus that someone else has been waiting for—seeing someone who is brave enough to stop accepting certain ways of being that counter their ability to truly embrace their authenticity.

Remember that a key factor in embracing our authentic selves is honoring both our strengths *and* weaknesses. You know you are not the only person in this world who is more successful at some things than others. I'm sure you're already playing the list through your head; what you want to improve at, what you wonder if you'll ever learn, what you think people must say when you attempt to do *X* task. So how about we try this instead? Can you think about your faults as FAULTS: *f*abulously *a*uthentic and *u*nique *l*imitations, *t*endencies, or *s*hortcomings? An acronym makes everything better, right? In all seriousness, not a single one of us is perfect, nor will we ever be. We should not spend *one more second* in pursuit of a version of ourselves that will not come to fruition. However, these fabulously authentic and unique limitations, tendencies, or shortcomings of ours provide an opportunity for thoughtful, productive self-examination as we consider reasonable goals and next steps.

Aren't you curious about what prevents you from making the changes necessary to improve your skill set, gather additional knowledge, or find ways to circumvent what is currently holding you back? Such honest conversations and reflections about who we are as compared to who we might *want* to be will deeply enhance our efforts to create authentic classrooms. I believe your personalized efforts will display courage and confidence to your students, thoughtfully nurturing learners who can self-examine with the same level of self-acceptance as you are growing to give yourself.

Take a moment to consider one of your current FAULTS. Now, determine if that fault is something you want to (and actually can) change about yourself. Then, complete the reproducible "Connecting to One of My FAULTS" (page XX), which poses the following questions, with that in mind.

- Which favorite or most compelling of your FAULTS (*f*abulously *a*uthentic and *u*nique *l*imitations, *t*endencies, or *s*hortcomings) do you want to address today?
- What has been getting in the way of you making a move forward?

- What additional knowledge, encouragement, or resources would get you to take the first step?
- Who will you seek out as your accountability partner?
- When will you begin?

As you pursue your next steps in acknowledging and accepting your authentic self, consider some additional strategies:

- Celebrate your strengths.
- Practice self-gratitude by listing what you're grateful for in your life each day.
- Forgive yourself.
- Accept your weaknesses and imperfections, and know that acceptance simply means you're accepting that something is a reality without passing judgment on it.
- Be kind to yourself, which includes taking care of your body and mind. When you're talking to yourself in a fashion that seems mean, ask yourself if you would talk to a friend that way.
- Don't compare yourself to others. For some, this may mean creating a healthy boundary with social media.
- Believe in yourself. (BetterHelp Editorial Team, 2023)

Although it can be challenging to simultaneously accept ourselves and express our true selves to others, we can be empowered by our efforts to simply do our best with what we have at the time. Consider this perspective:

> Truly humble people are able to offer this kind of gift to us because they see and accept their own strengths and limitations without defensiveness or judgment—a core dimension, according to researchers, of humility, and one that cultivates a powerful compassion for humanity. (Zakrzewski, 2016)

That is a powerful acknowledgment and space from which to grow.

Focus on Social Capital

A common question asked when I work with teams is: *How can I be vulnerable in front of my colleagues, given the risks of judgment, gossip, and being ostracized from them*? I respond to their question with a question of my own: "How are you currently growing your social capital within your team?" Most often, I get quizzical looks from the group. Let me explain.

Former associate editor of the *New School Economics Review* Will Kenton (2022) defines *social capital* as "a set of shared values that allows individuals to work together

in a group to effectively achieve a common purpose." While the idea is typically used to describe how humans are able to co-exist peacefully and fruitfully, there is a value in understanding the role of social capital within our school teams as well. In its simplest and purest form, social capital honors how people work together around a shared purpose for the greater good. School teams place high value on growing positive relationships with students from the beginning, and the same care and commitment applies to relationships among the adults dedicated to those students and their well-being.

Kenton (2022) further highlights research around two types of social capital: (1) bonding and (2) bridging. *Bonding* represents the connection within a group (think grade level or department), while *bridging* recognizes the connections built across groups (think across grades, departments, and roles). So how does this work in a school system? Building your social capital during unstructured moments throughout the school day is a safe, natural entry into growing relationships. Where do you see possibility in your environment for spontaneous connections with your colleagues? How can you show openness to sharing about yourself and getting to know others? Figure 2.3 shows an example, and the reproducible "Spontaneous Connection and Sharing" (page 77) is available for you to write in. Make sure to check out the ideas in the upcoming section, How Do I Get My Students Ready? (page 67), for building social capital with your students.

Ways to Encourage Spontaneous Connection	Ways I Can Open Myself to Others
Post a vision board or personal photos in your work space, prompting opportunities for discussion when people visit your classroom or office. Stand outside your classroom during passing times or before and after school to greet your colleagues, since your presence suggests your availability for conversation.	Make deposits that develop or deepen collegial relationships; reference something positive or affirming about your colleague. Speak up during a staff meeting; ask a question or advocate for or against a practice or decision. Suggest various wellness or socialization opportunities, such as walking the halls during prep periods or spending optional time together after school or during lunch.

FIGURE 2.3: Spontaneous connection and sharing.

Each of these strategies falls into that area of being easy to assert but hard to live by in the moment. About this, remember that "your additional confidence may also be a draw to the people you're trying to meet" (BetterHelp Editorial Team, 2023). I like the sound of that! It seems like a good space to start growing into and a mindset we can all bring to our collaborative teams.

How Do I Get My Team Ready?

The work to establish authentic, inclusive learning environments becomes a bit more complicated when you take it outside your own classroom walls and navigate these elements with all the members of your team, department, or grade level. And while trust is critical to collaboration, vulnerability—which is crucial to authenticity—is pivotal to establishing trust (Breuer, Hüffmeier, Hibben, & Hertel, 2019).

Talking with your teammates and colleagues about designing authentic classrooms will be most productive when the following two components are in motion.

1. You have authentically examined (or are in the process of examining) your own identity and have taken a step toward unconditional self-acceptance. This is a labor of love, and will likely be a journey for the rest of your life. But you have to be comfortable with who *you* are before embracing this discussion as a team. Use the reproducible "Self-Assessment: Embracing Authenticity" (page 74) as a place to start.
2. As a team, you mutually see value in having similar spaces of belonging and self-acceptance for adults and students at school. If all members of the team are willing to accept collective responsibility for the *academic* success of each student, you can focus on the precursory work of accepting that same collective responsibility for validating each student's and adult's *authentic identity and sense of belonging* in the school environment.

As noted, a critical aspect to this work is establishing trust on the team. David Horsager (2012), who writes about the concept, defines *trust* as:

> The natural result of thousands of tiny actions, words, thoughts, and intentions. It doesn't happen by accident, nor does it happen all at once. Gaining trust is work. Knowing that you need it isn't enough; you and I have to do the little things on a daily basis to earn it. (p. 45)

I refer to this definition often in my own work to support the development of collaborative teams. The part that resonates most often is *doing the little things on a daily basis to earn it.* Building trust—and keeping it—is more likened to a marathon than a sprint. It's an investment rather than an installment.

You may be familiar with the adage that trust is gained in drops but lost in buckets. As such, it's important to ask what attributes, behaviors, and attitudes represent the trust drops we implement with consistency to gain the investment we desire.

We, too, must lay the foundational pieces for trust to prevent us from going astray. Let's consider an example in practice.

Many teams and organizations love to kick off a new year with some kind of retreat, serving as an opportunity to network and foster personal connections between staff members around their professional shared purpose. It reminds me of a scene from the movie, *Remember the Titans*, when the head coach of a segregation-era high school football team leads his players through a grueling camp experience to work on the fundamental skills required to bring them a winning football season, while also demanding that his team come together to get to know each other as people. And you know what? It worked. The racial divides that had the potential to determine the team's fate were overcome, and the boys returned home from camp as a different group of players—until they weren't. When the boys reunited on the first days of school, it appeared as though the connections and fellowship developed during the course of camp were a distant memory. The stresses around the political implications of desegregating schools and friends suddenly feeling pressure to choose sides caused some players to retreat back into the comforting, familiar ways of the past.

There is a lesson for us in this example. What went wrong? What considerations or conversations, during the retreat, could have prepared the players for the realities that awaited them once they returned home? Fortunately, the team was able to lean into the bonds they created and were seemingly emboldened by the opportunities to leverage those connections to overcome the unique challenges presented—and they did indeed have a winning season.

As you think about the scenario, consider how often you and your teammates have experienced a similar dissonance. Everything is fine at "camp," but once you return to your classrooms and engage in the realities of a variety of student needs—with potentially not enough support to adequately respond—how does your confidence and dependency on one another represent the amount of collective trust you have built? Do you lean on each other or fall back into the isolation of your own classroom or office? In what ways can each of your voices be represented in the collaborative design and development of systems, structures, and strategies for the good of your team? The following sections present three actions to get the drops of trust flowing: (1) learn each student's name and needs; (2) connect with a four-square share; and (3) bridge with sentence starters.

Learn Each Student's Name and Needs

The notion of learning each student's name may seem obvious, yet this can prove to be difficult when you have more than two hundred students on your roster (or more than one thousand across the grade level). As a team, this practice is important and also connects to a relationship mapping exercise (page 99) that you learn more about in chapter 3.

Learning each student's name is challenging, but it's important because using students' names does the following:

> builds classroom community, increases student engagement by helping them feel more comfortable, makes students feel more accountable to the instructor, ensures students are comfortable seeking help, and increases student satisfaction with a course. (Cooper, Haney, Krieg, & Brownell, 2017; Murdoch, Hyejung, & Kang, 2018; O'Brien, Leiman, & Duffy, 2014, as cited in Poorvu Center for Teaching and Learning, n.d.b)

Make a point to ask students what they prefer to be called, including nicknames or monikers, and what their pronouns are (if law allows), rather than simply rely on what name appears on your roster.

In addition, ruthless equity leader Ken Williams (2022a) reminds us that "what you focus on grows" and all people grow when they are able to lean on and cultivate their strengths (p. 122). To learn about students' strengths and what conditions your students need to grow those strengths, consider asking students, in various ways and times, the following questions in support of establishing a learning environment grounded in support, reflection, and acceptance:

> What are you passionate about?
> How do you want to be recognized?
> What do you see as your greatest strength?
> What name do you want used when calling on you in class?
> What will a successful school year look and feel like at the end of the year?
> What are the characteristics or attributes you want in a teacher? (Pitler, 2017)

Think about how useful that information would be as you start a new year or semester with students. Furthermore, as it relates to students' needs, what information is typically included about each student when you receive your class roster? How is each person's name and need listed? For example, is the roster littered with labels that reinforce low expectations and further marginalize certain students, or does your roster invite you to be curious about what students *can* do, and how students will learn more because of the quality of your instruction and the scaffolds you provide along the way? As you embrace your responsibility to move each learner to and through proficiency, a clear message is sent to our students on how they are indeed meant for more.

Connect With a Four-Square Share

As you begin the process of accepting responsibility for each student's learning and feeling ownership for the team's work, learning about how each of you shows up in the workplace will be critical to maximizing your efficiency and effectiveness. The strategy presented here can be quite useful for newly formed teams or also for teams whose members have not yet spent much time together. It is one of my favorites because of the dialogue and discussion it evokes from the members of the team. Here are the steps.

1. Have all team members grab a half sheet of paper, divide it into four quadrants, and write one of these phrases in each box, as illustrated in the reproducible "Four-Square Share" (page 79): Assets, Misunderstood, Hot buttons, and Need.
2. Invite teammates to write their response to the following questions in the appropriate spaces (and let people know they will be sharing responses with each other).
   + What assets do I bring to this team?
   + In what ways might I be misunderstood?
   + What are my hot buttons (things that upset me during collaboration or professional learning)?
   + What do I need in order to be at my best?
3. Encourage teammates to share their information and record the collective thoughts from the group.
4. Look at your collective lists as a group, and use the following reflection questions to further define your purpose and potential as a team.
   + As you review your *Assets* list, which attributes are most connected or will be most beneficial to helping us achieve our mission?
   + As you review your *Misunderstood* list, how can we take steps to avoid these misunderstandings during our collaboration?
   + As you review your *Hot buttons* list, how might we acknowledge these concerns now, in order to prevent them from interrupting our work?
   + As you review your *Needs for being at my best* list, look back at the *Assets* list. Can someone's asset provide support for someone else's need? What skills and attributes do we already have on the team to create the most productive environment possible?

Review the sample Four-Square Share in figure 2.4 from a team of administrators I worked with; we used the tool to bridge the space between colleagues as well as build relationships across new members of the team.

Assets We Bring	Ways We Can Be Misunderstood
Humor Desire to improve Willingness to work hard Experience Idea generator Open to new ideas Good team player Build relationships Ability to work with others First instinct isn't "no" Hard worker Big heart Organized Detail-oriented Positive mindset Students first Systems thinker Embrace change	Flying the plane as I'm building it doesn't mean I haven't thought things through. I'm a multitasker; it doesn't mean I'm not paying attention. My conversations overlap with others'. Some think I overfocus on getting work done. Asking questions doesn't mean opposition to ideas. I hold back information because I'm protecting confidentiality. My facial expressions may convey negativity not intended. I don't always see other points of view because I'm in my own head. He's a rule follower. I need details before I can move forward. Talking too much doesn't mean I'm not listening or being insensitive.
Hot Buttons	**Needs to Be at My Best**
Disrespect to me or others Lack of follow-through or preparation "That's the way we've always done things" mindset Interrupting others or not letting every voice be equally represented Secrecy Not pulling own weight Lies or half-truths Lack of shared commitment Big, surprise mandates to implement or be excited about Not holding true to norms or agreements	Come prepared, and do your part Food! Idea generators Feedback on the ideas to make a better plan The why of the work Feel part of a team Slides and notes provided to know where I'm going Teamwork Honesty Feeling supported Have fun!

Source: © 2023 by Jolene Comer, Trisca Mick, Todd Schuster, Amy Shannon, & Tara Zehr. Adapted with permission.

FIGURE 2.4: Example four-square share.

You may also consider using the top half of the reproducible "Self-Assessment—Embracing Authenticity" (page 74) as a primer for identifying some of your own traits and qualities. As always, feel free to put your personal spin on this exercise as well.

Bridge With Sentence Starters

You may find that specific, concrete activities are best for nurturing an authentic, inclusive environment. Question stems that provide two options—*Are you this or that?*—or statements on index cards can present opportunities for impromptu yet intentional activities to ground and connect professionals as *people* first, which in turn connects us to their authentic selves (and to our own authentic selves).

Individuals can interpret the following sentence starters with whatever emotion or response they choose. Sometimes, it's a more serious sentiment and other times it's a laughing-so-hard-we're-crying sentiment. For example, you might pose the following fill-in-the-blank statements to your team as an impetus for dialogue and connection:

Sometimes, I wonder if I'm ______________________________ enough.

I'm hurt when people call me ____ because ______________________________.

I know I'm doing good work because ______________________________.

The reproducible "Engaging Every Voice With the Help of Sentence Stems" (page 80) offers examples of ways to engage every voice in a meeting space.

Another option is an activity called, Are You More? Each person draws a slip of paper and responds to the prompt on the paper. For example, some prompt options might include:

- Are you more sunrise or sunset?
- Are you more carnivore or herbivore?
- Are you more ocean or mountain?
- Are you more center stage or balcony?
- Are you more carry-on or checked baggage?
- Are you more email or snail mail?

No matter which strategy you choose (or create), the critical action of building social capital through trust on your team cannot be overstated. The initial time commitment and perseverance to do so yields long-term dividends for your collaborative opportunities moving forward.

How Do I Get My Students Ready?

Now that we have taken the steps to prepare ourselves and our teams to embrace authenticity, we are better equipped to walk students through this journey as well. DeLeon Gray (as cited in Bowen, 2021), associate professor of educational psychology and equity at North Carolina State University, explains, "When students feel a sense of belonging in the classroom, it can increase their educational success and motivational outcomes in multiple ways, and teachers can help create this feeling of belonging by building connections between classroom and community." Educator and author Tara Brown (2010) helps us further explore authenticity by differentiating between fitting in and belonging: *fitting in* is changing yourself to be liked by others, whereas *belonging* is about surrounding yourself with people who accept you for who you are. Telling someone "Just be yourself!" might be easy, but it may be difficult for students to actually *understand* what you are saying if they haven't been taught to authentically examine who they are in the first place.

One of the most important responsibilities we must accept is to serve as models of what we expect—in both language and action—so that students see us representing the authenticity we seek. Review the following four strategies and resources to assist in cultivating classrooms that are rich with confident, brave, and self-assured learners: (1) let students be the unique storytellers of their identity, (2) focus on students' strengths and prepare them to use mistakes as learning opportunities, (3) find common ground, and (4) let your students get to know you.

Let Students Be the Unique Storytellers of Their Identity

When we place labels on others or ourselves, we limit people from achieving what they are capable of. However, when we let students write their own narrative, they gain both self-efficacy and self-awareness. That happens as they determine what they want to share so they and others can further celebrate or nurture it. We explore how validating storytelling can be in chapter 3 (page 83) and learn how story can empower student voice in chapter 5 (page 153). However, storytelling is connected to our first *Meant for More* attribute of embracing authenticity because how comfortable our students (and staff) are at school impacts their ability to engage and invest in the learning environment overall. Consider that "when [student] voice is either heard or silenced, it has an impact on how the student engages in classroom activities and tasks" (Little, 2022).

Spoken-word strategies can nurture storytelling. While spoken word can include all forms of performance-style poetry (think of Amanda Gorman's 2021 presidential inauguration poem, *The Hill We Climb*), storytelling in this beautifully crafted, rhythmic modality captures a listener's attention and allows each story to be authentic and unique. The way we can encourage students to craft their verse, in order to lift their voice, develops a confidence in accepting and valuing both one's authentic self and empowering stories of authenticity from others as well.

Once we have begun collecting information on students' strengths, we can also learn more about what type of environment will enable each student to best nurture those attributes in the classroom. A brief survey, questionnaire, or profile form can be an effective tool for gathering this type of non-academic information from students; the trick, however, is to actually use the information you gain! Ask students to share about their hopes, hobbies, goals, interests, favorite things, likes, and dislikes. Use what you learn as informal ways to engage with your students and remember that:

> authenticity comes from having actions that match the words we say and not trying to be someone else to impress others. Authenticity helps us to feel confident in ourselves and it improves others' ability to trust us . . . It also helps us create strong friendships and is a very important part of wellbeing. (The Umbrella Project, n.d., p. 1)

The reproducible, "My Learning DNA (Desires, Needs, Assets) Inventory" (page 81) is a helpful tool to explore student authenticity. It not only asks students about themselves but also asks them about their preferred learning environment. (For example, just because you like to have the lights dimmed or music playing during work time doesn't mean that all students can be most productive as learners in that type of setting.)

Focus on Students' Strengths and Prepare Them to Use Mistakes as Learning Opportunities

Helping students identify their assets is an empowering step to creating authentic learning spaces. As we energize students about what they uniquely bring and can contribute for the greater welfare of others, we can highlight how valuable multiple perspectives, viewpoints, and opportunities can be to enrich our own life experiences—both inside and outside of the classroom.

Honoring students' strengths can prepare them to lean into their gifts, talents, and virtuosities when trying something new. However, many students are significantly underprepared to handle a mistake, a loss, or an unexpected result or event. As such, consider how you can design moments in your classroom where students can try new things that are low risk or low value for them, and then model strategies that demonstrate how to bounce back from a situation that didn't go according to plan.

Find Common Ground

Cultivating meaningful, authentic relationships with students can be difficult, but the return on that emotional investment far outweighs the energy and effort to get there: "When teachers are connected to their students, troublesome classroom behaviors actually decrease, as do the number of suspensions and school drop-outs" (Gonser, 2020).

Science teacher Lindsey Kervan (2023) explains her routine for establishing relationships with her students, highlighting a forty-five-second personal interaction and a survey to launch the year in a manner that allows her to pursue connection with each of her students right away. She greets each student at the door with a smile, hands them a short survey to complete, and lets them know there is a seating chart to alleviate any awkwardness from the start about where to sit. The survey poses questions about preferences (inside or outside? the book or the movie?) as well as open-ended questions for students to share information about their interests and learning styles and preferences. As they complete the survey, she plays music to soften the silence as she walks the room, asking students to introduce themselves to ensure she pronounces their name correctly. Kervan (2023) says that this simple, structured practice ensures that she has made a personal connection to each of her students within the first week of the school year, which establishes a space of belonging for her and her students right away; this practice improves her classroom culture because students:

> see you as a person and will be more likely to approach you with questions or issues, since they've already talked to you one-to-one. Students will feel safer and more willing to take educational risks. It allows for a clean slate to build a positive relationship with you, regardless of whatever reputation they came in with. (Kervan, 2023)

Once students feel comfortable in the learning space, they can begin the important process of becoming comfortable with each other. Educators ask students to learn from and with their peers during the course of their educational experiences, and that process will be much smoother if we allow students the time and space necessary to develop respect for and connection to each other.

Try the following steps to help students find common ground among each other.

1. Ask students to circle up and form small groups of three or four.
2. Have each group discover commonalities among them by taking turns asking each other questions—for example, *How many brothers do you have? Do you like football? What month were you born*? Students

should keep track of as many commonalities as they can in a brief, predetermined amount of time (two or three minutes).

3. Extend the activity (optional) by asking group members to share a few of their discovered commonalities with another group.
4. If you have time, mix the teams and play the game again. An even greater challenge would be to make larger group sizes.

For middle and high school students, consider asking students to write an essay about their values and principles or to create an identity chart, drawing their own portraits, with "half the face showing visible characteristics and the other half showing invisible characteristics" (Fleming, 2020).

Let Your Students Get to Know You

In one study, students reported authenticity when teachers were "approachable, passionate, attentive, capable, and knowledgeable" (Johnson & LaBelle, 2017). One way to model such authenticity is to have students provide questions they want to know about their teacher. As you select questions, be mindful that these moments—though intentionally designed—still have boundaries. Teachers, rather than throwing caution to the wind and fully opening their personal vaults, should intentionally engage with students as human beings, not just as their professional persona (Johnson & LaBelle, 2017). That said, just start small. For example, "sharing little personal snippets introduces and reinforces the notion that you have a life outside of the classroom without delving into anything too serious" (Sands, 2017).

On numerous occasions during my tenure as an elementary teacher, I saw shock from students when we crossed paths at the grocery store or other places in the community. My favorite was the incredulous look on the face of the little sister of one of my third-grade students as we saw each other at a concert. She stood behind her mom's leg, peeked around, walked over to poke at me with her tiny finger, and then ran back to her mom squealing with delight. After a few turns of her peek, run, poke, and squeal game, she started saying, "I simply can't believe it, Ms. Freese. It's really you! I can't believe it's you!" Sharing that story brings a smile to my face, and also serves as a joyful reminder to let ourselves be seen by our students as human beings as well as teachers.

Unfortunately, teachers now have to exercise much more caution about what they can and cannot discuss with students. How much connection to your personal life is too much? In addition to starting small, keep it light and considering how your stories might be shared with family members at home (Sands, 2017). Check out the

Meant for MoreMENTUM story at the end of this chapter (page 72) for a glimpse into how one middle school teacher is making it work in her classroom.

What Infrastructure Do I Need to Make It Happen?

Creating spaces that recognize the strengths, assets, and virtuosities of each adult and student in the learning environment has indeed proven more difficult than it seems. Perhaps this is because we have more consistently agreed on what it *shouldn't* look like than what it should. We are less versed in how to intentionally create spaces in our schools that not only notice but nurture each individual's identity. We want to do it, but we've never been explicitly taught how.

Do we know how to create schools that, by design, help individuals accept, behave, and feel confident demonstrating their unique authenticity as well as ensure others are equally as accepting of a person's true identity? Many times, we are nervous to ask others (students included) what they need because we are afraid we might not be able to give them what they ask for. We might fear we do not have the resources or do not yet have the skills needed to respond.

Try it yourself. Think truthfully about what, in your professional environment, you need in order to be the best version of yourself. Feel free to jot your thinking in the margins here or discuss with a colleague or book study partner.

Did you decide, *I need a million dollars*, or *I need the best parking space*? How about *I want the corner classroom with all the windows*, or *I want the best course load*? I venture that while you may *want* those things, they were not the first things that came to mind as you reflected on what you actually *need*. I imagine that the things you truly require sounded more like the following.

- I need permission to be my authentic self.
- I need permission to ask for help and not be judged for it.
- I need at least one co-worker I can trust and confide in.
- I need my team or supervisor to know that I am always trying to do my best work.
- I need to be given grace when I make a mistake.
- I need to find joy in my work.
- I need to be recognized as a value-add to my organization.
- I need a space where I feel like I belong.

Focusing on the intrinsic value of each student and how their unique identities bloom within your classrooms and learning space promotes an authentic *Meant for More* learning environment. Not just *allowing* but *inviting* students to share their stories of who they are, what they believe, or even what they need to be their best in the school environment, as well as celebrating their individual assets and leveraging those as gifts and virtuosities, to authenticate our classroom community.

Visit **go.SolutionTree.com/schoolimprovement** for a free reproducible "Chapter Summarization Tool to Inspire Action" and use its prompts to refresh your ideas and reflections from what you read in this chapter.

Meant for MoreMENTUM: Stories to Ignite Us

Mrs. Shantelle LaFontaine-Larson (more fondly known to her students and families as *Mrs. La-La*) pursued teaching after a first career in another field. The experiences of her twin daughters, who both were entitled to special education services, inspired a career change in her mid-thirties; Mrs. La-La knew that she simply had to become a teacher, if for no other reason than to do her part to ensure each student had access to a caring, compassionate adult.

She shares, "At my core, I try to be the teacher that I want my own children to have. As a parent, I didn't feel I had that with my own children. As I reflect on the time that my own daughters were in special education, I believe there were only two teachers who truly cared about my children. We'd be sitting at their IEP meetings, listening to people talk about my kids like they were talking about my car muffler! Indifferent, impersonal, and technical. But my daughters had personalities, dreams, aspirations, and goals. How did these adults see that in my girls? Where was the conversation about who my kids were as people?"

As a middle school language arts teacher, Mrs. La-La takes full advantage of her ability to impact students in their most impressionable years. She starts each year with a "Meet Ms. La-La" slide deck, sharing about her family and her dog, as well as some fun facts: her love of polka dots, her belief that there are two seasons in Minnesota (summer and buffalo plaid), and that Will Ferrell is her favorite celebrity. She reminds her students that she used to be a middle schooler once, and when they gasp in disagreement that it couldn't possibly be true, she shows them her seventh-grade yearbook picture. She talks openly about the kind of language she expects in her classroom, teaching with stories from her experiences and those of her daughters from their middle school days. And most importantly, she shares with her students, "If you think this stinks right now, remember that this is ***not*** the definition of your life. This is three years of your life, though, and I'm here to help you get through it."

One of the ways she shows her students that she is there for them is through an initial assignment. She asks students to pen her a letter. It serves two purposes: (1) it is a beginning-of-the-year writing sample, and (2) it shines a light onto each of her students. The letter has to be three paragraphs all about them, and that is the only requirement. The students get to pick the topic, and then Mrs. La-La uses that sample to help students set personal goals for their writing development over the course of the year. Some students share openly, and others are more reserved. Mrs. La-La comments, however, that this one assignment has helped her connect so deeply with students, learning about their triumphs and their losses, their energies and their fears. She writes personal responses back to each student, thanking them for their letter and making a connection or two to root the relationship for the months (and years) to come.

In addition, she introduces a changemakers project for her students. She uses the life and legacy of the late Supreme Court Justice Ruth Bader Ginsburg to describe the elements of this project to students; namely, because this one woman walked the earth, there are laws that help make the world a more equitable place for women. She then connects this assignment back to her social and academic expectations for her students: "We are each building our personal legacies every single day. We are leaving our mark on the world with each word, each thought, each action. We need to lift each other's voices to let our legacies be known. So, think: how do I want to be remembered?" (S. LaFontaine-Larson, personal communication, February 9, 2023).

"When we believe each individual has inherent intrinsic value, we demonstrate an understanding that each person is worthy of respect and dignity, can achieve their goals, and deserves to belong within the school community."

Self-Assessment—Embracing Authenticity

<table>
<tr><td colspan="3">Directions: Use the prompts to reflect on specific moments in your life that have helped you learn more about who you are and what is important to you.</td></tr>
<tr><td colspan="3">Think about a time when you helped someone else.</td></tr>
<tr><td>What qualities or traits do you possess that contributed to your success?</td><td>How did your success make you feel?</td><td>How did your success make the other person feel?</td></tr>
<tr><td colspan="3">Think about a time when you were proud or achieved a goal.</td></tr>
<tr><td>What qualities or traits do you possess that contributed to your success?</td><td>How did your success make you feel?</td><td>How did people you care about react to your success?</td></tr>
<tr><td colspan="3">Think about a time when you made a mistake or didn't get something you really wanted.</td></tr>
<tr><td>What reaction did you have when you were not successful?</td><td>How did not being successful make you feel?</td><td>How did people you care about react to your situation?</td></tr>
<tr><td>As you review your responses, list your favorite traits or qualities about yourself.</td><td colspan="2"></td></tr>
<tr><td>What do you notice about how people reacted to your situations, and how did that make you feel?</td><td colspan="2"></td></tr>
</table>

Given your responses, can you select or determine between four and six words that best describe who you are or what is important to you? Write them on the following lines. 1. ____ 2. ____ 3. ____ 4. ____ 5. ____ 6. ____
As you think about your responses in the preceding section, what parts of your identity do you choose to share with other people? Why do you prefer to nurture those parts with others?
As you think about your responses in the preceding section, what parts of your identity do you choose to keep private? Why do you prefer to keep those parts to yourself?
Is there anything about your identity that is hard for you to nurture? Why or why not?
What if a part of your identity that you want to keep private (or that is hard for you to nurture) was revealed to others? Consider the benefits and challenges of that situation. How would you react? What do you think you would do?

Favorite Parts of My Identity	Least Favorite Parts of My Identity

Who would be there to support you as you explore your least favorite personal attributes?

How do you know this person (people) would support you?

Circle something you wrote in the Favorite Parts column. You don't have to do anything with it right now. Just know it is there, waiting for you to notice and nurture it, when you are ready.

Connecting to One of My FAULTS

Which favorite or most compelling of your FAULTS (*f*abulously *a*uthentic and *u*nique *l*imitations, *t*endencies, or *s*hortcomings) do you want to address today?	
What has been getting in the way of you making a move forward?	
What additional knowledge, encouragement, or resources would get you to take the first step?	
Who will you seek out as your accountability partner?	
When will you begin?	

Spontaneous Connection and Sharing

Chances for Spontaneous Connection	Ways I Can Open Myself to Others

Four-Square Share

Assets	Misunderstood
Hot Buttons	**Needs for Being at My Best**

Engaging Every Voice With the Help of Sentence Stems

Sometimes, I wonder if I'm ______________________ enough.

I am hurt when people call me ______________________

because ______________________ .

I know I'm doing good work because ______________________ .

I find ways to persevere by ______________________ .

My greatest learning has been ______________________ .

I will never apologize for ______________________ .

I am a value-add to this team because ______________________ .

My ______________________ is my

hero because ______________________ .

I aspire to be ______________________ so that

I can ______________________ .

My Learning DNA (Desires, Needs, Assets) Inventory

Directions: This learning DNA inventory will help you and your teacher get to know your learning preferences. Please complete it to the best of your ability, then share it with your teacher. Hold on to it throughout the school year, adding, modifying, or deleting entries as you encounter new learning opportunities.

My Desires:

My future goals and aspirations are ________________________________.

My favorite activities and hobbies are ________________________________.

My favorite topics are ________________________________.

My favorite space to learn is ________________________________ because

________________________________.

My Needs:

I would like to continue to grow in my understanding of or ability to ________________.

One thing that challenges me is ________________________________.

I get stressed when ________________________________.

When I am stressed, I need to ________________________________.

When I am studying, I like it to be some place ________________________________.

My Assets:

I am interested in learning ________________________________.

I am interested in doing ________________________________.

My talents and personal gifts are ________________________________.

One thing I have learned about myself is ________________________________.

I know if I am to be a successful learner, I have to ________________________________.

Strategies I use to help me be successful when I need to study are ________________.

Strategies I use to help me be successful when I am confused are ________________.

Volume	Quiet	Loud
Light	Dim	Bright
Social Interactions	Private Just me alone in a room (in a coffee shop, for example)	Public A room full of people

Source: Erkens, C., Schimmer, T., & Vagle, N. (2019). Growing tomorrow's citizens in today's classrooms: Assessing seven critical competencies. *Bloomington, IN: Solution Tree Press.*

Chapter 3
Fostering Connection

I was once part of a conversation in which someone asked me if I could weigh in on some paperwork that had come home from his son's school. It was the start of a new semester, and the teacher had sent home a get-to-know-you form for students to complete. At first glance, the form appeared fairly neutral in that it asked students to share their passions, activities, likes and dislikes, and any personal hopes and desires to create an academically and emotionally successful classroom environment. At first, I didn't understand why he wanted my feedback. In fact, I was just about to tell him how excited I was that his son's teacher was intentionally gathering feedback from her students to create a place of belonging for her classroom when, visibly exasperated with me, he said, "Angie, look *here*! I mean, what is *that* all about?"

Under the space where students were to write their name, there was also space for students to indicate their preferred pronouns. Truthfully, I had simply scanned past that part of the form in my analysis of the other content. However, this father was upset that the school was "actively teaching" students that there were multiple pronouns. He indicated it was confusing to his son, who knew the individual-possessive pronouns as *she/he, hers/his,* or *her/him*. He didn't understand why it mattered and why the teacher couldn't just talk to "those students" privately about their preferences if they were different from what he called *normal*. The father then told me he had taken a picture of this form, posted it on social media with the caption, *Look what they are teaching these days in school!*

As you may imagine, there was a dynamic series of commentary that ensued. The father ultimately had to remove the post, as a few people began using the Comments section as a back-and-forth argument with increasingly hurtful and hateful language. The father, looking incredulously at me, said, "What do you have to say about all this? I mean, do you think the principal even knows what this teacher is sending home? Maybe I should just call the superintendent."

Take a moment to write your answers in figure 3.1.

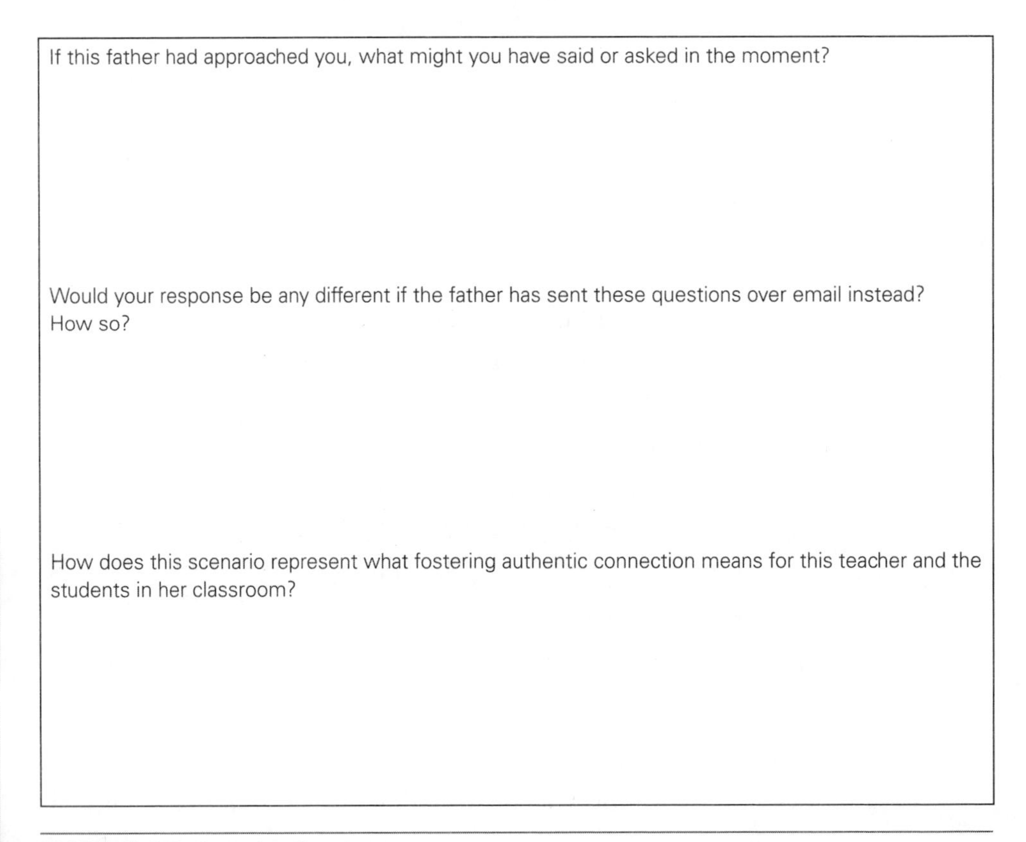

FIGURE 3.1: Story reflection.

To create a safe, inclusive environment where students truly feel connected to both the learning space and the people in it, we have to recognize that patterns of thought—like the one presented in the preceding story—are well established in our school systems. Jung (2023) affirms this reality by stating, "Policies, practices, and procedures perpetuate this exclusion and reflect the discrimination we see in society as a whole" (p. 36). As such, students, families, and colleagues across the globe stand ready, waiting for us to systemically create authentic, inclusive learning spaces where each unique individual can truly belong.

What Do We Mean by *Fostering Connection*?

Fostering connection may be rooted in both an understanding and demonstration of empathy. It may prove difficult for you to connect with one of your colleagues or students if genuine concern for their well-being is unsteady. Our students are looking within our schools as one place to find a sense of belonging and authentic connection with other people. Empathy is the ultimate counter-narrative to a culture where students feel there is only one "normal"; where they either need to adapt or figure out a way to survive.

One way you can define *empathy* is as a "concerned response to another person's feelings; it involves thinking, feeling, and even a physical reaction that our bodies have to other people when we relate to how they feel" (Harvard Graduate School of Education, n.d.). The assertion here continues that while we should recognize and embrace other people's feelings, we also need to show compassion toward them. While compassion and empathy are connected, compassion is a result of feeling empathy. This generally proves to be far more difficult than we imagine.

Yet the more we can honor and validate people's responses to their circumstances, the more empathic we are perceived to be. And most importantly, the likelihood of the development of a deep, meaningful connection will improve. Jung (2023) adds the following:

> Students need to be in an environment that is safe, embraces diversity of all kinds, one that is engaging and accessible, promotes belonging, and celebrates the many ways students can show their skills and understanding—no single way is "right" or "best." (p. 6)

Consider your student body's composition. Are there certain types of learners who you work harder to connect with than others? While it is unlikely that you will have a similar relationship with each student in your classroom, you can turn to some productive strategies in support of your efforts. The following sections outline three such strategies to honor within the *Meant for More* classroom: (1) prioritize students over content, (2) make deposits in students' individual emotional reserves, and (3) let students speak.

Prioritize Students Over Content

We know that our students lean on us for more than just academic content and knowledge. As we build trust with students, they will soon seek our opinions and guidance on all matters that affect their life. Whether it be world news or neighborhood news, it has become necessary to navigate these types of conversations when the details and emotions spill over into the classroom. We do not need to have all the answers to students' questions, nor should we try to. Instead, we can learn to create spaces where students can feel comfortable talking with you and in front of their peers about the issues, challenges, or conflicted feelings they may be experiencing.

The COVID-19 crisis exemplified how we grossly underestimated the impact of missing connections and relationships for our students. We've always been aware of the health benefits—both physical and mental—of engagement between and among students, and a global health pandemic certainly magnified the critical need for those social and emotional connections.

For example, when students return to school each fall, we may be deeply intentional about cultivating relationships, getting to know our students, and letting them get to know one another. However, those engagement exercises typically cease after the first few weeks. The good news is that we can continue prioritizing students' needs by way of our content delivery—planning, pacing, and yes, even assessment. We can leverage that content relevance so that students see themselves in the learning and understand how it connects to their own lives.

Make Deposits into Students' Emotional Reserves

In his book *The Seven Habits of Highly Effective Families: Building a Beautiful Family Culture in a Turbulent World,* Stephen R. Covey illustrates the concept of an emotional bank account and explains that:

> By proactively doing things that build trust in a relationship, one makes "deposits." Conversely, by reactively doing things that decrease trust, one makes "withdrawals." The current "balance" in the emotional bank account will determine how well two people can communicate and problem-solve together. (Covey, 1997, as cited in Wilson, 2018)

When we struggle to connect with our students, we could first reflect on our need to make more deposits into students' emotional reserves.

One of the easiest yet often overlooked ways to foster connection with students is to converse with them and provide positive feedback. While we can honor students' accomplishments and recognize their awards and achievements, we can also foster deeper connection with students by acknowledging what attributes, habits, or routines enabled them to arrive at the levels of success that they did. For example, "That was a great project!" as compared to, "That was a great project! I know you have invested a lot of time into your models and prototypes, and your efforts really showed." Notice how the specificity in the latter statement is more likely to connect with the student since the feedback was connected to observable behavior rather than an obscure reference.

Students are going to make mistakes. You are too. Yet because you have invested the time and energy to make authentic, purposeful connections with your students, you can more effectively maintain students' respect if and when you share more constructive feedback. We can make deposits that hold our students accountable without blaming or shaming them (Brown, 2015; Hamilton, 2017). In fact, "blaming hurts the blamer more than the one being blamed. It drives us apart. It pushes the responsibility off on someone else—and thus, removes any reason for us to improve or do better" (Hamilton, 2017). Consider opportunities to practice this type of deposit with your colleagues and students. Such language could include, "Even though it wasn't the outcome you wanted, you learned a lot along the way and know what to do next time to improve" or "Today, things didn't go according to plan, but let's try again tomorrow."

How much positive feedback does it take to overcome the negative? The answer, discovered in the 1970s by psychologist and relationship researcher John Gottman (1999), concludes the ratio is five to one. That means one hurtful turn of phrase can essentially unravel five previously communicated kind words or actions. Everyone gets richer when the deposits are made.

Hear What Students Have to Share

Sometimes your students just need someone to talk *at* rather than talk *to*. It is OK to set aside our personal agendas or advice we have learned along the way in order to simply let students *speak*. *Active listening* is a communication skill defined as being fully aware of and concentrating on what a person is saying with the goal of truly understanding and hearing what another person is communicating (Aguilar, 2016; Cuncic, 2022; Sudderth, n.d.). Active listening "involves going beyond simply hearing the words that another person speaks but also seeking to understand the meaning and intent behind them" (Cuncic, 2022).

By removing distractions and fully attending to students' language (verbal and nonverbal) in this space, you may see one of several things happen. Sometimes, students share details with you that enable you to get the right support systems in place. Other times, students talk their way through the problem and come to their own conclusion or solution (which then deserves your praise and acknowledgment!). On certain occasions, students' voices will demonstrate a pattern that enables you to respond and take action—for example, you hear lots of buzz throughout the day about an Instagram post from one of your students regarding the concern over some graffiti in the third stall of the bathroom on the second floor.

In addition, author and educational consultant Elena Aguilar (2016) states, "when we ask questions, and when we're genuinely curious about what students say, we are communicating an authentic desire to get to know who they are beyond their test scores and beyond what other teachers may share." Forming a habit of active listening can result in a better understanding of who your students are, what they need, and how you can provide support and encouragement. Your genuine interest in your students, as well as your validation and affirmation of what they have to say, fosters connection in the *Meant for More* classroom by dignifying the unique experiences they bring to your classroom.

How Do I Get Myself Ready?

As educators, one of the ways we can develop our own empathy is to actively seek and lean into other people's stories, particularly people who we are less familiar with or who have lived experiences outside of our normal socialization. We further realize how empathy is related to connectedness when reviewing the work of Daniel Goleman, author of *Emotional Intelligence* (2020), through the exploration of his description of three types of empathy: (1) cognitive empathy, (2) emotional empathy, and (3) empathic concern. Let's explore each type more directly.

- **Cognitive empathy:** This type of empathy honors one's ability to interpret and understand what someone else might be feeling or thinking. This awareness, however, is often rational or intellectual in nature and, as such, may not always result in an emotional response.
- **Emotional empathy:** This type of empathy honors one's ability to deeply connect with another person's feelings. Sometimes, this is also referred to as *affective empathy* because the connection or feeling is so overwhelming that the other person can be prone to accepting the feelings of the other as their own. Emotional empathy alone can often

be overwhelming to the individual if it is not also matched with an attempt to resolve that person's feelings.

- **Empathic concern:** This type of empathy is also referred to as *compassionate empathy* because it "involves not only having concern for another person, and sharing their emotional pain, but also taking practical steps to reduce it" (Mind Tools Content Team, n.d.). I, personally, connect with this definition as people's emotions or feelings are rarely satiated from simply acknowledging what they are going through. Empathic concern engages all people involved to act upon the situation and seek resolution to move forward. It shows someone that you care about them enough to engage in the repair and restoration required.

Consider these three suggestions for how to grow empathy in yourself and toward others: (1) be aware of your biases, (2) be mindful when asking questions, and (3) be an active listener.

Be Aware of Your Biases

Each of us has tendencies of bias or prejudice toward certain people or situations, whether or not we consciously identify with them. Our explicit biases are more visible; easy to name and recognize. Our implicit biases are more subtle, and often take intentional efforts to determine what they are and how they have developed. No matter whether explicit or implicit, paying attention to our biases requires deeper self-reflection. This awareness can wake us to our moments of strength and vulnerability as we seek to foster connection with others.

Another entry point for your personal reflections related to empathy might be engaging in a deeper examination of your biases. One such tool to help with this self-awareness comes from Project Implicit (www.projectimplicit.net), a nonprofit organization founded in 1998 that exists for the fundamental purpose of educating the greater community about individual hidden biases and implicit social cognition. The charge of the organization is grounded in "investigating implicit social cognition, or thoughts and feelings that are largely outside of conscious awareness and control" (Project Implicit, n.d.). The organization created the Implicit Association Test (https://implicit.harvard.edu/implicit/takeatest.html), which is an opportunity to respond to various prompts in order to gain insight into your attitude and beliefs about the topic you selected. There are fourteen different tests available, all free, including such topics as weight, gender–career intersectionality, disability, weapons, race, and gender expression.

Many districts have invited their educators to engage in Project Implicit, yet the purpose for doing so may be unclear. An important element of the tests is that the data are completely personal to the person engaging with the tests. Individuals can choose how to respond to the information they receive, which makes it a safe opportunity to gain additional perspectives about a variety of topics.

Be Mindful When Asking Questions

Despite our best intentions, sometimes all logic goes out the window when discussing a topic that is personal or meaningful. If either the content of the discussion or the desired outcomes are high value, the discussion can be laced with emotion. Being unaware of how our emotions can evolve during a discussion, our minds can soon become overwhelmed with defensive or protective responses. Clinical psychologist Madhuleena Roy Chowdhury (2019) connects research to these points:

> Self-regulation is all about pausing between feeling and reactions—it encourages us to slow down for a bit and act after objectively evaluating a situation. For example, a student who yells at others and hits their friends for petty reasons surely has less emotional control than a child who, before hitting or yelling, tells the teacher about their problems.

Such responses rarely enable us to pause and seek understanding, nor do they lead to a place of finding common ground.

In your hunger for clarity, be prepared to ask questions that guide you to answers rather than hold onto unverified assumptions about what another person may be thinking or feeling. Organizational psychologist Adam Grant (2021) poses thoughtful insight to aid our inquiry:

> A sign of intellect is the ability to change your mind in the face of new facts. A mark of wisdom is refusing to let the fear of admitting you were wrong stop you from getting it right. The joy of learning something new eventually exceeds the pain of unlearning something old.

As we seek to understand, two types of questioning strategies can minimize the chances that we evoke defensiveness and instead feel more productive.

1. *Adaptive* questions help clarify thinking (Garmston & Wellman, 2016).
2. *Restorative* questions are designed to heal relationships and foster community (White, 2012).

Using such models of questioning can build trust and promote safety among the participants in a discussion. Examples are given in table 3.1 for your review.

TABLE 3.1: Adaptive and Restorative Question Types

Adaptive Questions	Restorative Questions
What experiences have led to your thinking? I've never thought about it that way. Tell me more about how you see it. In what ways am I succeeding? In what ways can I improve? What will I learn from this experience? What steps can I take to ____________?	How have you been impacted by ____________? How have others been affected by ____________? What did you think when you realized what happened? What has been difficult to process as you reflect on the impact of this incident on you and others? What do you think needs to happen to make the situation right?

Be an Active Listener

Each of us has experienced a time when someone has asked us a question but then didn't seem too interested in actually listening to our response. That probably didn't feel good, and it may even have prevented you from engaging in other conversations or discussions with that person. Everyone wants to feel heard. *Active listening* is a "communication skill that involves going beyond simply hearing the words that another person speaks but also seeking to understand the meaning and intent behind them" (Cuncic, 2022). And, as you know from your work with students and adults, there is a difference between *hearing* and *listening*! This is an important attribute for fostering connection because "educators who seek to understand their students' perspectives are more likely to avoid misunderstandings that harm relationships" (Gehlbach, Brinkworth, & Harris, 2011, as cited in Nishioka, 2019). Your active listening helps determine whether students invest in the learning environment.

Table 3.2 (page 92) gives examples of seven active listening techniques to keep you engaged in a positive conversation with another person.

TABLE 3.2: Using Active Listening in the Classroom

Active Listening Techniques	Classroom Example
Be fully present.	Amid numerous students vying for your attention and plenty of distractions, you can show students you are fully engaged with them with behaviors such as eye contact, repositioning your body so your frame is facing the student, and trying to understand what the students is trying to communicate.
Pay attention to nonverbal cues.	Face-to-face communication can be difficult, especially if many students' conversations are happening over text or online. Students will need to practice observing your cues (gestures, eye contact, head tilts or nods, eyebrow raises), while also being able to practice observing and name nonverbal cues among their peers in the classroom environment.
Make eye contact (depending on the person's neurodiversity and cultural norms).	Depending on a learner's cultural norms or if communication is impacted by neurodiversity (autism, dyslexia, Tourette's) or social anxiety, eye contact can be one method to model your focus and attention when listening to students.
Ask open-ended questions.	Asking questions about the topic, or for more details on the topic, shows the person communicating that you are interested in what they are saying and also invites them to keep talking. Open-ended questions can also help you determine your role in the conversation; are you listening to gather information or to provide advice or guidance?
Reflect what you hear.	Paraphrase what students are saying to model your own understanding and show learners that you are paying attention.

Be patient to let the other person speak without interruption.	You might be tempted to jump into the conversation before the student is done speaking in order to either affirm what they are saying or offer solutions to a problem. Most often, students just need to be heard and sometimes they can reach their own conclusions simply from bringing their thoughts to the surface and speaking them out loud.
Withhold judgment in your responses.	Students are talking with you because they believe they can trust you. As such, unless the student is asking for your opinion or advice, be cautious in how you respond to what they are saying. Even the slightest nonverbal cue or gesture can seem like a rebuke.

Source: Adapted from Cuncic, 2022.

Listening requires patience and discipline. Rather than trying all the preceding strategies, choose one that you already believe you practice regularly. Then, be mindful of your actions in future conversations to confirm that practice is indeed in place. Add one new practice after you have secured the first. For example, I believe I make eye contact with others, when appropriate, and my visual engagement can help the other person know that I'm with them. Since that is a perceived strength, I would start there first, being more mindful of my eye contact during discussions to confirm consistency in that practice as well as recognize when it may be less impactful. However, I am also keenly aware of my tendency to overlap others in conversation, not because I'm trying to be rude or disruptive but rather because I *am* listening. I am excited about the topic of discussion and want to engage in more back-and-forth dialogue; however, that isn't always perceived in the same way I intend. This practice will take more time to nurture as I seek to model empathy in my focus on fostering connections.

Figure 3.2 (page 94) has reflective questions for each of the three practices outlined in this section and offers examples to get you started.

Questions for Self-Reflection	Initial Thoughts in Response
Be aware of your biases.	
What do I notice about my friend or peer group?	*A lot of "sameness," especially socioeconomically with the neighborhood I'm in, the people I work with, and family/friends.* *In day-to-day activities I probably feel most safe and comfortable with the "sameness" and the predictability that offers, but I also find it boring/monotonous. I don't know if I'm more comfortable but am drawn to people that are different than me.*
In which situations am I more comfortable: with people who are more similar to or different from me (including race, gender, ideology, or other social identifiers)?	*Situationally, I find myself most comfortable when there is either collaboration or a shared objective—those factors supersede anything related to similarities or differences for me. I like working with others to accomplish something.*
What do I notice about how I view others' decisions, lifestyles, or behaviors that don't align with my own?	*I am more judgmental toward those that are most like me (or that I *assume* are similar) especially when we have a difference of opinion. I'm generally accepting, curious, and open to those that I perceive as being different—culturally, financially, geographically, race, age, etc. I have much lower expectations of others' "alignment" with me when there are obvious or innate differences. I enjoy learning, listening, and working toward understanding people that are different.*
Be mindful when asking questions.	
When I have difficulty understanding another perspective or situation, how do I typically react?	*Logically, when I'm confident I'm right. I tend to try and persuade people with fact-based arguments. I react with curiosity when I'm not confident that I'm right. I'm a collaborative person who's genuinely interested in understanding other opinions because I think this leads to better decisions.*
In what situations do I have a more difficult time managing my emotional response?	*When I get impatient or feel like there isn't an attempt or interest in understanding my perspective. Also, when I feel a situation/behavior/decision may negatively impact someone I know, love, or work with.*
When I notice an imbalance in how I am feeling or thinking, what strategies help me reset and get back to "even"?	*I often need time. Time to return to balance but also time to process and work through what caused it. I tend to internalize, but venting or speaking the frustration to someone sympathetic to my situation can also help me.*

Be an active listener.	
When I'm talking with another person or group of people, do I listen to what is being said, or am I thinking about what I am going to say next?	This depends on my comfort level in the situation. I think I'm a good listener so I will call it 80% listen and 20% think by default. However, I am not good at being put on the spot so I will quickly move to the inverse of that (20/80%) if a situation or circumstance moves in a direction I was not expecting or anticipating.
What do I notice about the type of conversations that people want to have with me?	Generally, the conversations are analytical, logical, and practical. People appreciate that I listen and empathize/sympathize, but conversations are generally more academic/strategic than emotional/philosophical because those are my strengths. I also notice that while I feel others' emotions strongly, I don't show or share outwardly, so people see me as an even-keeled and rational person and seek that out from me.
What do successful conversations sound like with me? What can I learn from conversations that have been less successful?	I'm not sure what qualifies as a successful conversation, but I will answer two ways: 1. Productive! Clear movement, progress, or influence. I'm not a fan of small talk. 2. I've learned emotion-based conversations with people I trust and am comfortable with have been a significant benefit to my mental health. Having spaces to be vulnerable is important for me; it's healthy because it further strengthens my relationships.

FIGURE 3.2: Example responses on growing empathy and fostering connection with teacher peers.

The reproducible "Growing Empathy and Fostering Connection With Teacher Peers" (page 114) is a reasonable place to begin your self-reflection on your current tendencies for demonstrating empathy and being accessible to foster connections with other people. These moments you find throughout the book to self-assess or self-reflect are not binary; they are neither good nor bad, positive or negative, reassuring or adversarial. These moments of pause exist to support you in the determination of your starting point. And remember, you have full permission to be where you are; staying there is the issue. My hope is that you choose to keep engaging in the work and mapping each next step forward, wherever you may be in your own learning journey.

Continue digging into the questions in figure 3.2 (page 94) to reflect on your current circle, or community, of people you most frequently engage with. The Circle of Concern is an exercise derived through the Making Caring Common Project and was developed to reveal—in students and adults alike—an awareness of when, where, and for whom they may lack empathy. (Visit Harvard Graduate School of Education at https://bit.ly/410uIfP to learn more about this exercise.) The purpose of this tool can be intimidating and feel like something you wouldn't dare approach, yet intentionally examining the types of people, situations, and experiences most comfortable for you can further reveal your biases—however unintentional they may be—and empower you to grow from them. Through that growth, you will be able to foster truer and more authentic connections with your colleagues and students.

How Do I Get My Team Ready?

The conversations you had around embracing authenticity and creating space for each of your unique identities are foundational to this next step of developing teams and classrooms that foster connections. The following three sections examine how your team can: (1) reflect on biases, (2) model empathy, and (3) map student relationships.

Reflect on Biases

As discussed in chapter 1 (page 13), the presence of bias, explicit or implicit, is clear and present. We have some colleagues who are actively promoting safe, inclusive learning spaces and access to literature and resources that describe accurate versions of our national, provincial, or global histories, and other colleagues who are actively neutralizing those efforts. According to the 2022 Trust Outlook Global Research Study, although 89 percent of people believe that diversity is important for a high-performing team, only 24 percent of participants prefer to work alongside people who are different from them (Trust Edge Leadership Institute, 2022).

This large disconnect reveals an urgent need to have some conversation with the people you work alongside each day, if for no other reason than to clarify how each of your individual belief systems will or will not contribute to whether instruction is equitable and accessible. Associate professor and faculty director Tasha Willis (as cited in Bowman, 2020) states:

> By asking the questions and putting it into a public forum, I model that I'm continuing to push myself and asking for that kind of feedback in front of other people . . . That helps humanize me to other people around

me—faculty, staff, and students—and lets them know that this is just part of being human, and that we have all inherited the world as it is.

One idea for team discussion could be using a version of figure 3.2 (page XX) by having team members change the focus from their relationships with *adult peers* to their relationships with *students*. Figure 3.3 is offered as the reproducible "Growing Empathy and Fostering Connection With Students" (page 115).

Questions for Self-Reflection	Initial Thoughts in Response
Be aware of your biases.	
What do I notice about the students in my classroom? In which situations am I more comfortable: with students who are more similar to or different from me (including race, gender, ideology, or other social identifiers)? What do I notice about how I view students' decisions, lifestyles, or behaviors when they don't align with my own?	
Be mindful when asking questions.	
With which students do I have difficulty understanding their perspective or situation, and how do I typically react? With which students do I have a more difficult time managing my emotional response? When I notice imbalance in how I am feeling or thinking, what strategies help me reset for my students?	
Be an active listener.	
When I am teaching my students, do I listen to what is being said or expressed, or am I thinking about what content I need to cover? What do I notice about the type of conversations that students want to have with me? What does successful student dialogue sound like with me? What can I learn from the dialogue or conversations that have been less successful?	

FIGURE 3.3: Growing empathy and fostering connection with students.

Use this information to learn more about the tendencies of your team, build trust, and maximize the assets that diversity within your team or across your student population can bring.

Model Empathy

Referring back to Goleman's (2020) three types of empathy—(1) cognitive empathy, (2) emotional empathy, and (3) empathic concern—consider another strategy: modeling empathy in your interactions with students. As we learn about compassion and empathy, we have grown to understand that empathy is action-oriented. We are at our best as educators when we feel concern for others and then demonstrate empathy through our words and actions in response to that concern. We have already covered a number of these strategies throughout this chapter, but here is a quick highlight reel for your review.

- Respect and value differences by creating inclusive classrooms, assignments, and learning activities. Read more about inclusion on page 54.
- Widen circles of concern and show students how you are doing so. As a team, this links back to your reflections in figure 3.3 (page 97); are there certain students whom you tend to favor, and if so, how can you get to know other students and help them feel more included and connected with you as their teacher?
- Listen closely to others. As a team, this means practicing hearing what other people say and trying to understand what they mean (rather than listening for a pause so you can insert your perspectives). Read more about listening on pages 91 and 172.
- Honor and manage difficult feelings when they arise (anger, loss, frustration, competition). As a team, you can use your collective commitments, team norms, or school mission statements and values to navigate through difficult situations. Read more about helping others manage difficult feelings on page 245.
- Focus on nonverbal communication. As a team, this connects to the idea of being receptive through observation instead. Notice each other's facial expressions, body language, or positioning to determine the level at which you're in sync as a team. (Visit www.amle.org/the-power-of-positive-relationships to gain further insight about Tara Brown's Power of Positive Relationships strategy.)

Map Student Relationships

A final strategy for your team is more broadly known as *relationship mapping* (Harvard Graduate School of Education, 2023). Teacher-student relationships are an important protective factor, or resilience booster, for students. Administrators or teacher leaders can help each student in your school build a positive connection with at least one adult on campus (Gallagher, Dever, Hochbein, & DuPaul, 2019; Zolkoski, 2019). Rather than assume the presence of those trusting relationships for each student, relationship mapping brings intentionality to the process by identifying—student by student—the stable connections that already exist on the campus as well as revealing the students with whom we need to target our collective efforts.

Amazingly, the process doesn't take as much time as you might imagine (think: one staff meeting). Visit https://bit.ly/41n5Xua to read more about the relationship mapping strategy from the Harvard Graduate School of Education's Making Caring Common Project; read further for a quick overview of the process.

The following steps help staff identify students who may need extra support and ensure that all students at your school are linked to at least one caring adult there.

1. All staff review a roster of students enrolled at the school. They can do this on their own time and come together in step 4 to confirm all applicable students are identified and paired.
2. Each adult marks the students on the roster with whom they have a positive relationship, perhaps defined by that student's willingness to approach you, as the adult, with a problem or issue that needed resolution.
3. Staff follows the same process for identifying students who experience risk factors for dropping out or being retained in their current grade level, perhaps defined by students who display social, emotional, or physical needs that interrupt their ability to succeed at school.
4. Staff confirms whether each student in the school community is anchored to a trusted, caring adult.
5. Staff plan for students who are missing a connection. A teacher who is willing is assigned to reach out casually or formally to an identified student to begin the mentoring process.
6. Close the meeting by reinforcing the importance of each student feeling cared about in the school community and showing appreciation for staff participation.

You can also find strategies and lesson plans for grades 6–12 students as well as artifacts showing options for extending the strategy to include student identification of adults with whom they feel comfortable if they need help.

How Do I Get My Students Ready?

First and foremost, don't assume that your students are aware of or have experienced empathy in a manner that aligns with the environments you are attempting to create in our classrooms. As such, be explicit with your students about what empathy is (and what it is not) and why empathy matters. For example, you can teach young learners about empathy by reading stories and talking about the characters' faces or actions so they begin noticing physical displays of emotion in each other. As students get older, you can use language to engage in discussions about what someone is feeling, why they might feel that way, and if or how to respond when noticing others' emotions. You can also discuss empathy through current local or global events. Building bonds and forming alliances with students takes time, and those relationships most definitely need to be nurtured before students can feel capable of trusting teachers or even other students. The following sections offer three strategies to foster lasting, sustainable connections with students: (1) validate through storytelling, (2) develop a social contract, and (3) teach students to CARE.

Validate Through Storytelling

The essence of storytelling is personalization and humanization. A story can draw the learner in and, without much effort or consideration, soften the positional or authoritative space between you and your students. It can interrupt the distance between "the person who teaches my mathematics class" and "*my* mathematics teacher." Do you see the difference? While I am not advocating for you to cross the lines of your professionalism with tell-all tales of your life experiences, I do encourage you to consider the value of letting your students see a part of who you are that can help them better relate to you as a human being. As you model this vulnerability, without pretense or agenda, it will cultivate a space of belonging in which your students will continue to connect with, respect, and learn from you.

The Making Caring Common Project (2021) affirms the use of storytelling as a powerful means of fostering connection by piquing students' curiosity and generating interest in the lives of their peers. The project asserts that [storytelling] can be:

> Especially valuable in prompting students to reflect on their own identities and values, and to recognize that despite people's differing stories, we all

> share commonalities. Stories are a great reminder that we are all human and that we are all capable of bridging difference through understanding and connecting emotionally with others.

Similarly, storytelling is a highly effective strategy that can connect students through relatability and authenticity (Hughes, Oliveira, & Bickford, n.d.). When students have space to listen to their peers, they can more readily learn to validate the feelings, hopes, and lived experiences of the people sitting next to them in class every day. Think about how often students walk by each other in the hallway and have no idea what the other person is going through.

Develop a Social Contract

In addition to the validation strategies in the previous section, we can also take great care to integrate students' identities and experiences by involving them in the planning process for how some parts of our school operate (Marschall & Crawford, 2022). Before students can share their stories, it's critical to prepare our classroom culture in a way that makes it socially and emotionally safe for students to share. This culture creation does not happen overnight, and it also doesn't happen by chance. What does a safe classroom culture look like, sound like, and feel like for students? The answer lies within them.

Classrooms that foster connection are fundamentally grounded within a common set of guidelines and commitments, often known as a *social contract*—one that is often co-created with the students—in order to describe how their classroom environment will model acceptance and inclusivity for each student. These contracts "foster community in the classroom" (Edutopia, 2019). Our experiences may suggest that students want both autonomy and an opportunity to feel ownership in their learning environment, and co-constructing a social contract honors each of these from learners.

I suggest the following considerations as you plan for this discussion with students.

1. Establish the purpose and non-purpose of a social contract.
2. Set expectations for inclusive student engagement.
3. Brainstorm ideas with students.
4. Create a collaborative consensus workshop.
5. Resolve the discussion in order to make a decision.

Table 3.3 (page 102) further describes these conditions and provides suggestions for how to engage your learners in that development.

TABLE 3.3: Conditions for Co-constructing a Social Contract With Students of Any Age

Description	Process Instructions or Questions
Step 1. Establish the purpose and non-purpose.	
Share the purpose of the social contract and how it will be useful in your classroom. The non-purpose (what a social contract won't be or do) is equally as important.	Be sure to leave space for students to add their thoughts on how a social contract could benefit their classroom. Consider using a T-chart to describe the purpose and non-purpose of the social contract.
Step 2. Set expectations for inclusive student engagement.	
Provide your definition of inclusive engagement with students, as well as why this adds value to your classroom.	Do not hesitate to invite student feedback on your definitions, and be open to adding their insights.
Step 3. Brainstorm ideas with students.	
Organize students into dyads, triads, or quads (any larger and there is greater risk of someone dominating conversation) and reveal how brainstorming honors each idea with equal value.	Design an individual or collaborative structure to gather student responses to the following types of questions. You may consider using a graphic organizer to keep the discussion focused on the following questions. How would you like to be treated by me? How would you like to be treated by each other? How do you think I would like to be treated by you? How will we respond if one of us is not honoring the commitments we agreed on?

Step 4. Create a collaborative consensus workshop.	
Show students how to organize multiple perspectives to find patterns and trends (consistencies) in the ideas generated.	Ask students to cluster like ideas from the brainstorm into unique categories. The essence of the cluster can then be wordsmithed into a statement of behavior.
Step 5. Resolve the discussion in order to make a decision.	
Bring students to consensus by modeling a decision-making process that honors value, rather than volume, regarding the insights represented from the group.	Which statements represent clear agreement? Which statements need more clarity or discussion before we can make a decision? What happens when we make a decision?

Another excellent strategy emerges through the creation of *democratic classrooms*, which are learning spaces that promote shared responsibilities so students can actively co-create and sustain their communities. (See also table 5.3, page 184.) In this model, students and teachers co-create a classroom charter in which students specifically identify both their rights and their responsibilities as learners. (Visit UNICEF Canada at www.unicef.org/crc to access a global document that lists children's rights.) Visit www.unicef.ca/en/elementary-resources to learn more about that strategy, which works best for students in grades K–8.

Teach Students to CARE

The National Center of Safe Supportive Learning Environments (n.d.) has long honored the right of students to experience emotional safety at school, defining it as, "how safe a student feels in expressing their emotions in school." Empathy from, and connection with, peers can help create that sense of safety in students.

As a strategy for activating care and compassion in the classroom, Borba (2021) names the CARE acronym to support students as they learn to model empathy: console, assist, reassure, and empathize. She highlights the actions in table 3.4 to use (and role play) in our classrooms.

TABLE 3.4: Modeling Language When Teaching Students to CARE

Action	Examples of Language to Model
Console	"I'm sorry." "I know it's not true." "You didn't deserve that."
Assist	Run for first aid. Call others to help. Pick up what's broken. "Do you need help?" "Do you want me to get a teacher?"
Reassure	"It happens to other kids, too." "I'm still your friend." "I'm here for you."
Empathize	"That happened to me and I was so upset." "I know how you feel." "You're having a rough day!" "You seem [*feeling*]. Can you tell me about that?"

Source: Adapted from Borba, 2021, p. 90.

What Infrastructure Do I Need to Make It Happen?

Creating classrooms that foster connection involves intentional design and diversity of thought to ensure that the following three conditions, at minimum, are in place: (1) prioritize, (2) embed, and (3) notice (and respond) when things appear to be going sideways.

Prioritize School Culture and Climate

When we consider the possibilities for a school culture that focuses on authentic connection, it can feel overwhelming to invest in the development and sustainability of such a commitment. However, we should first take a breath and remind ourselves of two things: (1) we have been doing the best work with the tools and resources we have, and (2) we have to leverage what has already been working as the foundation for what comes next.

While most schools continue to define and describe their culture through their mission and vision statements, the culture actually evolves, as discussed, through the school community members' words and behaviors. For example, three important elements shape a school's culture and determine how people in it actually experience said culture:

- examining carefully the school's practices and policies to ensure that they embody mission and values
- gaining meaningful insight every year from students and adults about their experiences, being conscious of the outside factors—societal values, social media, college admission pressures—that can undermine a school's mission
- working to understand students' subculture, or the world of the young that is typically hidden from adults but that very much influences a school's overall culture. (Blodget, 2022)

As you can imagine, the work of developing a healthy, vibrant, inclusive *culture* of belonging as described here takes time, energy, and a commitment from each member of the school community. Whereas a school's culture is grounded in values, norms, and responsibilities, a school *climate* is often viewed as how those values are expressed relative to how people perceive and experience them.

Four widely accepted foundational elements are necessary for a positive school climate (Prothero, 2020).

1. Strong relationships among and between all stakeholders
2. High expectations with high levels of support
3. Consistent expectations for and responses to behavior
4. Regular feedback that inspires adjustments and actions for continuous improvement

Without these attributes, students and adults alike are simply going to a common space, having common experiences, and yet remain completely disconnected from each another.

In 2023, United States Surgeon General Vivek Murthy addressed the "epidemic of loneliness and isolation" by mapping a framework to intentionally advance social connection across the country. The COVID-19 pandemic catapulted us into isolation; global research on the effects of the pandemic related to connection, belonging, and loneliness demand an urgent response to preserve our safety and stability.

Consider the following four specific actions to consistently promote and sustain an inclusive school culture (Reeves, 2006).

- **Determine what will not change:** Take time with your staff to honor what practices and processes will remain because they have proven to be effective for staff and students in the past. The last thing any educator wants to believe is that they have spent precious time designing the "wrong" work. Preserve trust among your staff by stating what *is* working so that there is momentum for creating what is yet to be.
- **Understand the importance of action:** Be aware that what you say, what you hang on the walls of the school, or what you put on the school marquee means nothing to your students and families if it is not also represented in the actions—policies, procedures, decision-making processes—that define the infrastructure of your school.
- **Use the right change tools for your district:** Some tools help with culture, others help with leadership, and still others might support management. Make sure that the tools and processes you use to support the culture and climate development on your campus are actually designed for that specific work.
- **Be willing to do the grunt work:** Model your commitment to an authentic, connected learning environment by stripping yourself of your role and engaging in that nebulous "other duties as assigned" part of your job. Wipe tables in the lunchroom, wait with one of your scholars when their ride is late, or cover a classroom for a colleague who needs five minutes to recompose themselves after learning their best friend was just diagnosed with cancer. It takes each member of the school community to keep things steady, safe, and inclusive for our students.

Embed Learning Strategies That Promote the Culture You Want to Create

To create an authentic, empathic culture in our schools, we want to consider how the representation of that culture appears in the instructional delivery and engagement of students in the classroom. *Meant for More* classrooms will include activities, tasks, and communication strategies that are both collaborative and restorative.

COLLABORATIVE STRATEGIES

By *collaborative*, I mean that there are learning activities and processes within the classroom that actually allow students to work and create something together. Such experiences include helping students to develop the skills to effectively dialogue and discourse with one another, practice various roles and responsibilities in the classroom, and engage in collaborative thinking, discussions, and production of instructional tasks that best represent the work of a group. Consider the following examples.

- **Try brainwriting:** Instead of gathering the strongest, most self-assured voices time and again in your classroom, use brainwriting as a tool to ensure every student contributes. Pose a question to the class and then have every student write their response on a sticky note. Gather all ideas together and then have students read all the responses, finding common themes, new ideas, or wonderings to support a deeper understanding of the content being presented.
- **Give every student a voice:** Make sure that you have clarified the rules of engagement for classroom discussions or contributions in your classroom. In addition to the norms for dialogue, give students the language they need to clarify thinking, agree or disagree with another comment, summarize, or build on another idea. Phrases such as the following can be effective tools to develop a student's ability to communicate effectively.
    + "To be clear, you're saying . . . ."
    + "I see it differently because . . ."
    + "Adding to what [*student*] said, . . ."
    + "The overall point I'm trying to make is . . ."
- **Use zoom storytelling:** This isn't the Zoom meeting kind of zoom. The exercise works this way (Mulvahill, 2016).

1. With students in a circle, the teacher gives everyone a picture of a person, place, or thing. (You can use whatever aligns with your unit or curriculum.)

2. One student starts telling a story that includes whatever is on their picture. The next student continues the story, and so on around the circle. (Kindergarten and first-grade students might need help for staying on topic and such.)

The students, with teacher help as necessary, can curate the events of their story together with illustrations, actions, or recordings. The point of the exercise is simply to activate students' imaginations in a cooperative, collaborative way. Students can demonstrate they know how to listen to each other and also how to ensure the flow and evolution of the storyline as they create it together.

RESTORATIVE STRATEGIES

Restorative means that the classroom environment consciously monitors the words and behaviors of the learning community and intentionally (and with urgency) responds when part of the community norms or social contract has been compromised. Restorative practices have Indigenous origins: "Global indigenous communities have a long-standing history of living in alignment with what we now refer to as restorative justice" (Marsh, 2019). Whereas retributive practices seek punishment, restorative justice seeks healing and repairing the harm felt in a community (Marsh, 2019). Restorative practices adopted and employed in Western cultures are intended to support students in understanding how their actions affect other people and to, by design, learn from those actions and feel empowered in their own problem-solving efforts moving forward.

The *restorative* work is not equivalent to "I'm sorry." While apologies are part of restorative processes, they become more powerful because they represent specificity in acknowledging what happened, why it happened, what harm the action caused, and how it will be resolved. You can see how—different from collaborative strategies—restorative practices prompt (dare I say, *require*) educators to have robust training prior to attempting to implement such deeply personal work.

Here's a glimpse into the potential for restorative practices to enrich the culture and community within *Meant for More* classrooms. The following strategies (Collins, 2021) are consistently employed in restorative classrooms.

- **Restorative inquiry:** The intended result is to ensure that the initial form of questioning inspires each person to openly participate. This form of inquiry sets the tone for the discussion, in the spirit of seeking to understand rather than place blame, pass judgment, or prematurely determine an outcome. The International Institute for Restorative Practices (IIRP, 2015) affirms that restorative inquiry is designed in such a way to foster genuine listening from all involved participants. This will help any person sharing their story to feel respected and emboldened to speak more freely.
- **Restorative conferencing:** This strategy is a structured, controlled conversation in which the person who was harmed has an opportunity to confront the individuals who caused that harm. Contrary to the reactive nature of consequences imposed through zero-tolerance discipline for any offense, restorative conferencing provides an opportunity to clearly determine both how to best respond to what happened as well as best repair the harm that has been caused. Ted Wachtel (2016), founder of the IIRP, asserts that, "conferencing is a victim-sensitive, straightforward problem-solving method that demonstrates how citizens can resolve their own problems when provided with a constructive forum to do so" (p. 6). Restorative conferences can be used in isolation or as a supplement to historical forms of disciplinary action.
- **Restorative (community) circles:** While the restorative conference often occurs in response to an incident, restorative circles provide space for individuals to share their own story or narrative in an effort to build relationships and activate a sense of community. Circles can be employed for a variety of reasons—from conflict resolution to decision making to relationship development—and have a genuine, long-lasting return on investment. Restorative circles also adhere to a structure in that only one person can speak at a time and only if that person is holding the agreed-upon talking piece. The nature of this structure is rooted in the traditions of Indigenous peoples, and honors that each voice has intrinsic, equal value.

Most importantly, the use of restorative practices with students can ultimately enable them to bypass adults completely in their conflict resolution and empowers them in meaningful conversation with their peers. Restorative practices are not about taking sides but about utilizing strategies that engage multiple perspectives to create an accurate narrative that was collaboratively constructed by all parties involved. The effort required to foster connection may indeed feel frustratingly slow and with frequent setbacks, but that is normal. Building authentic connection is a labyrinth of intricately designed, meaningfully sequenced experiences that create a learning environment where students truly belong. That's an investment I contend we can each get behind.

Wilma Mankiller, recognized as the first woman Principal Chief of the Cherokee Nation, is quoted as saying, "One of the things my parents taught me, and I'll always be grateful . . . is to not ever let anybody else define me; [but] for me to define myself" (as cited in Brando, 2021). As we learn to take the time necessary to nurture collaborative and restorative practices within our school and classroom communities, we can foster conditions for empathy and voice to emerge from these connections.

Sarah Miller and Malik Peer, founders of Diversity Equity Outreach Consulting (www.datewithdiversity.com) and the Diversity Awareness Training Emphasis on Equity partnership, coach others for continued personal or team growth in areas such as equity, mediation, and restorative practice. They have also developed a framework for inviting adults and students to engage in discussion together. Caring and Committed Conversations (CCC) is a process they crafted to guide conversations that "value diversity, honor differences, and celebrate commonalities by elevating student voices" (S. Miller, personal communication, February 15, 2023). A CCC emboldens students to share about the lived experiences that have explicitly and implicitly impacted their lives in a structured environment, which offers safety and trust to all participants. These conversations leverage a circle formation, which is grounded in Indigenous recognition of how that arrangement promotes community, equality, and a balance of position or power. One way a CCC is different from other conversation models is that it encourages the listener not just to hear the story of another, but to open themselves to be *impacted* by that story, and then use the information and insight gained from that story to inform the listener's thoughts, words, and even actions moving forward. Sarah continues, "During the conversation, everyone has a chance to be seen, heard, and represented. Every*one* gets to experience every*one's* experience" (S. Miller, personal communication, February 15, 2023).

CCCs are, at their core, moments that seek to understand. They are not superficial connections or places for individuals to think they have "done something" simply because they engaged in one of these discussions. Rather, these conversations remind us that the journey is not a linear series of tasks to be completed. CCCs are crafted to help us see each other as human beings first. By hearing students' stories and insights, teachers have space to deepen relations with their students and are, as part of the process, encouraged to reflect on what they have learned. This new insight could impact the climate within a classroom learning space, types of learning activities, or revisions to protocols and processes within the school that could interrupt the issues or injustices communicated by students. The process elevates student voice by having the *student* take the lead on selecting a topic for discussion and crafting the message they want to share with the participants. When we offer students a space to speak, we develop their capacity to effectively advocate for their needs. The Meant for MoreMENTUM story at the end of chapter 5 (page 185) provides more narrative on this specific type of experience.

Notice and Respond When Things Appear to Be Going Sideways

Very likely, you have witnessed an uncharacteristic behavior from a student. The normally reserved student lashes out during whole-group discussion, or the previously self-controlled student hits another student during an argument. This is a cue. Because we have built positive, healthy relationships with our students, these moments become entry points of curiosity. Not every student wants you to get involved. They don't need to be rescued, and don't even *think* about hovering with "Are you sure you're OK?" But sometimes, students do need to know that you noticed. You see that they are struggling with something, and you are leaning into the strength of your relationship to say, "I'm here for you if you need me." Just notice, so that you can open the opportunity to nurture if the student wants it.

As you reflect on the students in your class, close your eyes for a minute. Picture a student with whom you found (or find) it difficult to connect. Was there a strategy or exercise in this chapter that you wish you could have utilized with them? Is there still a way to foster the connection or repair the relationship? What may have happened to turn the tables—in either direction? May that experience continue to both humble and inspire you to create the conditions that foster connection with each of your students in the months and years to come.

Visit **go.SolutionTree.com/schoolimprovement** for a free reproducible "Chapter Summarization Tool to Inspire Action" and use its prompts to refresh your ideas and reflections from what you read in this chapter.

Meant for MoreMENTUM: Stories to Ignite Us

Melissa Vogler, a seventh-grade social studies teacher in South Washington County Public Schools, fosters connection by creating a classroom environment where students feel safe to take risks and make mistakes because they know they will come out OK on the other side. This type of environment was a priority for her, given an experience she had as a sixth grader. She recalls being in a classroom where her teacher posed a question to the classroom, and no one responded. Melissa wasn't too sure of the answer herself, but she knew this teacher from first grade and decided it was safe to take the risk and offer a response. Melissa shared her answer, and knew immediately, given the look on her teacher's face, that it was wrong.

The teacher shouted, "No!" in a tone that Melissa interpreted as, "My goodness, child, what are you thinking?" Melissa had been humiliated by a teacher who had known her for five years. For the remainder of the year, Melissa bent her head and did her work, but she didn't openly offer participation in another lesson. When she became a teacher, she vowed to never make a single student feel the way she had.

As such, she takes great care in cultivating a learning environment in which students feel comfortable putting their voice in the learning space. She opens every period of her seventh-grade U.S. history course with a bellringer, an opening activity intended to provoke thoughtful discussion between peers. Since Melissa encourages choice in seating arrangements, the students are often seated in different chairs each day, which means that occasionally students are asked to engage with a peer that they may not know very well. However, because Melissa knows her students so well, she can recognize where discussions may need a little bit of her support; she hovers around certain student pairings to affirm their comments, drop new questions in this space, or perhaps invite a neighboring pair to join and keep the conversation propelling forward. Though her students perceive these moments as informal, Melissa is quite intentional about her organization and structure so students can feel a certain way when they walk into her classroom.

She shares, "It's not that complicated. If students like being in your classroom and they like being with you, then classroom management and student behaviors are not an issue." One of the ways that Melissa gets her students to open up to her is by creating classroom conditions grounded in mutual respect. She knows that her middle school learners understand the purpose of school and also recognize that a majority of their day is going to be spent interacting with their peers and teachers. She starts "with the positive presupposition that my students know what they are supposed to be doing and as they acknowledge what are currently doing, they are fully aware of whether or not that is aligning with the expectations of my classroom or school in general." As such, when students need her grace—because they didn't do their homework, turn in a project yet, or are inappropriately working in groups—she provides students with the grace of asking students "What's your plan?" or "What's your next move?" Just because students don't always do exactly what they are supposed to doesn't mean they don't deserve your grace when they make mistakes.

What is Melissa most proud of as an educator? She shares how her recent school year had been her hardest yet; the United States was emerging into a less rigorous phase of the COVID-19 pandemic, and students were simply not ready for full days of in-person school. It was as if they had forgotten how to treat each other, and Melissa had to completely help rebuild her students' understanding of how to function in a classroom community. It was rough. But Melissa reports that those same students who had detached themselves from school and all the responsibilities that come with it began regularly finding her in the hallway or swinging by her room to say hello. Her insistence on connection reminded her students what they deserve, both from themselves and from each other (M. Vogler, personal communication, February 15, 2023).

"Listening requires patience and discipline."

Growing Empathy and Fostering Connection With Teacher Peers

Questions for Self-Reflection	Initial Thoughts in Response
Be aware of your biases.	
What do I notice about my friend or peer group? In which situations am I more comfortable: with people who are more similar to or different from me (including race, gender, ideology, or other social identifiers)? What do I notice about how I view others' decisions, lifestyles, or behaviors that don't align with my own?	
Be mindful when asking questions.	
When I have difficulty understanding another perspective or situation with students, how do I typically react? In what student situations do I have a more difficult time managing my emotional response? When I notice an imbalance in how I am feeling or thinking during student situations, what strategies help me reset and get back to "even"?	
Be an active listener.	
When I'm talking with another person or group of people, do I listen to what is being said, or am I thinking about what I am going to say next? What do I notice about the type of conversations that people want to have with me? What do successful conversations sound like with me? What can I learn from conversations that have been less successful?	

Growing Empathy and Fostering Connection With Students

Questions for Self-Reflection	Initial Thoughts in Response
Be aware of your biases.	
What do I notice about the students in my classroom? In which situations am I more comfortable: with students who are more similar to or different from me (including race, gender, ideology, or other social identifiers)? What do I notice about how I view students' decisions, lifestyles, or behaviors when they don't align with my own?	
Be mindful when asking questions.	
When I have difficulty understanding another perspective or situation, how do I typically react? In what situations do I have a more difficult time managing my emotional response? When I notice an imbalance in how I am feeling or thinking during student situations, what strategies help me reset?	
Be an active listener.	
When I'm talking with another person or group of people, do I listen to what is being said or am I thinking about what I am going to say next? What do I notice about the type of conversations that people want to have with me? What do successful conversations sound like with me? What can I learn from conversations that have been less successful?	

Chapter 4

Cultivating Curiosity

During a conversation with Katie, an educator friend of mine, we—as anticipated—effortlessly toggled between personal and professional stories as we shared a Sunday morning Zoom call. However, one story especially piqued my interest as she talked about a past learning activity she facilitated in art with her ninth-grade students.

Katie had tasked her students with creating a work of art that would elicit an emotional response for the viewer. Students could choose any method or medium with which to work. Katie first facilitated a whole-group brainstorm of provocative topics, from reproductive rights to the Holocaust, and then, as each was ready, students set off to let their artistic representations unfold. My friend shared joyful memories of what her students were able to create—even beyond her own expectations—and then paused as she recalled how difficult this task was for one of her students (we'll call her *Julie*).

Julie was quick to let Katie know how much she just *loathed* the idea of this project; upon reflection, Julie presented a disdain for this particular course in general. Julie was a highly accomplished student, knowing how to pursue and accumulate points in her quest for the grades she desired. This assignment in Katie's course, however, didn't have a recipe per se. There were, in fact, fewer boundaries regarding how the project should be done, and students were being called upon to invite personal creativity and perspective into how they approached and created their final product. Katie had numerous conversations with Julie, attempting to draw out her reservations and determine how to best help her student navigate such visible discomfort with the task. Julie revealed how she could not tap into her own creative potential because she felt more confident when she simply had to *re*produce something that had already been done before. Julie had been able to proficiently "do" school in part because she had learned the formula: complete this specific assignment, using this specific criteria, in order to acquire this specific number of points, which will result in this specific grade. Her struggle was with the idea of producing something entirely new.

Julie couldn't see how to use the information she had learned about how to approach a new challenge nor could she work through an experience that may be familiar but had a new twist for how it was to be done. Julie had a comfort zone from which she knew she could perform well. Her past success hadn't required her to be creative or curious. She simply didn't know what to do when she had an open-ended starting point with goals that felt unfamiliar.

Take a moment to answer the questions in figure 4.1 and write your answers.

Which students in your classroom or on your campus remind you of Julie?
Why should we be concerned about students who feel like Julie does?
What connections can you make between certain teaching styles and moments of student apathy toward learning? Between certain teaching styles and moments of active engagement in student learning?

How can we, as educators, stay curious about different ways for students to complete a task or approach a problem to be solved?

FIGURE 4.1: Story reflection.

Think back to Julie. Here she was, following the rules, adhering to the conditions for success, and drawing the metaphorical line from point A to point B. In her mind, that's what she needed to do. And those behaviors and patterns of thought at school had largely enabled her (and many other students) to be successful as measured by grades. But what Julie had not yet been taught is that learning can also be a beautifully messy process. It isn't binary and it certainly doesn't function in a straight line. One intent of this manuscript is to bust the myth that schools are places where teachers explain things to students, rather than places of curiosity and wonder where students can explore. Terrell Heick (2021), founder of TeachThought, affirms:

> In school, we tend to "schoolify" things so that they "work" in a classroom. This often means that whole and full and interesting "things" lose their heads and tails so that we can squeeze them into a timeframe, assessment form, or the like. By returning some content to its more natural "state," curiosity can be encouraged.

This chapter explores how to initiate curiosity in your classrooms so that students can chase their interests and discover their true passions.

What Do We Mean by *Cultivating Curiosity*?

Inquiry-based learning, *passion projects*, or *learner-driven content exploration* are terms and phrases you may have come across in your educational career. You may have even been part of a school or district that latched onto this student-centered concept, decided to implement it (without adequate thought or intentional design), and as it became overwhelming to plan, manage, and resource, *inquiry-based learning* was ceremoniously added to the list of things doomed with the fate of *this too shall pass*. This is unfortunate, however, because the idea of designing classrooms where students have the resources and space to wonder and be curious, in order to help them pursue their demonstration of mastery of content, should not be something seen as a fad or the next big thing in education. Honoring and dignifying student curiosity through connection and relevance to content is a natural, respectful, and sustainable way to heighten learner engagement as well as promote academic growth and achievement. For example, when children are curious, they demonstrate an openness to new ideas or new ways of thinking, are more willing to take risks in learning, and become creative problem solvers (Bakkegard, 2023; Borba, 2021; Price-Mitchell, 2021).

It doesn't take more than anecdotal observations of any daycare, classroom, or playground to recognize that children are inclined to be learners by doing rather than learners by listening. Developmental psychologist and researcher Marilyn Price-Mitchell (2021) confirms, "Curious children spend time reading and acquiring knowledge because they sense a gap between what they know and what they want to know—not because they are motivated by grades." The Pedagogy of Play research team at the Harvard Graduate School of Education studied the impacts of play when intentionally built into the learning environment (as cited in Mardell et al., 2016). While observing middle school students at the International School of Billund in Denmark, the researchers saw students drawing a map of the world—on an orange. Students were utilizing the resources in the classroom, such as atlases, maps, and globes to then draw their representation of the world on a three-dimensional sphere. Then, students peeled their orange to see how the view changed when the Earth's surface was flat. When the researchers asked students about the experience, they honored moments of confusion, laughter, attention, and—most importantly—engaged, active learning. In response to their observations, the research team asserts:

> Creating and operationalizing such a pedagogy [of play] requires a school culture where playfulness is celebrated, examined, made visible, and better understood as a powerful pathway of learning. Indeed, bringing play into a central role in a school entails creating a culture that values the core tenets of play: taking risks, making mistakes, exploring new ideas, and experiencing joy. (Mardell et al., 2016)

Our students are regularly exposed to simultaneous, competing stimuli and are quickly learning how to adapt and navigate as part of their development. They are self-regulating and selecting options that provide them joy, laughter, and security while also becoming quite proficient in decision making. Our students' apathy and disengagement in some types of learning environments at school may be symptomatic of two distinct elements that not all learning environments can accommodate: outside of school, (1) students have a broader level of access to whatever they want to learn about, whenever they want to learn about it, and (2) students regularly engage in an emboldened decision-making process, which enables their confidence to advocate for choice about their learning pathway.

As educators, our continued quandary is how to balance the requirement of having students learn the essential content for each course or grade level while also delivering the instruction in a manner that is relevant to each group of learners. Without purposeful collaboration (*what* we mean [and don't mean] by classrooms that enable students to pursue their passions, *why* this is a pathway worth pursuing, and *how* to effectively design and implement such a learning environment), this type of thinking can feel more like a free-for-all instead of a thoughtfully designed, engaging learning model for our students.

Meant for More classrooms are not solely inquiry- or passion-based. That's not what this chapter is about, and there are plenty of other resources available, like those listed here, if you are interested in exploring this topic more deeply.

- *Hacking Project-Based Learning: 10 Easy Steps to PBL and Inquiry in the Classroom* by Ross Cooper and Erin Murphy (2016)
- *Teaching for Deeper Learning: Tools to Engage Students in Meaning Making* by Jay McTighe and Harvey F. Silver (2020)
- *"PBL Is for White People": Debunking Lowered Expectations* by Charity Moran (n.d.)
- *My Students (of Color) Aren't Ready for PBL: 6 Examples of Implicit Bias* by Joe Truss (2022)
- *Thinking Through Project-Based Learning: Guiding Deeper Inquiry* by Jane Krauss and Suzie Boss (2013)

However, embedding time and space for this purposeful collaboration is a productive means for teachers to learn about students' interests, learning styles, and preferences so that deeper levels of student engagement and achievement can occur. We explore ways to provide explicit instruction to remind students how to be curious and reignite their *inner kindergartner;* the playful spirit that once defined how they actively learned about the world around them. This construction of self-awareness in students gives them a frame of reference to make informed choices about what, when, and how they can demonstrate mastery of content when such opportunities are presented in the learning space.

Think back to the story of Katie and Julie in this chapter's introduction (page 117). Katie's request of her students was not something she pulled from her passion-based or project-based learning drawer. It was, however, an intentionally designed and executed lesson in which students were able to make their own meaning and relevance of the content as they thought through how to display what they had learned in a way they found personal and meaningful. Katie shares further:

> I don't want my students to approach a creative task with the idea that they are going to simply replicate something they can already create. I worry that kids are learning to reproduce things that they have already done before, but for a new audience—like a new teacher—and that they will just continue to apply skills that are already quite well-honed and create products or performances that are familiar to them. That's the challenge of creativity; people often want to sit in their own pocket of comfort—which is OK, we want to encourage that—but there has to be a catalyst that disrupts their thinking. (K. White, personal communication, November 13, 2022)

If we continue to administer instruction and develop learning environments based on the status quo, our students will be ill-equipped to see the possibility of what could be; as a result, they will inevitably demonstrate a heavy reliance on what they already know to solve their problems. For example, Katie asks students to engage in another art project using acrylic paint on paper. But before they begin, she asks her students to go to the back of the room and choose five things to first affix on their paper with glue, then paint over the whole page with one solid color and *now* create their project on top. It's a similar task, but now students must consider how to navigate around the new textures.

Students are actively problem solving in new ways to map out how they planned to use their papers. For example, a student says, "I want to paint a bowl of fruit and had planned to put the orange in the middle, but now I have this doily over here, and so I'm rethinking my composition." This type of critical thinking can flourish when the classroom environment is designed for creativity: accepting errors, promoting risk taking, and—perhaps, most importantly—involving humor and laughter as part of the learning experience (Dow & Kozlowski, 2020).

Imagine this type of learning experience as opposed to asking students to only review selected samples from Pierre-Auguste Renoir, Vincent van Gogh, and Paul Cézanne to *recreate* a bowl of fruit. Organizational psychologist Adam Grant (2017) affirms this thinking: "If no one ever argues [with what has always been], you're not likely to give up on old ways of doing things, let alone try new ones." I assert that it would indeed be dangerous to continually promote status quo thinking and ways of being as productive approaches to the challenges and issues facing our ever-evolving world.

Is this the generation of scholars we need—students who simply reproduce examples of what's already been done, engaging with problems that have already been solved, and using thinking that further perpetuates a narrative of stagnancy? I think not. Instead of either/or thinking, let's explore the concepts of both/and. A *both/and* experience is when multiple experiences or feelings, which often are perceived to be in conflict with one another, are simultaneously sensed or faced, making both things true (Buck, 2020; Epstein, 2021). For example, you can *both* love being a parent *and* cherish the time you have to yourself. Both sentiments can be true. The both/and concept connects to the strategies and stories to come in this chapter; we can have consistent, highly reliable teaching strategies and instructional methods, *and* we can offer unique, relevant pathways for students to demonstrate their learning. We can teach high academic standards *and* employ heightened relevance, creativity, and curiosity for how students approach tasks. This chapter provides information that can equip you to make choices about how to break through this tiring narrative of either/or and instead generate ways to deliver both/and experiences.

Even if you do not yet have the capacity to engage students in the pursuit of their intellectual passions and curiosities, creating environments where students are encouraged to ask meaningful questions and actively pursue their answers is linked to our previous learning on embracing authenticity and fostering connection in *Meant for More* classrooms. As the following sections demonstrate, *Meant for More* classrooms can cultivate curiosity if we choose to (1) value inquiry and investigation, (2) build student capacity for self-advocacy, (3) provide structure, and (4) have fun.

Value Inquiry and Investigation

In an era of instant access to almost any information we need or desire, we literally have knowledge at our fingertips. You can ask students to extend their concentration and study a topic in order to engage in (and learn to love) the anticipation of finding an answer to a question. The late Romanian-French playwright Eugène Ionesco (as cited in Wells, 1998) famously said, "It is not the answer that enlightens, but the question" (p. 15).

We want to ignite a passion in students that makes them hungry to know something, and then be motivated by the new questions that emerge from those answers. We can leverage that perspective in our context of curiosity in the *Meant for More* classroom, citing how "questioning, critical thinking, and the creative development of new knowledge through inquiry are as important (if not more so) to learning as information finding through research" (Britannica Education, 2016). How might you consider ways to set aside time for students to explore an area of curiosity? For example, Google expects their employees to dedicate 20 percent of their work time toward the development of new knowledge or skill sets (Clark, 2021). Imagine if schools functioned under the same mindset. What possibilities can you see for collective or individualized student exploration in your classroom?

Review some examples to engage learners of all ages in inquiry and investigation.

EARLY ELEMENTARY SCHOOL

Many students at this age are what I call *walking wonderisms*. They are curious about most anything and everything, asking questions that start with "How come . . . ?", "What would happen if . . . ?" or "Why does . . . ?", among other things. Harness this wonderment by praising and encouraging it.

You can collect student questions about a topic using digital tools such as Nearpod or Padlet, or students can sketch a version of their question (or have a teacher dictate it) on an anchor chart in the classroom.

One of the primary challenges teachers face, however, is what to do with all those questions that their students are asking. Occasionally, you may sometimes feel it is easier not to allow students to ask questions because either you don't have enough time to respond to everything or don't know how to find the answers. Push through that feeling and engage your students. Learning happens all the time at school—whether or not someone is asking questions—but when students have a chance to learn about something of interest to them, we can improve engagement and rigor simultaneously.

UPPER ELEMENTARY AND MIDDLE SCHOOL

At this age, students may show a refinement in curiosity. This includes the normal yet sometimes frustrating demonstration of skepticism. As they grow their independence, consider leveraging their natural doubts by modeling *positive skepticism* (Price-Mitchell, 2023). For example, during a seventh-grade critical thinking course, students needed to advocate for a position (for or against) regarding an identified issue. One student was assigned to defend cosmetic testing on animals. It was difficult for her; while she acknowledged her limited understanding of this practice, she was adamantly against it. After researching, she learned about the reason for the practice, as well as the resulting impacts and discoveries. She explained that she would not personally advocate for the practice, but understood why it was happening. Through her investigation, she was better equipped to empower her voice (more on this in chapter 5, page 153) and show the reasoning behind her thinking through the use of evidence, rather than relying on unexplored information to craft her thoughts. Her skepticism was actually strengthened, through inquiry, into valid argumentation.

MIDDLE OR HIGH SCHOOL

You might feel apprehension about inquiry's messiness, lack of structure, or free time, but:

> the more voice and choice students experience in the classroom, the more structures and processes the inquiry teacher utilizes to best support students with having more agency over learning. Whether these structures are student check-ins, 1-on-1 conferences, Google Forms reflections, or small teacher-led seminars to introduce a needed skill or understanding, structure is a critical feature in the inquiry classroom. (MacKenzie, as cited in Burns, 2018)

Students can brainstorm topics of interest or relevance and research them during dedicated time in the classroom. Rather than promoting inquiry as a what-to-do-when-you-are-finished-with-the-work-assigned strategy, you can embed this type of learning into unit and lesson plans and include a culminating project to present their findings.

Also, consider feedback's importance since "When you praise students by describing how their questions, explorations, and investigations are contributing to their own or classroom learning, you let them know that they are valued for their motivation, regardless of the grade they achieve" (Price-Mitchell, 2021).

Build Students' Capacity for Self-Advocacy

During a walk through any classroom, from preschool to high school, you are likely to hear, "Does anyone have any questions?" or "Does anyone need help?" but no response. You know some students would benefit from some extra support or information, yet no students raise their hands. You ask again, this time highlighting a specific part of the task that has been problematic for others in the past, hoping your encouragement will prompt at least one voice. Still nothing, but you know they have questions. For example, maybe one student needs to review the directions privately with you. Another student may need to remind you that she requires scaffolds for this assignment, per the accommodations listed on her IEP. These students need help learning how to advocate for themselves.

To self-advocate, students must find their own voice to effectively communicate what is essential to or important for them. This skill has lasting impact, since "People who know how to self-advocate are more likely to do well in school, work, and life. They often feel confident in what they're learning and doing" (Lee, n.d.). Building self-advocacy in students brings such value to the classroom. While it is important to define what *self-advocacy* means in general, we also want to define how it can look and feel in the classroom environment. Although it may not necessarily be part of your required standards or instructional resources, a resulting impact of self-advocacy is that people who demonstrate this skill can describe what they want and develop a plan for how to get it.

These principles of self-advocacy become clear with a relevant student scenario:

> If you're a strong self-advocate, you **understand** that taking notes is going to be a challenge for you. You **know** that support like pre-printed notes may help. You **communicate** your challenge to the teacher and ask for pre-printed notes. If the teacher says no, you know you can reach out to a counselor or other person for help. (Lee, n.d.) [Bold in original]

This example honors a student's ability to recognize a need, consider what might help them to resolve that need, and then let others know about the need so they can help. This can be particularly important for students who already feel marginalized, including students of color, LGBTQ+ students, students who are gender nonconforming, students suffering under the stress of living in poverty, students who are suffering from anxiety or depression, or students who have varying abilities within the classroom. Jung (2023) reminds us that "to reach all, we must reach each." Building healthy, sustainable relationships with each student to honor their unique strengths (as discussed in chapter 2, page 49) and foster deep connection (as discussed in chapter 3, page 83) can also pave the way for students' capacity for self-advocacy.

Students who can self-advocate not only feel more control over their learning environment, but also provide themselves with the authority to make decisions that will best enable their success. Look for more on this concept in chapter 5 (page 153). To get you started, here are some possible strategies for your consideration. You'll find that some of the strategies listed in the table have been highlighted in previous chapters—and some are yet to come. In addition, you can easily adapt the strategies in table 4.1 for any age group.

TABLE 4.1: Age-Appropriate Strategies for Teaching Self-Advocacy

Preschool
Give students language to ask specifically for what they need: For example, instead of "Can I use that marker?", students could ask, "Can I use that yellow marker? I'm drawing a picture for Ms. Kennedy and I need to color the sun yellow."
Provide opportunities for independence: Although it would be faster to zip up that jacket, tie those shoes, or put on mittens for your students, build some time into the schedule to allow them time to complete such tasks on their own. A little productive struggle is important; children build confidence while also learning to recognize when they just need a little more time versus when they actually need support.

Elementary School

Role-play situations and practice what to say: If a student needs more time to complete an assignment because it is a struggle, you could model this interaction for students or even use a student or two in your classroom to role-play the scenario with you. Anticipating students' needs and proactively using role-play or modeling can be a passive form of permission, so to speak, giving students the confidence to ask for what they need because you have modeled that it is safe to do so.

Provide agency with decision making: Providing choice to students, within reasonable and appropriate scenarios, is integral to supporting a student's ability to advocate for themselves. For example, you could ask students to determine whether they want to work alone or in pairs, or work at their seats or find a more comfortable place in the room. We explore how to partner with students for decision making in chapter 5 (page 153).

Middle School

Let students know you're on the same team: Students are flexing their independence more consistently at this age, and sometimes they get tripped up in those first moments when they go it alone. As such, remind students that you are their biggest advocate and will engage in a conversation with them when it's needed or requested (and that you won't always get that part right). It's appropriate to let them know that you are still figuring out how and when to support them.

Praise students when they do speak up: Students may hesitate to speak up in front of peers. For example, a student across the room from you is tapping a pencil. You hear it, and one glance at the students sitting close to the pencil tapper suggests they hear it, too. As the noise continues, one student puts her hand over her ear and keeps writing with the other, one shifts in his seat, and a third keeps glancing at the person tapping the pencil. Finally, the third student walks over to you and communicates the issue and what he needs. You praise the student for advocating for himself and ask if he would like to ask the other student to stop or if he would like your help doing it. This small affirmation emboldens him to address the other student directly. The student who was tapping the pencil is apologetic and ceases doing it. You later praise the self-advocating student again, sharing how, in this case, going directly to the student was both brave and productive.

High School

Volunteer, work, or be a community helper: Students can practice self-advocacy skills when operating in a different, less comfortable environment than school or home. Learning how to balance your own needs as you recognize the needs of others (including your boss) can be beneficial for navigating social groups or workplace environments and cultures in the future.

Teach (and model) determination: It's important that students set goals, understand how to achieve those goals, and then demonstrate a tenacity to start and finish. Self-advocacy is a set of skills that develops over time, but we can help students by providing clear expectations and time and space for them to determine their next right moves.

Source: Adapted from Borba, 2021; Lee, n.d.; Schreiner & Falardeau, 2020.

However, we cannot be naïve enough to think that students will only harness their self-advocacy in ways that will please us. Students can also demonstrate their self-assurance through unwillingness or even opposition to learning; for example, students can claim self-advocacy by saying they shouldn't have to complete an assignment because something else is more important to them. You may even recall a moment where the beautiful, multifaceted spirit of self-advocacy was fully on display in your classroom. Perhaps you thought, "Well, he is actually making a good case," but the pressures of your team's decisions, curricular pacing, or other factors prompted you into saying the always-unpopular, never-motivating reply, "You have to complete this task because you need to know the material for the test." In these situations, it can be difficult to muster a productive reaction in the moment. You may consider giving students choices in how to complete a task, extending the due date, or—perhaps, most important—talking with the student privately to determine if there is an underlying concern.

Despite all this, self-advocacy isn't always about asking for help. Sometimes, students need more time. Sometimes, they just need a few minutes alone. Sometimes, they need you to notice that they did something to your liking without being reminded. Practicing self-advocacy can help students become more aware of their strengths and therefore establish boundaries that support their success. Remember that, "Self-awareness is a key component to being able to self-advocate—if we're aware of what we want, we can take steps to fulfill these needs" (Schreiner & Falardeau, 2020). As such, if we hear rhetoric in our community that devalues the presence of social-emotional learning in the classroom, we can cite the value of curiosity, innovation, and independence as critical societal markers for promoting self-advocacy.

Provide Structure

If the ambiguity of discovery—coupled with uninhibited exploration and play—are essential ingredients to cultivating curiosity, then where do boundaries and structure fit into this recipe? A common interpretation of structure in the classroom might evoke images of rigidity and adherence to established rules. And while those elements might feel counter to curiosity, let's uncover how structure might actually foster new, rich ideas to explore and interrupt predictability. Routines are important, but:

> You want a process that gets you out of the habit of seeing the most experienced person as the one with all the answers . . . If we can create a culture in which we're not expecting that at all, then we tend to listen much more inclusively to the whole range of people who are participating in an active way. (Eppinger, as cited in Walsh, 2022)

For example, one of your opportunities as an educator is to create an open learning environment to encourage and facilitate the sharing of new ideas and then balance those new ideas with space for them to marinate for a while. Letting a question sit for a minute can create even more anticipation for what is to come! It is reminiscent of the scene from *Mary Poppins Returns* when Georgie wants more details about which game they are going to play next with Mary Poppins. She replies that they are beginning an adventure and to refrain from spoiling it by asking too many questions. While we definitely want our students to *keep* asking questions, the connection here is that Georgie (like Julie from this chapter's introduction) wants to know all the answers and see the full pathway before even starting. Is the content taught in your classroom challenging enough that mistakes will occur, with regularity, or is your classroom a place where students only engage in the work if they know they will succeed?

What's important is to find the balance in your classroom. Describe the nuances of the academic architectural blueprint for your students and then let their emerging ideas for structural design unfold. You see many uniquely shaped buildings in your community, and while they may look different on the outside, they all follow the same rules and principles of design in order to remain standing. Establishing a structure for creativity and innovation can help students better focus their thinking, which promotes an increased likelihood that they will uncover information that moves them closer to resolving their questions.

How can you create the necessary framework for cultivating curiosity in your classroom? "Create boundaries, explain why they exist and enthusiastically encourage your people to innovate within those boundaries. This will increase creativity and provide direction" (Brost, as cited in Forbes Coaches Council, 2020).

Have Fun

The idea of having fun might speak for itself, but the brain appreciates fun so much that it learns better when it's enjoying something (Wicaksono, 2020; Willis & Willis, 2020). Learning something new is not boring. Do a quick check-the-facts mental reflection on your own practices; how often are students talking to each other about what they are learning? How often are they laughing, doing, creating, and any other productive *-ing*? And how many of those *-ing* activities are parts of the curriculum that can manifest through true moments of fun and leisure, which capture interest and bring joy into the learning space? Catherine Price (2021), author of *The Power of Fun: How to Feel Alive Again*, states, "if we want to change our defaults and take back control of our leisure time, we need to expand our repertoire of passions, hobbies, and interests, and make these activities as accessible as possible" (pp. 204–205). Don't be afraid to model that behavior and work on your own exploration right alongside your students. They will be curious about what you are doing and may be more inclined to follow your example.

How Do I Get Myself Ready?

Let's first get clear on what we are actually trying to create and how that may look, sound, or feel different from before. We attempt to design an environment that ignites curiosity while honoring an adherence to rigorous academic expectations, yet creates room for additional moments of unscripted, unplanned, completely organic inquiry and wonder in response to what our students bring into the learning space. Oh, and we should be able to do all that while also maintaining emotional stability, safety, and belonging for each student. It makes sense that you (and your students) feel suffocated!

Remember the idea that we can make a shift to both/and? That's what we explore in this chapter. The following sections offer three ways you can get yourself ready: (1) determine what passions, curiosities, and interests you hold; (2) open your heart and mind to should-free learning moments; and (3) learn how curiosity connects to peers, passion, projects, and play.

Determine What Passions, Curiosities, or Interests You Hold

You deserve to stay curious yourself. Curiosity not only promotes happiness, elevates interest and excitement, and improves decision making, but demonstrating your curiosity in front of students models its connection to intellectual, emotional, and social wellness (Campbell, 2015; Latumahina, 2023).

I always appreciated the opportunities to get to know my colleagues well enough that we could talk about our lives *outside* of school. I was shocked by how many of them, however, did not have any consistent interests or activities outside of school. As I moved into an administrative role, I became even more aware of the absence of this type of self-care. How could we give ourselves permission to turn off the work mode and refresh our capacity as educators through regular, intentional moments of our own types of productive play? It soon became a regular topic of conversation and practice with my staff.

Children are often quick to name several things they are interested in or want to do for fun, but it turns out that adults, particularly those who have become mired in the daily grind of responsibilities, pressures, and expectations, can have more trouble defining what they are truly interested in. Would you be able to make a list of things you like to do for fun or things that you want to know more about? Maybe it's learning a new language, starting a new physical activity, or deciding that, now in your forties or fifties, you want to sign up for guitar lessons. The prompts in figure 4.2 activate your thinking.

Prompt	Your Response
I'm interested in learning to ________.	
I'm interested in learning about ________.	
I'm curious about ________.	
I'd like to try ________.	
I'd like to get better at ________.	
It might sound silly, but I'd love to ________.	
When I was a child, I enjoyed ________.	
Things I used to ________ with my free time but don't anymore.	
I always say I want to ________ or learn more about ________, but to date I haven't found time for it.	
I feel alive when I ________.	

Source: Adapted from Price, 2021.

FIGURE 4.2: Prompts to evoke interest, curiosity, and fun.

After connecting with a few of the prompts, perhaps you can engage (or re-engage) in a curiosity that brings satisfaction into your life. Let go of fears that something new might be hard, or that you might make a fool of yourself. Personally, I rekindle my belief that I am meant for more on a daily basis by engaging with something or someone to truly make my heart happy. I encourage you to give it a try as well.

Open Your Heart and Mind to *Should-Free* Learning Moments

As discussed in previous chapters, pre-determining what students *should* explore or steering them away from a passion can stifle their curiosity and impede their desire to ask questions or take risks in future learning scenarios. *Should-free moments* are times and spaces in which adults and students can display enough mutual trust in each other to let one another choose a path that will lead to a satisfactory result.

A few examples of such should-free moments in our schools follow.

- Not telling a student how a game *should* be played at recess
- Avoiding structuring every writing activity as five paragraphs because it *should* look like that (because that's how it's always been done)
- Not telling a student that she *should* or *should not* take a particular course
- Relaying to a student that he *should* have completed the task using the same process as all the other students

Of course, there will be moments when you do need to provide structure (as noted throughout this book) and you indeed *should* guide students with direction or boundaries to keep them safe or meet the intended rigor. You have a lot to accomplish with students and not nearly enough time to do it. However, if you can leverage something like pre-instructional unit planning to proactively create access in your classrooms for students to grow their knowledge of various skills, as well as how they can apply those skills, you model ways for students to learn not just how to think, but how to think *differently*. The late author David Foster Wallace, in his 2005 commencement speech at Kenyon College, posed:

> learning how to think really means learning how to exercise some control over how and what you think. It means being conscious and aware enough to choose what you pay attention to and to choose how you construct meaning from experience.

In what ways *should* our students learn how to think? Let's create space for that answer to unfold as we approach the next section, which aligns curiosity and engagement with productive play.

Learn How Curiosity Connects to Peers, Passion, Projects, and Play

Educators have historically spent an incredible amount of time monitoring students' academic abilities and stamina. While both intelligence and effort are indeed critical to student performance, research suggests that a third element—curiosity, or a "hungry mind"—is also pivotal for academic achievement and growth (von Stumm, Hell, & Chamorro-Premuzic, 2011). Other research bolsters the evidence, revealing how curiosity not only improves academic performance in learners of all ages, but also points out that the chemistry of our brain changes when we allow it to stay engaged and curious (Eva, 2018).

In her book, *Thrivers: The Surprising Reasons Why Some Kids Struggle and Others Shine*, Borba (2021) shares observations from her visit to the Media Lab at the Massachusetts Institute for Technology. She concludes that student successes are grounded in the curiosity principles described in table 4.2; through peers, passions, projects, and yes, even play.

TABLE 4.2: Curiosity Connection to the Four Ps

Element and Concept	Considerations for *Meant for More* Classrooms
Peers	
Students who Borba (2021) interviewed shared that it's hard to get to know other students in class—or even their teachers—due to the regularity with which students are asked to do individual work. Borba (2021) states, "Curiosity flourishes when people—regardless of age—collaborate and build on another's work" (p. 163).	What do you notice about the ways in which students are asked to think together, learn together, and create together in your learning environment? This perhaps means we would need to expose students to various perspectives as well as provide intentional moments for collaboration (which also may yield opportunities for instruction on what collaboration is and how it can benefit deepened understanding of content).
Passion	
In spite of breakdowns or epic failures, students in the labs were not daunted. They were simply able to dust themselves off and try again, and again, and again (Borba, 2021). The students were fueled by their failures, not debilitated or defeated by them, because they were grounded in their passion.	Does this reaction happen by chance, or is this by design? A 2019 Gallup report finds that most students did not regularly engage in activities that allowed them to be curious; nearly three in four said they spend too little time choosing what they learn in class, and more than four in ten said they spend too little time demonstrating what they have learned in creative ways or trying new ways of doing things.

Projects	
Projects, when centered in topics that students are excited about, provide something to rally together around. Borba (2021) shares, "Active engagement increases curiosity; passivity reduces it. Projects ignite curiosity; worksheets stifle it" (p. 165). Borba's observations convey that collaboration and innovation were so abundant at MIT because every single student wanted every other student to be successful and actively encouraged them to do so. Projects can build communities where curiosity can thrive.	What do you observe about how students talk with and support each other during collaborative work time within your learning environment? This principle may be the most demanding since *authenticity* and *connection* are essential for such a learning space. Whether you organize students into collaborative work groups or promote individualized innovation, securing a cooperative classroom culture where risk taking, active engagement, and innovation can work together is paramount. Students are best served in a classroom culture where the tone and language they use with each other, as they rebound from setbacks, is positive, productive, and promotes improvement and the capacity to try again.
Play	
Engaging in free play could be one of the most impactful ways to interrupt the mental health challenges that students face because it can help them "decompress, learn to enjoy their own company, and make sense of others and their world" (Borba, 2021, p. 114).	Different areas of learning are quite interconnected and "playful learning experiences can be particularly effective ways to foster deeper learning and develop a broad range of skills and an understanding of academic concepts." Play can promote greater confidence, problem-solving skills, resilience, advocacy, and self-regulation (Lego Foundation, 2022). Use games, cooperative learning, discussion, and discovery to enhance play.

Source: Adapted from Borba, 2021.

Curiosity piques interest, which can inspire students to think creatively, build or design something new, or spark the feeling of "What more can I learn about this?" By partnering with peers, pursuing their passions, designing projects to fulfill wonderment, or even engaging in play, *Meant for More* classrooms create spaces where students can actually learn *how* to learn.

How Do I Get My Team Ready?

My hope is that you are feeling more equipped and more deeply inspired as a result of that self-exploration into your personal curiosities and interests. I wonder if you might already be scheming up ways to add a curiosity corner or even embed interactive play in your instructional design, using the information in table 4.1 (page 126). The most curious thing about curiosity is that we often feel we need permission to be so. Curiosity can be difficult to teach because students have limited experience being asked what they want to learn, why they want to learn it, and how they should learn the information they seek. As we pull away from antiquated practices, we may notice students hesitating to share what really piques their interest. As such, some direct instruction may be required here. You may also need a little nudge as well, particularly if you find yourself no longer asking questions about how to improve your practice.

Consider the following three strategies for engaging with colleagues about how to embed inquiry in your classrooms: (1) brainstorm ways to support students' curiosities, (2) enhance content relevance, and (3) study the high-operational practices (HOPs).

Brainstorm Ways to Support Students' Curiosities

Students need support to stay curious because not only does curiosity prepare the brain for learning but it also makes ensuing learning more rewarding (Stenger, 2014). Can you recall a time when anticipation had you on the edge of your seat, eager to know what was coming next? Now, think about the last time your students experienced that same feeling in your classroom. Aren't those the moments that bring you joy as an educator? Those moments when you have your entire class in the palm of your hand are just—ah. So good. Let's explore how to bring even more of those into the classroom.

Students in *Meant for More* classrooms grow their desire to find out. Perhaps it would be easier for them to say, "I don't care that much" or "I don't really need to know or understand that part of it" but instead they are driven by their desire to seek, explore, and wonder. In Lewis Carroll's (2009) renowned 1865 novel, *Alice's Adventures in Wonderland and Through the Looking Glass* (now more commonly referenced simply as *Alice in Wonderland*), there is a moment in which Alice asks the mischievous Cheshire Cat for directions. The Cat is the only character in the novel who actually listens to Alice and—albeit, in a roundabout, colorful way—tries to help her out of the adverse situation in which she has found herself.

Their dialogue represents a beautiful piece of advice we could use as we approach a curiosity conversation with our team:

> "Would you tell me, please, which way I ought to go from here?" asked Alice.

> "That depends a good deal on where you want to get to," said the Cat.
>
> "I don't much care where—" said Alice.
>
> "Then it doesn't matter which way you go," said the Cat.
>
> "—so long as I get somewhere," Alice added as an explanation.
>
> "Oh, you're sure to do that," said the Cat, "if you only walk long enough."
>
> (Carroll, 1865/2009, p. 56)

As with most good intentions, intention only transforms into implementation if there is both shared development and purposeful creation of a plan. When teams put that plan into action, then they begin to see the resulting impact of their intentionality. What learning experiences could your team design differently for students that would keep students curious? Why do you want to pursue those enhancements right now? How could you build the pedagogical and instructional bridges to getting there?

Patrick Brown (2023), who is executive director of science, engineering, technology, and mathematics in Fort Zumwalt School District, describes a four-part explore-before-explain method to help teachers develop a curious mindset in the classroom.

1. Planning backward
2. Engaging students' ideas
3. Enhancing understanding
4. Promoting reflection on learning to guide teachers through this type of curricular design and instructional delivery

The specific element of engaging students' ideas, for example, highlights instructional planning behaviors you are probably already familiar with: starting a lesson by finding out what students already know or wonder about the topic, predicting what might be learned or what might happen, and then developing pathways for exploration to guide students' curiosities, unveil their misconceptions, and then help them draw evidence-based conclusions that deepen their conceptual understanding.

Revisit the four principles of curiosity listed in table 4.2 (page 133)—(1) peers, (2) passion, (3) projects, and (4) play. Plan ways to learn more about those ideas. Map out a first step with your team *and* make time to review and reflect on the productivity and effectiveness of your collaborative implementation. This could become actionable for you and your team by adding a four Ps checklist to your unit plans and determining how the instructional component or activity aligns to one of the curiosity elements. For scaffolding, you could work through the elements one at a time; focus on peers one month and passion the next, for example.

A more technical consideration can be found in figure 4.3 regarding the different types of questions that can be taught and posed within the classroom environment. You will notice the scaffolded nature of the questions increase in rigor as you work your way from top to bottom in the figure. Use of these types of questions opens student thinking to possibility through *what if* or *what could be*. In addition, be sure to include student feedback and input when reviewing your planning as well. Their voices and ideas may improve the efficiency of your design and the overall process.

Question Type	Question Stem
Clarifying Questions	What do you mean by . . . ? What is an example of . . . ?
Debate Questions	What would another perspective look like . . . ? What is the counter argument . . . ?
Innovation Questions	What if . . . ? How might we . . . ?
Causal Questions	How does that connect to . . . ? Why did that happen . . . ?
Analysis Questions	What would have changed if . . . didn't happen? What were the contributing factors to . . . and how did that affect . . . ? What is the relationship among these components . . . ?

Source: Erkens, Schimmer, & Dimich, 2018.

FIGURE 4.3: Types of questions to promote dialogue.

Enhance Content Relevance

With all the demands and legal mandates about what students must learn, as well as requirements for how learning is measured, it becomes essential for educators to unleash some creativity to link academic content to student relevance. Relevance is important because "When students see the relevance of the curriculum, they are more likely to remain engaged in their learning, and therefore, more likely to achieve academic proficiency" (Denby, 2023). How to introduce creativity? Instead of having them measure lines on a photocopied piece of paper, take them outside or through the building to find three objects they can measure (and introduce comparison of objects). Also, have them dialogue with friends about the data they are gathering.

You could teach argumentation in theory, or you could let your class choose a relevant topic, make a claim and counterclaim, take sides, and outline their justifications with reasons and evidence to support their thinking. Rather than solely teaching the facts and figures of a significant historical event, task learners with hunting down the potential causes for an event and determine a cause that, if it had never occurred or had occurred differently, would have changed not only the entire sequence of events but the ultimate outcomes as well.

During the COVID-19 pandemic aftershocks, we noticed that some students struggled to be interested in anything we had to offer in the classroom. Anecdotal stories from teachers indicate that the displays of apathy, disengagement, and disinterest are rising. Polls confirm this:

> Engagement is strong at the end of elementary school, with nearly three-quarters of fifth-graders (74%) reporting high levels of engagement. But similar surveys have shown a gradual and steady decline in engagement from fifth grade through about tenth grade, with approximately half of students in middle school reporting high levels of engagement and about one-third of high school students reporting the same. (Gallup, as cited in DeFuria, n.d.)

In addition, a 2018 Gallup survey reveals that students were thirty times more likely to be invested at school if they strongly agreed with the following two statements: (1) "My school is committed to building the strengths of each student" and (2) "I have at least one teacher who makes me excited about the future" (as cited in DeFuria, n.d.). What is *exciting* about these data is that both statements represent elements of the school or classroom that we can actually control. Using figure 4.4, brainstorm and write ideas for how your grade-level-, department-, or campuswide team can prepare students to strongly agree with those sentiments.

Statement	What Our Team Would Have to Learn, Say, or Do to Make This Statement a Reality for Each Student
My school is committed to building the strengths of each student.	
I have at least one teacher who makes me excited about the future.	

Source: Adapted from Gallup, 2018.

FIGURE 4.4: Adult actions to build engagement in our students.

The splendor of curiosity is that you never know what might result from it! Did you know that these inventions came from school-age children (Milbrand, 2023).

- In 2014, a fourteen-year-old invented a sensor as a measure to prevent parents from leaving their children in hot cars, in response to the prevalence of news stories about these accidental occurrences.
- A fifteen-year-old invented Braille in 1824, due to an injury that left him blind at age three.
- In 1963, a six-year-old invented the toy truck from bottle caps.
- In 1930, a sixteen-year-old invented the trampoline because he thought it would be cooler if trapeze artists could bounce back up from their safety nets.
- An eleven-year-old developed the popsicle in 1905, after accidentally leaving soda powder, water, and a stirring stick outside—and it froze overnight!
- An eighteen-year-old invented water skis in 1922 to combine his love of water and aquaplaning.

The point is that enveloping students in environments that empower them to be curious learners will inevitably lead to students creating something new. (Or, at minimum, think of how interested your students would be in learning about inventions from other kids, people of color, or persons with disabilities.) Your team can help your students feel a part of something special as they explore and discover the content you yourself are so passionate about.

Study the High Operational Practices (HOPs)

Yvette Jackson (2011), in *The Pedagogy of Confidence*, asserts that *each* student should have access to attributes of what has historically been limited to gifted education programming, such as identifying and activating students' strengths, situating learning in their lives, or amplifying their voice. She further claims that students and teachers who collaboratively engage in more reciprocal relationships simultaneously build confidence on both sides. Jackson (2011) describes an impetus for her continued work:

> Time after time I have witnessed teachers being stimulated by the identification of their students' strengths and the potential these strengths testify to, and, like teachers of students labeled as gifted, they are motivated to remember that this belief in potential is why they went into teaching. The challenge for these teachers once they remember this motivation and begin to focus on strengths is to stand up against the current deficit culture with confidence in their ability to inspire, elicit, and build on these strengths,

> enabling the high intellectual performance that encourages self-directed learning and self-actualization. This is the Pedagogy of Confidence. (p. 4)

Jackson (2011) defines high-operational practices (HOPs) that have emerged from her research, which affirm the exact pedagogical practices utilized in gifted programming are "essential concepts of any program for reversing underachievement and realizing the intellectual capacity of school-dependent students" (p. 86). It was important for me to specifically highlight the work of Jackson here because of the intersectionality of race and perceptions of students' academic potential. For example, the elements of *identifying and activating student strengths*, *situating learning in the lives of students*, and *amplifying student voice* are conditions for success in cultivating curiosity in the classroom.

Table 4.3 represents a brief summary of all seven high operational practices; while there is far more depth to these practices than I can unfold for you here, interpretation of what these HOPS are and why they matter will aid your team to cultivate curiosity in *Meant for More* classrooms.

TABLE 4.3: Jackson's (2011) High Operational Practices

High Operational Practice (Jackson, 2011)	What It Is	Why It Matters
Identifying and activating student strengths	Uses intentional plans for instructing students on how to recognize and make meaning of their strengths.	When we start from a place of strength, students' motivation to perform, set goals, and actively engage in their learning creates a reciprocal response in teacher motivation as well.
Building relationships	Involves careful, mindful development of a mutually personal connection between teacher and student.	People are far more likely to work hard and stay committed with someone they know cares about, respects, and is compassionate toward them.

Eliciting high intellectual performance	Involves multiple forms of complex thinking, including ways for students to expand ideas, make connections, or create new ways of thinking	Neuroscience research (Fueurstein, Fueurstein, Falik, & Yaacov, 2006); Sasmita, Kuruvilla, & Ling, 2018) indicates that new neural pathways are established and activated when the brain is presented with complex or challenging tasks.
Providing enrichment	Enables the learner to use spaces or opportunities to more deeply connect with the development of their strengths and personal goal setting or motivation.	*All* students need access to enrichment to cultivate their gifts and talents. Access to enrichment is not a privilege afforded only to those who have completed or shown mastery of a given task or standard.
Integrating prerequisites for academic learning	Secures foundational learning elements and acquires adequate background knowledge; planned for in advance of instruction.	Having all the information and tools needed prior to engagement in a task reduces stress and increases the likelihood of success.
Situating learning in the lives of students	Uses knowledge of the lived experiences, interests, and passions of our students in order to match the rigor of the content with personalized relevance.	There is more likely to be a connection to or engagement with content that feels purposeful and meaningful. (This includes play!)
Amplifying student voice	Provides opportunities for students to co-create learning activities, procedures, assessments, and other development aspects within the classroom or school community.	The mutual sharing of ideas and perspectives fosters respect between all members of the classroom community, as well as contributes to students' cognitive and social development of self-advocacy, empathy, and respect for alternative perspectives. Students need purposeful moments to collaborate.

The strategies presented here—brainstorming ways to support student curiosity, enhancing content relevance for students, and studying the high operational practices—are intended to feed dialogue and discussion among your team. Use what you already know about the gifts and talents of the members of your team in order to determine which strategy seems most purposeful for this moment, with your current students.

How Do I Get My Students Ready?

Advancements in technology afford our students more immediate access and opportunities to information, such that they can immediately fulfill many of their needs, questions, and wonderings on their own. And now that we have the capacity to update information in real-time, some of the methods we used as students to learn about new ideas are antiquated or obsolete, such as recitation, copying information from the whiteboard, or searching through volumes of encyclopedias.

While technology has enhanced our lives in some ways, we must be mindful of how our brains are being retrained to respond to constant stimulation. Neuropsychologist William Stixrud and test-preparation expert Ned Johnson (2018) found that technology diminishes the types of interactions our brains need most. For example, we need to reinforce face-to-face interactions to build trust and foster a sense of comfort. (This sentiment links back to chapter 3, page 83, about fostering connection and alludes forward to chapters 5 and 6, pages 153 and 189, regarding collaboration and nurturing relationships.) The authors conclude that students "need to learn to work successfully within the world they will inhabit, not the world you were raised in" (Stixrud & Johnson, 2018, p. 208). That's an important point to remember as we move forward.

As teachers, we nurture an underutilized source of energy when we define and explicitly teach students how to be curious as well as understand how developing perseverance means learning to dig deep, pursue and research answers, and interpret and make sense of evolving information. Through these actions they can enrich their lived experiences. The following sections offer three ways to get your students ready for these moments: (1) differentiate between an *interest* and a *passion*, (2) allow students to explore their own curiosities, and (3) create safe spaces for students to persevere through and learn from mistakes.

Differentiate Between an *Interest* and a *Passion*

Although it may seem as though interests and passions are interchangeable terms, it is important to clarify the difference for students by primarily focusing on how students choose to prioritize their time and thoughts. I can be interested in learning how to crochet, for example, and decide to spend a Sunday evening teaching myself how to begin. But when Sunday evening rolls around and my friend calls and says, "Let's go for a hike!" (something I am passionate about doing), I throw in the towel on my crochet attempts in favor of hiking. I'm interested in learning how to crochet, but I am passionate about hiking. It fuels me. It drives me. I love how I feel before, during, and even after a hike. I am truly passionate about it.

- An *interest* represents a task or activity that you would give time and attention to in your spare time, and it brings you enjoyment. However, time spent engaged in an interest could be temporary, particularly if a new interest arose or there was a setback that impacted your ability to continue spending time with it.
- A *passion*, however, is your engine. It wakes you up. A passion drives you, and—if possible—you would want to spend all your time, attention, and energy focused in pursuit of growth and perfection in this area. Robert Vallerand, psychology professor at University of Quebec, who studies the concept, explains that "'Passion is a strong inclination towards a self-defining activity that people love, that they consider important, and in which they devote significant amounts of time and energy'" (as cited in Bradberry, 2016). No matter how many setbacks you may have, a passion fuels you emotionally and resourcefully.

Why does this differentiation even matter? Consider the existence of solid research proving the link among curiosity, engagement, and achievement. Additionally, author and educator Dr. Jackie Walsh, who researches use of effective questioning to advance learning, asserts (2022), "The teacher controlled, fast-paced rhythm of classrooms provides little opportunity for students to make a 'bid' to interrupt the flow with a thoughtful (but potentially time-consuming) inquiry." Cognitive scientist Elizabeth Bonawitz (as cited in Boudreau, 2020) explains that although we can't truly see what is happening inside a student's brain, we can empower students to believe their curiosity will be worth the pursuit; for example, "children won't act on their curiosity because they might not feel confident in their ability to resolve their curiosity." And truthfully, we may not feel we have the time or energy to allow students to dive deep into their curiosity—particularly when they need to stay focused on what they need to complete right now.

To create space for students to pursue the things they are curious about in class, whether something they choose or something you are guiding them through, first look at your master schedule. Is every single minute of your instructional day filled with predetermined content? When you look at your schedule, do you see potential for flexibility? If it is planned down to the minute, consider learning more about how to leverage the four Ps (page 132) or the high operational practices (page 139), so that learning is situated in relevance and empowered through student curiosity.

Allow Students Explore Their Own Curiosities

We do a great disservice to students when adults tell them who we think they are (or should be). We then, as my friend and colleague Ken Williams would say, "With love in our hearts" proceed to share what we think they should do with their lives, as though we have a deep, personal view into their future and have seen how their path has already been written (K. Williams, personal communication, November 14, 2018).

And we share well-intended but potentially curiosity-stifling insight freely and boldly. It's as if—again, with love in our hearts—we should expect our students to be singing thanks for our foresight. Instead, consider how to find specific moments throughout the course of the school year (or the schooling experience) to help students see the possibilities in what they are capable of and could become. Encourage them to think about how they might leverage their current gifts and talents to formulate new or deeper ones.

Most teachers want to get past the "teachers ask, students answer" way of doing things, but aren't always sure where to start. One idea is to teach students why questions are so important in the first place. Walsh (2022) shares that when we communicate our expectations to students that they should ask questions in the classroom, and explain why that matters, we can then work on helping them develop the skills to generate questions to advance their own learning. Consider the following sentence stems as a starter self-assessment of sorts for students to react to (and visit https://tinyurl.com/46nakp37 to find more information).

- I ask myself questions to monitor my thinking and learning.
- I pose questions to clarify and deepen my understanding of academic content.
- I use questions to understand other perspectives and to engage in collaborative thinking and learning.
- I use questions to channel my curiosity and spark my creativity. (Walsh, 2022)

Findings from a collaborative study, which included researchers from Australia, New Zealand, and the United States, conclude that curiosity makes progress feel more satisfying (Sheldon, Jose, Kashdon, & Aaron, 2015). In other words, "when you meet a goal that is driven by your authentic desire to learn, you may get a more lasting boost in well-being . . . your academic goals become less about performance and achievement and more about personal growth" (Eva, 2018). You could then show students what type of learning is required to pursue such pathways and what opportunities are in place for them at school to support their curiosity and inquiry.

If curiosity is a natural brain response to information (Boudreau, 2020), then in order to get started we need to find out what our students are indeed curious about. Fortunately, several inventories and strategies are available to use with all ages. The reproducible "All About Me" (page 151) is an example of a self-awareness inventory for upper elementary and middle school students because it uses statements like, "I'm very interested in or good at . . ." and "Things I'd like you (or need you) to know about me . . . ". The reproducible "I Try to Be Creative, But . . ." (page 152) is an example of a self-assessment tool that helps students from elementary to high school identify roadblocks to creativity. With elementary-age students, asking questions of wonder as well as documenting their predictions can help you model inquiry. For example, when reading Caldecott Medal-winning picture book, *A Snowy Day* (Keats, 1962), you could ask students, "Do you think the snowball will be safe in Peter's pocket overnight?" and tally student responses of *yes* or *no* in a T-chart, or, "I wonder what will happen if Peter leaves the snowball in his pocket overnight?" When we model wonderment with our students, we make it safe for their curiosity to emerge in the learning space as well. You can start the discussion with middle or high schoolers using this reflection from Albert Einstein (as cited in Gray, 2013): "It is not that I'm so smart. But I stay with the questions much longer." What questions are your students asking themselves over and over again? What ideas do they keep coming back to? Get the conversation started, and see what unfolds from there.

Moving forward, we can be mindful of the curiosity balance in our classrooms. Do students spend as much time asking their own questions as they do answering yours? If not, consider the following:

> Questions can be extraordinary learning tools. A good question can open minds, shift paradigms, and force the uncomfortable but transformational cognitive dissonance that can help create thinkers. In education, we tend to value a student's ability to answer our questions. But what might be more important is their ability to ask their own great questions—and more critically, their willingness to do so. (Heick, 2017)

Finding ways for students to discuss and explore their own questions normalizes curiosity in the classroom.

Create Safe Places for Students to Persevere Through and Learn From Mistakes

Anecdotal stories from teachers and educators in the field indicate that the most significant observed barrier to inviting curiosity and pursuit of passion into their classrooms is actually the students. Many students demonstrate such fear of failure that any potential threat to the stability and security of what they know can manifest into a legitimate mental health crisis (Ginsburg & Jablow, 2020; Lahey, 2015; Stixrud & Johnson, 2021). Accumulation of points is more important than acquiring proficiency on the expected learning. Sharing a wrong answer in front of a classroom of their peers can induce such anxiety for some students that they begin to have difficulty managing the physical symptoms (Prentiss, 2021).

Consider a middle school student describing a mathematics lesson on comparing fractions. The teacher asked, "How would we accurately compare $\frac{5}{6}$ and $\frac{7}{8}$?" The teacher continued by communicating the first step in the process or finding common denominators. As she was doing this, the student raised her hand to contribute. When called on, the student shared: "I understand what you're asking, but you could also notice that both fractions are only missing one part to complete their whole. So when I visualize the pictures of the fractions in my mind, I just know that, in this case, the fraction with a greater denominator, $\frac{7}{8}$, will cover more space than $\frac{5}{6}$. So $\frac{7}{8}$ is the larger fraction."

Her teacher replied, visibly frustrated, "Yes, that may be true. But I'm trying to teach something different here."

The student said she caught eyes with some of her peers, and fortunately, none of her classmates poked fun at her after this tense interaction with the teacher. The teacher turned back to the whiteboard and finished completing her process for the students to see. Although the teacher admitted that it was a longer way to do it, she told her students it was the right mathematical procedure and the best way of checking it.

Was the teacher reasonable to ensure students understood a technical process for comparing fractions? Yes. Was the student reasonable to share an alternative approach to solving the problem? Also yes. When I asked her how the teacher's response made her feel, she said:

> I understand she was trying to teach a process since some students weren't getting the concept. But she had been teaching it that way for two days already. Maybe teachers should be open to all ways of students being able to show they know something, especially in math when we can actually prove it!"

Some of you may know from experience that arguing with a middle schooler is an exercise in futility, but in this case, there truly was nothing about this student's response with which I *could* argue. I complimented the student on her ability to bravely share an alternative perspective and represent a different way of thinking. However, the student told me that after this interaction, no one else spoke up for the rest of the class period. After class, another student told her that he approached the problem in the same way that she did, telling her, "My brother already warned me this teacher likes when our work looks exactly how she taught it in class."

The scenario is a non-example of creating a safe space to cultivate curiosity and wonder in the classroom. This is *not* how we want our classrooms to sound nor how we want our students to feel when contributing to or solving problems within classroom discussion. However, consider yourself in that situation. Would you have reacted in the same way? It's OK to say yes here. It's also OK to admit that you have reacted that way in the past. Remember, since the start of the 21st century (particularly in the United States), we have been conditioned to explain content to students and make sure they can show us they have learned it in a specific way. How can we break free from this cycle of telling and doing and move into a space of asking and innovating? Let's walk through some strategies for creating such an infrastructure in our classrooms.

What Infrastructure Do I Need to Make It Happen?

Classrooms that cultivate curiosity and discovery do not do so at the expense of rigorous learning experiences and high expectations for student achievement. In fact, due to the rapid nature with which the world is evolving, classrooms must become learning spaces where students not only ask questions, but pursue alternative methods to explore, solve, and innovate responses to those questions. In fact, since 2016, when The World Economic Forum started writing about the top skills required for the future, reports have been published every two years to stay relevant with which skills are required in the global community (Eich, 2022). There is conjecture that "employees at all levels need to develop their innovation skills. These include competencies like *creativity, critical thinking, communication, strategic thinking,* and *problem solving* to find and develop creative solutions for the complex world we live in" (Eich, 2022).

Earlier in this chapter, we previewed the seven HOPs that emerged from a belief system that *all* students deserve pedagogical practices that "elicit high intellectual performance to motivate self-directed learning and self-actualization" (Jackson, 2011, p. 86). Additionally:

> Positive verbal feedback is an excellent way to bolster this message. Imagine the impact of a teacher statement such as, "I really appreciate the thoughtful question that Maria asked earlier. I am curious to know if others of you have wonderings of your own'" (Walsh, 2019).

Leverage your belief that students *can* and *should* wonder in order to design learning experiences and expectations so that they *will.* The future of our society to innovate and evolve depends on it.

Visit **go.SolutionTree.com/schoolimprovement** for a free reproducible "Chapter Summarization Tool to Inspire Action" and use its prompts to refresh your ideas and reflections from what you read in this chapter.

Meant for MoreMENTUM: Stories to Ignite Us

Brian Eberhardt is a middle school life science teacher at Lake Middle School in Woodbury, Minnesota, with fifteen years of teaching experience. Although initially swept into traditional teaching practices by his first teammates, Brian quickly mastered his content knowledge and found himself confidently transitioning back to the student-centered pedagogy he learned in college. This is as science should be: grounded in inquiry, discovery, and possibility.

Brian's classroom is an example of cultivating curiosity in that he constantly models and expects inquiry within the learning environment. From a structural design, students have base tables in the classroom, where they start with their peers to initially discuss the day's prompt or scenario. Students are motivated to engage together because they know they will soon be taking the key points from their table discussion

to their new working groups to implement the day's lesson. From a learning design, Brian is regularly shuffling student groups and fostering networks to have students hear multiple perspectives and interact with various personalities and learning styles over the course of a unit. He specifically commented on how the design of his learning environment keeps students' levels of engagement authentic and real; he states, "Students enter my classroom with the predictability of, 'I am going to be interacting today.'"

Brian was offered an opportunity to design STEM and engineering lessons aligned with NGSS standards that revealed the true power of phenomenon-based instruction. Brian saw the possibility of how he could activate student engagement, and promote their natural inquiry, by keeping students at the center of his lesson design. The more he grew his content expertise, the less he had to worry about student-centered activities devolving into chaos. Behind the scenes, he was incredibly meticulous in the details; organizing materials, planning how students would physically flow through the classroom, and preparing his responses to anticipated student questions. This intentional preparation created space for him and his students to navigate each lesson—still focused on the standards and the intended learning targets—with curiosity and excitement.

He further commented how the days of him talking all the time are gone. Brian prides himself on being very organized and knowing his content inside and out. This content expertise, paired with his classroom routines and organization, provide him the freedom to promote student exploration and inquiry. He smiles as he shares, "I've never had a sense of burnout. I know my content inside and out, and even when things go bad, I can quickly recover. There is no build up of, 'What am I going to teach tomorrow?' And if I find myself getting bored or dissatisfied with our current activities, I know I am 100 percent in control to make it more exciting." This confidence enables him to feel that his own workload is actually less because students have lead ownership in the lessons.

Brian shared that he built students' capacity to ask questions through direct modeling and creating safe environments in which questions could be brought forward. He poses to students, "If you wanted to find out more, what types of questions would you need to ask?" Then he invites students to respond privately, on a post-it note, or electronically, offering the opportunity to cluster questions by topic or idea. Student reviews of those questions tend to stimulate even more questions, as students feed off each other's thinking. Often, Brian assigns each group of students a different question to explore as part of their inquiry for the lesson. He then nurtures the value in each student's responses, even when a student's response is off base or when a question is not directly related to the topic at hand. Instead, he uses his content knowledge to connect that idea to previous learning or experiences. These displays of grace extended to students preserve their dignity while empowering voice in the classroom. (B. Eberhardt, personal communication, February 9, 2023)

"You deserve to stay curious yourself. Let go of any fears that something new might be hard."

All About Me

Name: ______________________________ Date: ______________

Complete the prompts in each column to describe yourself.

All About:				
Words that describe me	**My favorite books or stories**	**Things I like to do with my friends**	**My favorite activities when I'm alone**	**My favorite activities when I'm with my family**
			Favorite activities: Other activities:	
I'm very interested in or good at . . .	**Things I'd like you (or need you) to know about me**	**My hopes and dreams for myself**	**The easiest ways for me to show what I know**	**One thing I would like to do better**
Shhhhh! My greatest fears are:				

Source: White, K. (2022). Student self-assessment: Data notebooks, portfolios, and other tools to advance learning. *Bloomington, IN: Solution Tree Press.*

I Try to Be Creative, But . . .

Removing the Blocks That Hinder Me

If I knew I couldn't fail, I would create ______________________________.

Even if I couldn't fail, what sometimes holds me back? ______________________________

How do I sometimes stop my own creative process with my thoughts? Select from the following sentences what you have heard yourself say in the past. Then, try to create alternative messages that might open up your creative thinking.

Self-Talk About Me		
	What if people think I'm stupid?	If I want to be more creative, what messages must I say to myself instead?
	I'm not creative or innovative.	
	I'm better off if I play it safe.	
	I'm not that interesting.	
	I could never do that!	
Preferences to Be Practical		
	It's already working. Why fix it?	What's the worst that could happen if I were less practical? How could I block my practicality from inhibiting my creativity?
	I've never done it that way before.	
	I tried it before, and it didn't work.	
	Why reinvent the wheel?	
	There's no need to change.	
Preferences to Be Critical		
	Here's why that idea won't work.	How can I become more of a daydreamer and risk taker?
	Others won't appreciate that idea.	
	It's not possible because . . .	
	As I see it, there are many problems with this because . . .	

Source: Erkens, C., Schimmer, T., & Dimich, N. (2019). Growing tomorrow's citizens in today's classrooms: Assessing seven critical competencies. *Bloomington, IN: Solution Tree Press.*

Chapter 5
Empowering Voice

Michael was so excited! His school had finally replaced the rusty, broken, and outdated playground equipment over the summer, and the final piece—a new gaga ball pit—had been delivered and installed over the weekend. He had just dominated during recess—only getting out of the game once!—and some of the students were high-fiving Michael on the way inside for lunch. Everyone was heading to their lockers to put their jackets away, but Michael stopped at the bathroom first. When he came out, his classmates Jada, Trevor, and Henry were standing there. These kids didn't like Michael very much and made sure he knew it. Since second grade, they had been calling him names, taunting him, and using various racial slurs on the playground, all outside the earshot of teachers and other adults. Michael said, "Why are you standing there?" The group looked nervously at each other, and then Jada, referencing their time at recess, said, "You know we aren't going to let you dominate at all the games, right?"

Michael, surprised by this comment, said, "What do you mean? We were just having fun out there! Well, maybe you weren't, but everyone else was laughing and having a great time."

Trevor chimed in, "Well, it wasn't fun for us. And we've decided we aren't going to let [racial slur] like you play anymore." Michael, visibly startled, said, "Whoa, what did you just call me?" Henry stepped toward Michael and chimed in, "You heard him, Michael. Or did your tiny [racial slur] brain not understand what he was saying?" Jada and Trevor started acting out the slur. Michael took a deep breath and said, "Whatever, guys. Just because you three have a problem with my awesome skills doesn't mean I'm not allowed to play tomorrow."

Michael started to walk away from them, toward the lunchroom. As he left, Jada said, "Hey *boy*, where are you going?"

Michael stopped in his tracks. He was all too familiar with certain gestures and sounds, but this language from Jada was humiliating. He tried to stay calm, but what had that done for him in the past? He had told his teacher, who empathized with him, but she didn't know what to do other than report it to her principal. The principal was no help either, unfortunately; he just reminded Michael that Henry's mom was the president of the PTA and contributed a lot of time and money to improve the school, including most of the funding for that gaga ball pit.

But Michael decided, at that moment, he was done staying calm. He was done letting these kids walk all over him, talking to him like he was garbage. He turned around and shouted, "That's enough! You don't get to talk that way to me!" At that moment, a teacher in a nearby classroom heard the commotion in the hallway. She saw Michael and said, "Why do you always have to be so loud? Just calm down. Jada, Trevor, Henry—you guys get to the lunchroom. Michael, you come with me." Michael started to cry. He was so frustrated that, once again, these students were going to get away with their behavior. And to make matters worse, he was going to get in trouble for breaking a school rule: quiet voices in the hallway. Jada, Trevor, and Henry saw Michael's tears and started giggling, making more inappropriate comments as they ran down the hall to the lunchroom.

As you reflect on the story, consider the questions in figure 5.1.

What are your reactions to the experience shared in the story?

What caused it to go sideways?
What could have reconciled the situation?
Take yourself back to a similar moment in your career, when you responded before gathering all the information. What was the situation?
What could be done differently for students to ensure an accurate narrative is heard?

FIGURE 5.1: Story reflection.

Students deserve to feel safe to express their emotions or protect themselves during (and from) any situation, especially at school. Teaching them how to use their voice also means that we must be prepared to encourage them and then listen to what they have to say.

What Do We Mean by *Empowering Voice*?

You may have noticed phrases such as *voice* and *choice, student agency, autonomy,* or *letting students speak* emerging throughout your professional learning mediums, referenced as powerful practices. Although the phrases carry unique nuances, each center around a desire to intentionally develop skills in which students learn how to utilize their voices for self-advocacy and meaningful change. Research from the Harvard Graduate School of Education states:

> When schools give students the agency and the tools to speak out, the effects can resonate across students' lives. The process of becoming engaged as active partners can give young people a set of strategies they can use to create positive change in future classrooms or communities. And when they form authentic partnerships with teachers and school administrators, it can set the stage for lasting bonds and important mentoring relationships. (Shafer, 2016)

We embolden students in the classroom setting when we share influence over what happens and how it happens in the classroom environment (CASEL, n.d.; Safir, 2023; Talbot, 2021).

But what does all that mean? How would it impact my classroom? And what would it mean for students? A current challenge to activating student voice in schools and classrooms is that we do not yet have a shared understanding of what it is. The following quotes are a sampling of definitions or interpretations of *student voice*. As you read, annotate or jot notes in the margins to highlight words or phrases that resonate strongly with you.

> The complete integration of youth into the systems that govern them, allowing the meaningful leadership of students in educational systems, encouraging student agency in defining their learning environments, and honoring the authentic experiences that define students as people. (Brennen & Kahloon, 2021)

> Authentic student input or leadership in instruction, school structures, or education policies that can promote meaningful change in education systems, practice, and/or policy by empowering students as change agents, often working in partnership with adult educators (Conner, Ebby-Rosin, & Brown, 2015)

> Students actively participating in decision-making at school on things which shape their educational experiences. Student voice is more than just students 'having a say' and 'being heard'. To be successful, schools must value the perspectives and opinions of students and act on them in a way that genuinely shapes learning and decision-making at the school. (New South Wales Government—Education, n.d.)

> Sharing thoughts and ideas in an environment underpinned by trust and respect, offering realistic suggestions for the good of the whole, and accepting responsibility for not only what is said but also what needs to be done. (Quaglia, Fox, Lande, & Young, 2020)

> It refers to the expression of values, opinions, beliefs, and perspectives of individuals and groups of students in a school and to instructional approaches and techniques that are based on student choices, interests, passions, and ambitions. Listening to and acting on student preferences, interests, and perspectives helps students feel invested in their own learning and can ignite passions that will increase their persistence. (St. John & Briel, 2017)

You can see common themes across each of the posed definitions, as well as room for interpretation. In addition to the patterns described, empowering voice, in the context of *Meant for More* classrooms, means intentionally providing opportunities for students to be equally aware of their voice and how to use it as well as being given moments in which to do so. Due to the evolving body of information, including research, ideology, and philosophy, on cultivating and empowering student voice, I encourage you to keep learning about and refining what practices could nurture the capacity of your team to best support your uniquely powerful students. The following section gets you started by highlighting three ways in which *Meant for More* classrooms empower voice: (1) ensure students see themselves within the learning activities and environments, (2) partner with students to co-construct learning experiences, and (3) foster trust and normalize risk taking. Let's explore how to support these opportunities for each student (and adult) in our schools.

A key component of empowering voice is that we are—by design—creating spaces that allow learners to grow into who *they* want to be because they know how to productively advocate for their needs and display a tenacity to engage, even in moments where their voice is being diminished.

Ensure Students See Themselves in the Learning Experiences and Environments

I discussed the connection between students' sense of safety in the classroom as well as their emotional well-being and academic performance at school in chapter 3 (page 83). The same premise rings true for lifting students' identities and cultures into the learning environment. Creating identity-safe classrooms are linked with culturally representative classrooms.

A mindful place to start is by examining three things: (1) our own culture, (2) how we see evidence of culture in our classroom (for example, what is on the walls, your procedures and expectations, and the opportunities for collaborative learning activities), and then (3) how evidence aligns with the identities and cultures of the students we are blessed to serve. Gholdy Muhammad (2020), a professor, author, and thought leader who is reframing conversations about excellence for students who have been historically underserved, reminds us that "we have so long prescribed what others think is best for youth in schools, all while leaving out of the picture the ways communities of color have historically acquired and used literacy" (p. 15).

In what ways do students have power and authority to determine what hangs in your classroom or what is painted in the hallway? Do students have access to information that is representative or expressive of how they see themselves? Consider how your current design—from games and toys to classroom décor to book accessibility to guest speakers—connects to the lives of your students.

Katie Novak (2022), a thought leader in the application of Universal Design for Learning principles, asserts that:

> all students, regardless of identity, must have equitable access to inclusive classrooms with grade-level peers, equitable opportunities to learn aligned to grade-level standards, equitable expectations that they can be successful when provided with the appropriate support, and equitable feelings of belonging and hope. (p. 25)

That said, educators are likely to continue having a difficult time creating inclusive, authentic learning spaces for their students with limited access to the knowledge and perspectives that most accurately reflect our global society. Representation in literature is essential. Despite global book censorship being at an all-time high, when students see themselves in the stories they read, the visual displays in their classroom, or the learning experiences and activities they engage in, feelings of authenticity (chapter 2) and connection (chapter 3) emerge (Garcia, 2023). Consider this:

> Children from dominant social groups have always found their mirrors in books, but they, too, have suffered from the lack of availability of books about others. They need the books as windows onto reality, not just on imaginary worlds. They need books that will help them understand the multicultural nature of the world they live in, and their place as a member of just one group, as well as their connections to all other humans. In [the U.S.], where racism is still one of the major unresolved social problems, books may be one of the few places where children who are socially isolated and insulated from the larger world may meet people unlike themselves. (Bishop, 2015)

Child psychologist Jody Carrington (2020) reminds us to consider "connection before direction" (p. 124). We can create moments in our classrooms to learn more about who our students are as *people*, to ensure they believe that the partnership you are seeking will be realized. This means agreeing to hear their feedback and putting their input into action in the formation of the learning environment. For example, Cleveland, Ohio's Facing History New Tech High School lockers feature student graffiti art. (Visit www.youtube.com/watch?v=PZ1IG9EwJs4 to watch a video clip of their youth voice and empowerment efforts.) They can determine a welcoming ritual—a physical or verbal greeting or a list of their favorite songs to stream as they enter your classroom. (You can ask students to write the title of a favorite song on an index card, collect the cards, play one song at the start each class period, and have students guess whose song it is.) If student feedback and input are counter to the

district's or school's mission or would be dangerous for them, speak directly with students to ensure they understand the rationale.

Learners in *Meant for More* classrooms are more inclined to take ownership of their learning once they see themselves mindfully represented in the design of the learning experiences and environments. As discussed in the next section, student partnership in the creation of learning can yield powerful results.

Partner With Students to Co-Construct Learning Experiences

While student voice is an important component of classroom decision-making opportunities, it can also activate a student's sense of agency—as an individual or among a cohort—to meaningfully contribute on a larger scale. For example, consider the high school assistant principal who is reviewing data with her attendance clerk. The data show an increase in student tardies to first period, which is startling as it revealed a new problem. The assistant principal reviews camera recordings and talks to other teachers and students about the issue, only to realize that the parking lot updates, made over the summer, compromise the flow of entry. New medians, crosswalks, and entry points create a disruption for students who were getting used to the changes. The assistant principal took the issue to the student leadership team, who, in partnership with adults, brainstormed a viable solution for the problem. The students created a slide deck with videos that described the new patterns necessary for drivers, bus drivers, walkers, and drop-offs (including examples of safe and unsafe behavior) to be shown during the Advisory block. They also found some neon vests so that students and adults could volunteer for "traffic control" each morning for the next week. When the assistant principal reviewed the data again two weeks later, there had already been a significant drop in tardies.

The response to the tardy issue could have gone two ways: (1) the adults alone could respond to the tardy data by doling out detentions and putting other punitive measures in place or (2) the adults could work in partnership with the students, gather information about *why* the issue was happening, and engage students in a decision-making process to lead their ideas (and actions) toward a resolution. If this situation had happened in your school, which way would it have gone? Do the adults tend to dominate responses to situations by conferring together and displaying authority? Or do the adults seek understanding by involving the people who are mostly closely impacted by the issue (which in this case, was the students and teachers)? Propelling student voice to the center of the issue can be both efficacious and rewarding.

As you involve students in genuine decision making, it will be important to consider how students using their voice can result in deeper understanding and empathy as well as more just, inclusive, and equitable ways of being. If we invite students to explore a topic, issue, or injustice, and then seek their insights and gather their perspectives, there must also be space to ensure our students respond to what they've learned from exploration. Students may wonder if their efforts are futile. We want to create moments where students can see the impacts of their feedback and insights. Sadly, although some students "are well-informed, innovative, and future-focused key stakeholders in their education, they rarely have an actual say in it" (Fontein, 2022).

A group of high school seniors, when asked about the types of decisions they make at school, shared that the decisions were technical and operational; attending school, completing homework, preparing for tests, and who they hang out with at lunch (Quaglia Institute, 2020). When asked how their voices could impact the learning environment in their classrooms, however, these students suggested the following:

- I could explain why students cut particular classes.
- I could tell you why everyone likes classes with Mr. X.
- I could help teachers see why some students feel school doesn't matter.
- I could actually help teach any class that relates to computers. (Quaglia et al., p. 98)

Student voice isn't just for the older students, either. Data gathered from over half a million students in grades 3–5 over the course of a decade indicate that when they feel like they have a voice, students are three times more likely to experience self-worth, five times more likely to be engaged, and five times more likely to have a sense of purpose in school (Quaglia Institute, 2020).

We have already discussed how voice is connected to both trust and respect. Most students need time to feel comfortable with you, the room, and their peers. That trust has to be carefully nurtured with and between each one of you in the classroom. When we take time to build these trusting relationships with our students, respect simultaneously emerges in the learning space. This includes words and behaviors such as listening to each other and others' ideas, working together to make improvements to their daily routines and life at school, and creating rules to keep everything predictable and safe.

The data in table 5.1 demonstrate the urgency of lifting students' voices in the learning environment.

TABLE 5.1: How Students Feel About Having a Voice in their Learning Environments

Percent Agreement for Students in Grades 3–5	Percent Agreement for Students in Grades 6–12
42 percent of students see themselves as leaders.	48 percent of students believe that adults at their school listen to student suggestions.
31 percent of students believe that other students listen to their ideas.	54 percent of students feel that adults and students work together to make their school better.
43 percent of students believe that teachers learn from students.	51 percent of students agree that students work with adults to find solutions to school problems.
94 percent of students believe that it is important to follow rules.	46 percent of students feel that they have a voice in decision making at school.
39 percent of students agree that students help make classroom rules.	48 percent of students agree that students develop programs that improve the whole school.

Source: Adapted from Quaglia Institute for School Voice and Aspirations, n.d.

As you review the data, what inspires your sense of urgency? Which data points are most relevant to you and your student body? Consider the following suggestions for partnering with students of various age groups in decisions that support co-constructed learning experiences or environments.

- **Early childhood:** When, how, and where to share; how to help each other keep materials organized; self-management strategies; student work displays on the classroom walls; or play time
- **Elementary:** How to keep the school safe and clean; how to respond when someone gives a wrong answer or makes a mistake; or solving problems or issues with friends
- **Secondary:** Commitments for behavior in collaborative learning spaces or use of personal technology; input on school lunch menus; clubs and enrichment offerings

Partnering with students in this way allows them to develop and refine decision-making skills to strengthen their ability to self-regulate and allows them to trust their own voices.

Foster Trust and Normalize Healthy Risk Taking

We reviewed aspects of trust and risk taking in *Meant for More* classrooms in previous chapters, and your thoughtful investment of this principle within your classroom infrastructure also paves the way for students to utilize (and grow) their voice inside and outside of the classroom walls. Kindness and respect go a long way to cultivating the kind of relationship that enables authentic vulnerability in the classroom, and relationships "are the connective tissue that makes learning possible for students and adults. If you want people to take risks and grow together, you have to invest in cultivating trusting relationships" (Safir, 2017, p. 82).

Read the following two scenarios from students that represent non-academic moments of empowerment at school. Notice ways the school environment has cultivated trust with students, preparing them to take risks, solve problems, and be confident in doing so.

Scenario one: Tommy leaves the safety of his peer group during class to publicly stand up for Max, who is being hassled about his choice of clothing. Tommy is then ridiculed on social media for defending Max, whom the other students are calling a gay slur. As students arrive at their advisory period the next morning, the carryover from the social media posts dissolves the agreements that have been created to ensure a safe classroom. Everyone is saying things about Tommy., using the same slurs. Like a bad game of telephone, rumors are spreading. Briana timidly raises her hand and calls out the homophobic language some students are using as counter to their classroom agreements. She hears an affirmation from another student in class behind her, which bolsters her confidence. She boldly follows the commitments for navigating behaviors that breach their classroom social contract by requesting that the class process the situation using the restorative practices they have agreed to. More students voice their affirmation. The students who were name calling drop their heads and apologize, saying they got caught up in the drama; they agree to restore the classroom balance as well. The teacher pauses the intended lesson for the morning and turns leadership of restorative circles to Briana and the rest of the class.

Scenario two: Gabby knows that Chrissy uses the bathroom after lunch to make herself purge. Today, the two unintentionally lock eyes as Chrissy comes out of the stall, and in that moment, she knows that Gabby knows. Gabby asks Chrissy if she is OK, but the latter simply walks away. Gabby isn't sure what to do. Chrissy would be mad if someone told the teacher what was happening, but this is worrisome behavior. Gabby takes a deep breath and knows exactly which teacher she can trust with this information. She goes back to class but requests a pass to see the teacher immediately, explaining that it's important and can't wait. The teacher raises an eyebrow out of concern. She can tell from the look on Gabby's face that this is significant. The teacher doesn't pry, knowing Gabby will tell her more if and when she's ready. She hands the young girl a pass and Gabby heads out the classroom door.

In these two scenarios shared, where do you hear evidence of trust? What about evidence of risk taking? What actions do you think the adults in the school community have taken to secure any kind of emotional safety and security for their students?

Before moving to the next section, consider how prepared students in your school are to respond if faced with similar types of challenges. They might be younger than the students in these scenarios, but, regardless of their age, do you think each one knows how to speak up about an injustice or infraction, or how to find a trusted adult when they see another student hurting? Take a moment of pause to reflect and write here before reading on.

How Do I Get Myself Ready?

Individuals who join this profession are full of hope and tenacity, with a deep desire to engage every child. Some are nurtured in environments that allow autonomy in how they craft their classroom communities, lessons, and meaningful relationships with students. Teachers in these spaces have a voice. They have control over how to inspire students and to leverage the rigor of the academic, social, and emotional learning standards in relevant ways. Here, there is safety in the school community because there is mutual care and respect for the humans in it.

Other teachers are handed documents that prescribe the infrastructure to be followed, page by page, rule by rule. Teachers in this position have no voice, no autonomy, and perhaps most egregious of all, no joy. Taking away a teacher's voice is like sucking the air out of a room. Research from the National Education Association reports:

> Respecting the knowledge and opinions of educators to help regulate and improve the profession in which they work is a sign of respect and a necessary step to ensure that transformation efforts are long-term solutions and not short-term, feel-good activities. (Jotkoff, 2022)

Learning to find your voice, both in and out of the classroom, is not a singular event. It unfolds and evolves over time as a result of life experience—celebrations and sorrows, fulfilled hopes and empty promises, moments of prideful reflection and others where we are left to wonder, "If only I had . . . ?" I anticipate this reflection will be incredibly personal for you, and as such, I am hopeful you will take the opportunity to just sit in the space for a while. Two valuable ways to utilize and balance your own voice as an educator include (1) notice how you currently empower your own voice and (2) relax your control.

Notice How You Currently Empower Your Own Voice

Empowering our own voices in the school community is first and foremost built on trust and respect. It can manifest more fluidly when leaders and peers create an environment to honor each member's intrinsic value. Employee voice at school can take various forms, such as having autonomy over lesson planning, providing suggestions to resolve a current challenge or need (that are taken into serious consideration or implemented), advocating for opportunities for personal and professional growth or wellness, or participating in school board elections. Even taking the time to learn about the policies and procedures in your school or district (as discussed in chapter 1, page 13) gives you access to knowledge and information to increase your confidence and use your voice in the first place.

Most of us feel more comfortable bringing our voice into a space when we are confident it will be gracefully received. Your places of comfort might be outside the school walls, in your home, community, or peer group. It is far more difficult to lift your words into a space that feels emotionally unsafe or unstable, especially if you experience an environment where voices have already been silenced by hostile feedback, dismissal, or inaction. Finding your voice and then lifting it might be hard if you tend to be a people pleaser, striving to please others and sacrificing your own wants or needs (Villines, 2022a) or were are encouraged to stifle your expression.

In the workplace, research suggests certain attributes help employees' voices be better received, including the following (Brykman & Raver, 2021; Jotkoff, 2022).

- Making sure your ideas or opinions are based on evidence
- Ensuring your suggestions are attainable and practical while also displaying a fresh perspective or approach
- Showing how your contributions would advance the mission and goals of the organization

In addition, Gonzalez (2021) encourages us to find others who share our voice and collaborate, as we may find greater success (and momentum) when we work together. Figure 5.2 helps you engage in the work of emboldening and leveraging your voice when you have something important to say. Or, if you want to do a little more self-reflection first, use figure 5.3 (page 166).

Key Question	My Thoughts
What am I trying to say?	
Why does saying that matter to me?	
Does this matter to anyone else in the same way it matters to me? If so, who? If I'm not sure, how can I find out?	
What could happen—good or not so good—if I speak up?	
Are the potential risks of speaking up worth the benefits?	
If the benefits outweigh the risks, when will I speak up? If they don't outweigh the risks yet, how can I build more self-confidence in what I have to say?	

FIGURE 5.2: Emboldening and leveraging my voice.

When do I feel confident elevating my voice and when do I feel uncomfortable?

When am I letting others speak for me?

How do I feel when that happens?

Who are my models for empowerment, and what can I learn from them?

Who do I want to be a model of empowerment for? What action can I take toward becoming that model?

FIGURE 5.3: Empowering personal voice reflection.

Relax Your Control

As we consider ways to lift our voices into the learning environment, we can also balance the use of our voice by partnering with our students. We are proud of the effort to equip students with the knowledge, skills, and dispositions they need to be productive, competent, and capable citizens, instilling in them the presence of mind to make informed, responsible choices that guide their future. And these points of pride may be coming at the expense of our own capacity. As a cohort, many of us feel exhausted, frustrated, burnt out, and near (or at) our breaking points (Jotkoff, 2022). We may find ourselves out of patience, perhaps even out of a desire to keep engaging in this meaningful work because we have nothing left in the tank to address the inequities and blockers to our success.

Let's remember to give students the chance to actually use those skills and competencies we are so proud of. In these moments, it's vital to understand how and when to just release our metaphorical grip on making sure everything happens exactly as we want it to. In these fragile moments, both you and the learners deserve space to relax and then lift each other back up into emotional safety (as opposed to inadvertently using our voice to diminish the voices of others). This type of regulation and awareness enables the right tone of voice to emerge when it is most needed.

Consider this insight from Patricia Wolfe (n.d.), who notably applies brain research to education: "The person working the hardest is learning the most." Who is working the hardest in your classrooms? My guess is your answer would lean toward the adults. Would you be willing to give yourself permission to let go of *all* the control? Would you consider regaining time and patience when you realize you've been doing things for students who are quite capable of doing these things for themselves? When you are open to realizing that you are not the only decision maker in the classroom, you can elevate the voices of your students to help you find the best way forward. To enable the elevation of voices, there must be an environment in which the sharing of insights, asking of questions, or suggestions for improvement are not only heard, but valued.

A growing body of research, some of which are cited in table 5.2 (page 168) explains how to elevate and empower student voice, with such information continuing to evolve as this book goes to publication.

TABLE 5.2: Research on How to Elevate and Empower Student Voice

Promising Practice	What It Is	Who It's For
Youth Participatory Action Research at https://yparhub.berkeley.edu	"An innovative approach to positive youth and community development based in social justice principles" (Youth Participatory Action Research, n.d.). "A cyclical process of learning and action—research is done not just for the sake of it but to inform solution to problems that young people themselves care about" (University of California Berkeley, n.d.).	Anyone! It's a focused approach for young people who may be experiencing various forms of oppression or marginalization.
Student SEL Data Protocol from CASEL at https://tinyurl.com/2827844h	"A structured way for educators to engage in meaningful data reflection conversations with students and elevate their perspectives when interpreting data and making school-level decisions" (CASEL, 2022).	Students and teachers, working collaboratively
Democratic Classroom Practices at www.edutopia.org/article/power-democratic-classroom or *Worldwide Learning: A Teacher's Guide to Shaping a Just, Sustainable Future* (Marschall & Crawford, 2022)	"A classroom that promotes shared responsibilities so that students are engaged in their communities . . . [it] engages students in living democratically by promoting values such as inclusion, voice, representation, and participation" (Marschall, 2021).	Students of all ages, in partnership with their teachers

When multiple perspectives and voices are invited into a space, be aware of how the conditions have or have not been created for both students and adults to learn how to make empowered choices and how and when to use their voices. To that end, examine some ideas for preparedness with others.

How Do I Get My Team Ready?

Educators across the globe are more actively acknowledging the value of student voice and intentionally designing opportunities to bring student perspectives into school- or classroom-level decisions (Holquist, 2019). Bringing student voice into these moments requires educators to make sure that students know *how* to make decisions to begin with.

Gauging student readiness could happen in the classroom by proposing scenarios to hear how students respond. Examples appear in figure 5.4.

Grade Level	Potential Scenario to Present to Students
Preschool	You really want to play with a toy at recess, but someone else is already using it. What do you do?
Elementary School	You decide to wear a short-sleeved t-shirt, sweatpants, and no jacket to school, even though you know it's only fifteen degrees Fahrenheit outside. How might your decision impact your comfort at the bus stop?
Middle School	You want to have a sleepover for your birthday. You want to invite eight of your friends, but your mom said you can only have three over. How do you choose? How will you respond if someone feels left out?
High School	A girl you have been working up the courage to talk to just invited you to a party at her house tonight. It sounds fun and you're excited to go, but then you overhear some kids from the soccer team talking about sneaking alcohol into the party. You're in season for lacrosse, and she plays for the tennis team; both of your athletic eligibility would be at risk in the presence of alcohol, as would the eligibility of the members on the soccer team. How would you handle the situation? What choice do you make yourself? For your friend?

FIGURE 5.4: Scenarios to gauge student readiness for making decisions.

Elementary teacher and social-emotional learning author Peyton Curley (2021), shares, "To demonstrate responsible decision making, students need to learn skills in critical thinking, open-mindedness, sound judgment, reason, problem solving and identifying solutions." The preceding scenarios provide students with the opportunity to demonstrate such skills and can reveal to students the impact of using those skills to make decisions. Their reactions can target your instructional efforts in order to focus on the decision-making elements that require more attention.

As you open yourself to the possibility that all members in our classroom community could assist in making decisions for the betterment of the *learning* environment, let's consider three strategies and discussions to ask our teammates to share in the work of: (1) acknowledge the power dynamics in your classroom and determine how to create more balance; (2) listen, learn, and lead; and (3) commit to being students' fiercest advocates.

Acknowledge the Power Dynamics in Your Classroom and Determine How to Create More Balance

Have you ever watched a young child who is learning to tie her shoes? Cute, right? Except when that child is your *own* child, and you're already ten minutes behind schedule, and it would just be *so much easier* to bend down and tie the shoe yourself. And you know from experience that your desire for efficiency, however urgent it may have been, squashed the feeling of competence in your child.

Can you think of a moment where that same squashing has happened to a student or to one of your colleagues in your school? As we unlearn the conditioning and push back against the implied pressure to yield to specific pacing, focus on higher test scores, and adopt mile-wide, inch-deep curriculum coverage, we can re-learn how fostering hope and joy in our classrooms means students are involved in the process of learning. This effort can position us as teachers to better notice moments for choice in order to intentionally nurture them through our designed learning experiences. Research indicates that in addition to allowing student choice in their work, "students need to develop the ability to self-reflect and assess their different learning opportunities . . . students [need] practice in problem-solving and decision-making and help . . . [reflecting] on and [making] decisions about what they need" (O'Rourke, 2022).

One way to model a shift in the balance of power is to intentionally design a lesson in which you can talk with students and model how they can be partners in creating the classroom community. Katie Novak (2022), a former teacher who helps educators implement inclusive practices and Universal Design of Learning principles, suggests that if we do not believe our students are able to reach targeted academic or social-emotional goals, our isolated decisions about classroom setup, lesson planning, and learning activities will simply reinforce those low expectations—and ultimately promote deficit thinking and a lack of efficacy within our students. She continues, stating:

> If we offer students a remedial curriculum or run a classroom that allows minimal freedom, we are unconsciously preparing our students to aim low. When students are not given freedom of choice or taught critical thinking skills, they are less likely to develop the tools they need to fulfill their career aspirations later in life—whether that is in the professions or the trades or some other path of their choosing. That's not what we want for our kids. Providing options and choices for our learners helps us co-create a learning environment that ensures that we don't communicate these types of hidden messages to our students. When we set the bar high and provide students with options to reach it, it sends them a message that we expect big things from them and we believe in them. (Novak, 2022, p. 67)

Sample opportunities for students to co-design experiences—including how they look, feel, and sound—can begin neutralizing the dynamics of power, removing the teacher as the sole position of authority in the learning space. Students can help make decisions around time, materials, and space, as well as relationships and interactions between peers and adults.

In addition to normalizing a balance of decision making between teacher and student, you also may notice that some students appear to have more control over the learning environment than you (or your students) may be comfortable with. Iesha Small, (2022), author of *The Unexpected Leader: Exploring the Real Nature of Values, Authenticity, and Moral Purpose in Education*, says, "Power dynamics between your pupils could be limiting their learning potential." Have you ever noticed how some students in your classroom dominate discussion while others can sit without saying a word? This could be an example of power imbalance between your students. Think back to the discussion on social contracts as a positive tool for realignment (page 101).

Here are more examples of question stems you might pose.

- How does it feel when you get to make a decision on your own?
- Which decisions should I make in the classroom as your teacher?
- Which decisions should you make as students?
- Are there any decisions we should make together?

In addition, consider implementing the following inclusive strategies from international thought leaders Carla Marschall and Elizabeth Crawford (2022), who specialize in global education through the development of who they call worldwise learners. In this framework, the authors ask students to integrate the heart, the head, and the hand in their active learning experiences. The authors propose the fostering of a democratic classroom, a learning space where teachers and students toggle between control, in which "students actively practice democratic values, understand their rights, and take responsibility for their behavior as both individuals and members of a community" (Marschall & Crawford, 2022, p. 37).

- **Early elementary:** Students create a peaceful place in their classroom, which is defined as a quiet space where they can retreat to reflect on their feelings, work out a challenge with a friend, or find a sense of calm. Students use a Y-chart to brainstorm what a peaceful place in their classroom would sound like, look like, and feel like. Students then use the ideas generated to determine the best location in the classroom to establish a peaceful place. Students can build and decorate that space, promoting a sense of agency. The teacher partners with students to model examples of how to use the peaceful place well, in adherence to the norms and commitments previously created by the students. The teacher also finds moments over the course of the year to check in with students by asking how it's going, confirming whether the space needs any improvements, or celebrating their responsible use of the space.

- **Upper elementary and middle school:** Like Mr. Eberhardt's modeling in the Meant for MoreMENTUM story shared in chapter 4 (page 148), try the sort, group, name strategy. Students generate questions about a topic or issue they have discussed and then sort those questions into categories; rows or columns work best so that all questions are visible. Finally, students name the categories with single words or short phrases. This process teaches students about the power of a question, leading to meaningful learning through student-driven inquiry. Students have sufficient content knowledge to develop open-ended questions for exploration rather than yes/no questions to which answers are simply found.
- **High school:** Students identify a challenge in order to develop a collaborative inquiry-based project on which they could take action. They might try learning about a problem in the community or an issue in current events. Students use a protocol to develop outcomes, a timeline, and a list of resources needed to complete the project. They form teams and utilize strategies they have learned in class, such as note-taking, collaboration, perspective sharing, and solution generation.

Similar to the child learning to tie his shoes, when students are involved in decision making, it might take longer to get things done. However, keep in mind that "Students use their identities, prior knowledge, and deep understanding to engage critically with problems in communities at various scales. They view themselves as able to produce positive change" (Marschall & Crawford, 2022, p. 5). That is a moment well worth the wait.

Listen, Learn, and Lead

My most humbling experiences as an educator were during my times of reflection after knowing that I had taken a royal misstep with my students. These missteps were often due to the absence of student voice and perspective in my decision making, which led to flaws in my isolated interpretation of a situation or—worse yet—erroneous assumptions that there was an issue to be resolved in the first place.

But how can we prepare ourselves for the moment students actually do or say something that hurts us or someone else? It's important to connect as a team in order to make sure everyone has a shared understanding of why you are asking for student voices to emerge in the first place. Then, together, you can determine some potential sentence stems or plan collaborative co-led activities with students. For example, you could share a mock scenario with students: "Student A said something to Student B about Students C and D. Now, Student A is feeling left out by all three of the students."

Ask students what they would do if the situation happened to them.

- "How can Student A figure out why Students B appears to be upset with her?"
- "How could we help Student A fix her behavior with Students C and D?"
- "What did we learn from this situation that can help us with our own friends?"

In a real situation, you could pose questions such as, "What could I have done differently?" or "What am I doing or saying that is making it difficult for us to work together?" You could also lean into previously suggested exercises of developing a social contract, utilizing restorative circles, and using the power of story to invite and gather thoughts and information from students.

Another useful strategy is known as an inside-outside fishbowl. Students form an inner circle and an outer circle; for example, students on the inside of the circle are having a discussion about an event or academic prompt, and students on the outside are listening and taking notes because eventually students will be able to change positions. This activity cultivates an authentic, inclusive environment that empowers voice because students have both a speaking and listening role, which creates heightened ownership in the content of the discussion (Learning for Justice, n.d.). Additionally, reflective questions such as the following can further deepen student connection to the activity.

- How did it feel to share your thinking out loud knowing that your peers were paying attention?
- Were you able to communicate better when you had notes in front of you, or when you were responding on the fly, in the moment?
- In what other situations can you be heard and validated as you share your perspectives?

- Now that you have participated in this experience, what are you most proud of related to your contributions? What would you like to do better next time?

Quaglia Institute (2020) affirms, "We view voice as a process that leads toward collective action; *listening* to what people are saying (and not saying), *learning* from what is being said, and *leading* together on what actions need to be taken." Review the example scenario in figure 5.5 and access the reproducible "Listen, Learn, and Lead Process Outline" (page 187). This team-friendly structure provides an accessible frame for teachers to approach the various concerns or issues we might face with our students.

Current Campus Issue or Idea Needing Resolution: *Students are not completing their homework assignments.* Current Adult-Driven Solution: *We will implement a scaffolded set of consequences, starting with notes or calls home, then after-school detentions, and progressing to zeros or incompletes in the gradebook for these assignments.* Evidence That the Adult-Driven Solution Is Ineffective: *Homework is still not being completed.*
Listen: *What are my students saying? What are they not saying?*
"Homework isn't completed because we don't understand what we are supposed to do, and there isn't enough class time to clarify with the teacher before it's due." *"My teacher only has office hours before school on Tuesdays and Fridays, but I ride the bus, so I am unable to come early."* *"I just don't like this teacher, and I am not interested in working hard in that class because I know my teacher doesn't care about me anyway."* *"Different teachers have different expectations."* *"I have lots to do at night outside of school. My teacher doesn't even bother to review my homework for accuracy (or at all!), so why should I spend my time doing something that doesn't feel valuable for me?"*
Learn: *What do I know now after hearing what students had to say?*
We need to re-clarify the purpose of homework and reduce or eliminate its use as singular evidence of learning in the gradebook. *We need to find alternate times to be accessible to students who need help with their assignments.*

We need to strengthen relationships with students, especially those who may be uncomfortable asking questions of adults with whom they have unstable relationships.
Lead: *What actions can students take—as a cohort or in collaboration with adults—to move toward resolution?*
We could bring a cohort of students together to review the data on missing or incomplete homework and provide potential reasons for the issue. *We could conduct focus groups with students to determine solutions.* *We could ask students directly about the perceived relevance of homework and co-generate solutions to develop a shared understanding between students and teachers.*
Additional Notes or Considerations: *We also need to revisit our homework and grading policies across the campus to ensure consistency across classrooms and content area teams. We should review the data to notice which students are having trouble in certain classes and which students are having trouble completing work across the board.*

FIGURE 5.5: Example listen, learn, and lead process outline.

In working with teams, departments, and districts all over the U.S., I have heard about countless hours of discussion where adults have gathered in an effort to resolve a situation involving students. Sometimes, that approach is necessary. However, in many cases, the adults are able to arrive at solutions more efficiently and more effectively when the perspectives of the people who are closest to the issue (in this case, the students) are intentionally sought.

Commit to Fierce Advocacy for Students

Educators are a bold, fierce, driven, compassionate, and humble cohort. Quiet and graceful at times, tenacious and steadfast in others. We engage in the daily grind because we deeply understand that the enormity of our potential for impact is striking. Stop for a moment and consider: Who do you work hard for? I would hardly imagine that you choose to work hard for people who constantly tell you all the ways you are messing up or things you are doing wrong. Students want you to be in their corner. Some of them actually *need* you to be. Catharine Biddle, Lyn Mikel Brown, and Mark Tappan (2022) state:

> To understand children's needs, particularly children who, because of systemic injustice and inequity experience school on the margins, we must create spaces and opportunities for them to speak about their experiences, to explain what isn't working, to ask for what they need, and to share what excites them and nurtures them.

Your belief in them is critical. But it's not enough. Strategies in the previous sections prepare both teacher and student voice. Now, let's examine the magnitude of our conviction. Consider the questions in figure 5.6. How is your advocacy not only inspired, but ignited, through this reflection?

How will you commit to teaching students as they are and equipping them with the tools and strategies they will need to make informed choices in their lives?
How will you stand beside them, in partnership, instead of always leading from the front?
What will you do and say to show them that you mean it?
How will you behave so that students believe that you *value* what they have to say?

FIGURE 5.6: Student advocacy reflection.

Visit ***go.SolutionTree.com/schoolimprovement*** *for a free reproducible version of this figure.*

Another potential moment for empowering voice can emerge through your feedback delivery. Consider this: feedback should never *hold* students back, and it must always feed the learning *forward*. For example, when communicating to students about their learning, making it a process where you first identify what the student did well, focus on what they need, and partner with the student to describe what's next for them as a learner is far more effective than generic feedback such as "Good job!" or "Needs fixing." Teacher Angela Di Michele Lalor (2022) shares her reflections, stating, "The more comprehensive feedback can empower students because it's individualized to the student, leverages students' assets, interests, and learning preferences, and builds students' confidence in themselves." In addition, student-led conferences, peer-to-peer feedback, and collaborative group work can build shared understanding of what success can look like and even strengthen work sampling (because the learners have been meaningfully and purposeful involved in generating the criteria for performance).

Remember that the presence of voice is a legitimate fundamental right of any child. Article 12 of the United Nations Convention on the Rights of the Child "establishes the right of every child to have a say in matters which affect them, whether in or out of school, as well as to be involved in decisions that affect them" (United Nations Human Rights Office of the High Commissioner, 1989). Creating conditions for student voice empowers a sense of belonging, a sense of citizenship, and a sense of care and compassion toward others. Our collaborative efforts as teacher teams provide the best vehicle through which to drive this *Meant for More* attribute into practice.

How Do I Get My Students Ready?

In *Meant for More* classrooms, students will best develop (and refine) their voice when provided with learning experiences that actually enable them to *use* their voice. Gretchen Brion-Meisels (as cited in Shafer, 2017), a faculty member at the Harvard Graduate School of Education, echoes the need for student voice representation at all levels with the system, stating, "Principals should leave space for students on school leadership teams, improvement teams, or equity and diversity teams. In meetings, participants should treat students as full members of the team, not just observers."

But as noted in the introductory vignette to this chapter, we cannot cultivate and empower voice in our students and then continue to implement classroom policies or procedures that leave students voiceless. Research affirms that when we tokenize student voice, meaning we ask for it but don't consider it, students share they feel detached from the school and classroom communities and rarely seek opportunities to share their voice in the future (Brennen & Kahloon, 2021; Holquist, 2019; Rademacher, 2015).

Consider the following three suggestions as entry points for both teaching and lifting your students' voices in your classroom or school: (1) co-construct feedback for improvement, (2) share examples of what empowering voice looks like at school, and (3) let students speak.

Co-Construct Feedback for Improvement

Let's start with an example. You recently implemented a new routine for bathroom use in your classroom, and it isn't having the effect you intended. As a high school teacher, you noticed a pattern of students using the bathroom more frequently during guided practice time, after the core content of the day's lesson had been delivered. You have been allowed by your administrator to employ your own bathroom policies in your classroom. (Side note: this is *not* something I would advocate for as it creates imbalanced conditions for students and teachers alike.) You have not had "rules" about bathroom use in the past.

You believe that students can self-regulate their time and needs and have trusted them to do so. Yet based on recent observations of an increase in student bathroom requests—and after having a conversation with your department chair—you decided to implement a new approach, stating that students would only be allowed four opportunities during the semester to use the bathroom during your class time. Students have not said anything to you directly, but you have felt tension in the space. The positive, trusting relationships you have had with students seem newly strained, and student participation during your lessons has plummeted.

You don't understand what has gone wrong; after all, you're just trying to make sure that students stay in your classroom during guiding work time because you find that time to be helpful for formatively assessing your teaching effectiveness as well as allowing students to complete the required work (and avoid *home*work). Yet you decide to pause today's lesson and figure out why everything has gone sideways. You address your students as follows: "I'm noticing some tension in the classroom lately, and I feel like things have changed since I announced our new bathroom policy." You notice heads nodding in affirmation, acknowledging this is the issue. You continue, saying, "To be honest, I'm not sure I understand what all the fuss is about. Can you help me understand the problem?"

Ask and you shall receive, right? Students were hesitant to share at first, but it didn't take long for that boulder to start rolling. Students shared how they felt slighted by a new policy without understanding that there was a problem in the first place. They shared that, because this class was after lunch, there was going to be an increase in bathroom use. Students stated they were actually showing you respect by *not* using the bathroom during your actual lesson because they found that time highly critical for their understanding of what to do during their guiding work time. You heard their responses and integrated their voices to let the conversation flow, using additional guiding questions such as, *Why does it matter so deeply?*, *What needs to be different?*, or *How can we make that happen?* Ultimately, you built a shared understanding of each other's perspectives and were able to generate a shared, mutually agreeable outcome for moving forward. Remember what we discussed earlier in this chapter? Partner *with*, not do *to*. When issues arise, invite students to help you understand before making assumptions and moving to action. They will tell you; you just have to ask.

Share Examples of What Empowering Voice Looks Like at School

There is a glaring disparity between the shared desire among teachers, parents, and students alike for empowering voice and its capacity to be meaningfully cultivated in our classrooms and schools. For example, most people want students to be able to express themselves as well as demonstrate confidence in their opinions and independence in their thoughts and communication. Yet, some schools remain places where teachers and students alike are told exactly what to wear, how to act, and what to learn without any input or opportunity to provide feedback. We cannot expect students to develop empowerment skills when we give them no opportunity to practice.

If you feel this tension in your classroom and your interactions with colleagues and families, Quaglia Institute (2020) promotes the urgency for changing this dynamic:

> Student voice challenges the current norm where the state, district, and teachers decide what students will learn, direct how they will learn, and dictate the assessment of that learning. Meaningful student voice requires students to play an active role in all that a school does, from instruction to assessment to curriculum design.

How can we make this happen? When can students lead? Where can they meaningfully advocate for their needs?

Consider this example in practice. When students in a pre-algebra course were demonstrating difficulty graphing and interpretating data, the teacher and assistant principal decided to incorporate real data from their school to illustrate the concept. They collaboratively shared recent student discipline referral data with students regarding classroom disruption. Students looked at the data, and quickly determined that a valuable piece of information was missing: why students were creating disruptions in certain learning spaces more than others. These students—who were demonstrating difficulty with the clinical task of graphing irrelevant data (scenarios of pre-populated information from the textbook) were now highly engaged in reviewing the data of their peers by noticing patterns and trends, and were hungry to find out why the data was presenting in this way. This classroom of students created a survey to invite any willing participants to respond to a set of questions (developed as a class), reviewed and graphed the collected data, and then used the information gathered to provide suggestions and alternate solutions to reduce the number of classroom disruption referrals to the office. The administrative team on this campus reviewed the class suggestions and insights, determined a reasonable solution, and then shared their findings and decisions with the student body as a whole regarding the renewed policies and expectations for students and teachers alike.

At the elementary level, this concept of empowering voice also links back to the content in chapter 2 (page 49) and chapter 3 (page 83) on empathy and fostering connection. Connection and voice are interdependent when students display assertiveness, such as naming behaviors that intentionally exclude or tease a classmate or pausing during academic situations where collaborative group work is expected but not everyone is contributing equally. Neuroscientist Judy Willis (2020) states, "Assertiveness practice starts with building children's recognition of situations when it is appropriate to feel concern for themselves and/or others, even if what to do or how to do it is not obvious." When we anticipate these moments and provide explicit instruction, students can begin to gain confidence in their skills independently because they have used the same skills under the supervision of an adult in their classroom.

An empathy map is one example of such explicit instruction. Use the map in a variety of situations, from having students learn about historical events by aligning with a person or a role and identifying that person's feelings, thoughts, and actions, to students identifying their own social-emotional needs and desires for a successful school year. Author and SEL educator Jorge Valenzuela (2021) recommends using empathy maps when determining the right instructional strategies or scaffolds for students, in order to avoid unproductive frustration in the learning experience. An example empathy map is in figure 5.7. You can adapt the reproducible "Empathy Map" (page 188) to the specific needs of your students.

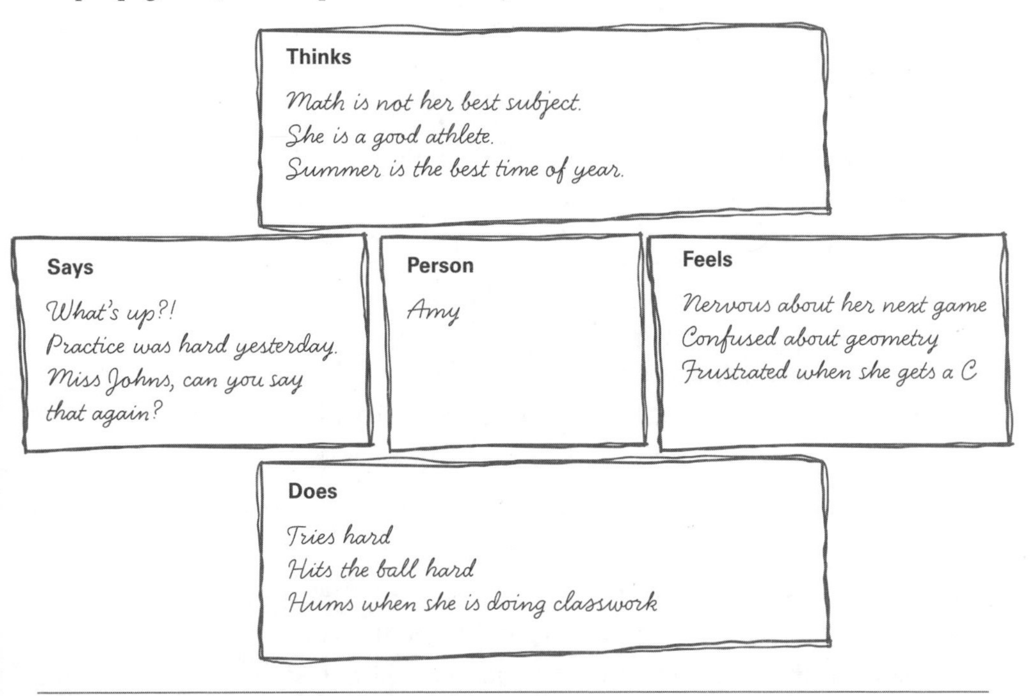

FIGURE 5.7: Empathy map frame example.

I love these stories and examples; when we engage students in moments of partnership, and then show students how we value their feedback with a meaningful response, we increase the confidence of students to use their voice in the future. As you read those examples, hopefully you can generate similar possibilities for the students you and your teammates currently serve.

Let Students Speak

Circling back to a comment earlier in this chapter, it is difficult for students to use their voices if they do not believe that you actually want them to. One way to help students *learn* to speak is by activating their ability to make choices for how to best demonstrate their learning. For example, if you have students organized into book clubs, for the intended purpose of reading a book together, discussing the book together, and then summarizing the book together, perhaps you could let students select the medium or modality in which they share what has been learned.

Instead of asking each book club team to provide a summary via a traditional written report, try offering alternate ways for students to demonstrate their ability to summarize, such as creating a comic, writing a blog post, producing a video commercial or advertisement about the book, drawing a marketing poster or crafting a poem or song lyrics to accurately communicate the summarization. You could be tight on the criteria, such as What does success look like? and What components must be included in your summarization? Then, let students take it from there. I remember being wonderfully surprised by the quality of student work when I released common expectations of how their learning had to be represented; their creativity oozed into my classroom, and more often than not, student representations far exceeded my expectations and more deeply represented their understanding of the content.

Be mindful of places where our good intentions can go sideways. Opportunities to gather student voice can quickly lose integrity if it doesn't also include compassion. Here are *non-examples* of engaging student voice (Holquist, 2019).

- Allowing students to speak before a school board meeting, but preventing them from hearing adult discussion on the issues or the rationale for a decision
- Asking students to complete a survey but not sharing results (employing transparency)
- Requiring students to use a script for what to say or how to say it in public forums or meetings

During my administrative tenure, I witnessed several open forums at school board meetings, but one still sits with me. This particular evening, we were continuing a discussion on the projected closure of a school due to projections regarding future enrollment. Although we were using reliable data, the community was lit with deeply passionate advocacy for the school remaining open. Many young students registered to speak and shared their thoughts and feelings with members of the district and school board. While their passions were appropriately placed, it was difficult to watch some of these brave students, quivering at the microphone, glancing back at family members, stumbling over words that someone else had written, and ultimately crying when afterward some adults told the students they "didn't say it right" or "didn't read it like we practiced." This is an example of misalignment to *Meant for More* student voice definitions; during that meeting, students may have felt *tokenized*, meaning they were "manipulated when asked to share their voice in a decision-making capacity" (Holquist, 2019). Let their voice be *their* voice, in their own words, where their unique, authentic personalities can be genuinely on display.

What Infrastructure Do I Need to Make It Happen?

Before we begin this next section, let's put some real talk out there: intentionally designing opportunities to elevate student voice may be tougher than we think. Like many attributes of the *Meant for More* classroom, the value of student voice is simple to understand (and believe in) but far more complex to actually implement (Mayes, Finneran, & Black, 2019). Brennen & Kahloon (2021) state, "Students spend upwards of thirty-five hours a week in a classroom and yet, they are rarely consulted when it comes to improving our schools." Might our struggle to invite students' voices into the fold stem from the fact that our voices as educators may also be muted, uninvited to the table for insights and input when decisions are being made that would directly impact us? The infrastructure for this attribute again focuses on the behaviors of adults; this chapter discusses investing in a culture of belonging and amplifying educator voice as two considerations to elevate this powerful practice in our schools.

Invest in a Culture of Belonging

Writer and teacher Toko-pa Turner (2017), an immigrant to the United States, writes, "There are many different kinds of belonging. The first . . . is the feeling of belonging to a community, or to a geography . . . and the belonging [that] we yearn to feel in a purpose or vocation" (p. 15). As a former English as a second language teacher, I wanted to cultivate a space of belonging for each of my learners. To me, this meant creating a place where students felt safe, could make mistakes without fear of being teased, and continued to celebrate their native languages and traditions.

I always aspired for students on our campus to say "That's *my* school" and "Those are *my* people," with pride, rather than "Oh yeah, that's just where I go to school." I wanted to create a deep and rich culture where students felt pride and ownership in what they were doing, how they were learning, and why it all mattered. Research from ASCD (2004) indicates "students are eager to serve as role models in leading change once they have been empowered by a learning community that acknowledges their sense of individual responsibility and facilitates the acquisition of leadership skills." Additionally, self-determination theory claims that every person really wants a sense of autonomy, competence, and *relatedness* (Ryan & Deci, 2018). This connects back to earlier learning throughout the book regarding both authentic identity expression (Brennen & Kahloon, 2021; Safir, 2017; Wamsley, 2021) and the importance of belonging (Brown, 2010; Novak, 2022).

Students can feel connected to, or as though they belong, in our school when we make the learning experiences engaging, relevant, and meaningful. Sometimes, we need the voices of our learners to be successful in this endeavor! In one district, an elementary student happened to notice the volume of vehicle traffic surrounding the intersection next to his school and how inattentive drivers were creating a dangerous situation for the crossing guards and students alike. This student signed up to speak during an open forum at a school board meeting to share his observation and provide a suggestion to redesign that intersection with a roundabout (instead of a four-way stop). The student's ideas were recognized and validated, and a board member suggested the student sign up for public comments at an upcoming city council meeting. This lone empowered voice generated momentum with his ideas and garnered additional voices of support; today, that intersection has been redesigned as this student envisioned. This student's sense of belonging—he cared about people in his school, and they cared about him—provided an opportunity to use his voice and to see its productive power.

Authorize Teacher and Administrator Voice

Educators want their students' voices to be heard and valued. Yet it will be more difficult for teachers to create learning spaces that empower student voice if their own voices are muted or even discredited. "Administrators can contribute to faculty emotional well-being by "allowing teachers to have a voice in regards to issues in the school" (Lambersky, 2016, as cited in Polite, 2020). To go even further, study participants report feeling improved engagement, commitment, and morale "when principals allowed teachers to have a voice" (Lambersky, 2016, p. 399).

Teachers and administrators alike benefit from regular status check moments embedded in staff meetings. We should regularly seek feedback on what's working and what isn't. Dialogue about why specific teaching efforts have or have not been successful help us avoid inadvertently pulling resources from an area of success. The people who are closest to the impact of the decision need a seat at the table (a voice) as that decision is being made. We need to normalize the seeking, gathering, and organizing of educator voice to ensure that our students can learn how to best use theirs as well.

Table 5.3 represents those ideas for partnering with students to make decisions and also highlights their connection to this component of our *Meant for More* infrastructure.

TABLE 5.3: Designing Decision-Making Opportunities for Students

Model Type	How It Could Work	Example
Adult-run, active listening	Adults seek input from students and gather their insights, then incorporate that feedback into decisions being made.	A teacher administers a survey to students, asking them to give feedback on the lesson activity.
Adult-run, shared decisions with students	Adults ask students to share their feedback in front of a decision-making body, such as the school board or community leadership team, and then involve students in the decision-making process.	A school principal interviews a group of students about the increase in bathroom vandalism. The students have some ideas to curb the behavior and want to be part of the solution. The students prepare a presentation for the school board to communicate their ideas and needs in effort to resolve the issue.
Student-run, shared decisions with adults	Students organize the activities or experiences, and adults provide final approval.	The student council has been asked to plan the school dance and given a budget.

Student-run, limited influence from adults	Students are able to make decisions on school climate, wellness, activities, or clubs (since students cannot be given full school authority on all operational or instructional planning).	Students plan activities (such as author visits and food trucks), community involvement, and service projects to promote a partnership between the school and members of the community.

Source: Adapted from Holquist, 2019.

Check out the Meant for MoreMENTUM story to read about a rural Minnesotan community, displaying the student-run, shared decisions with adults model of decision-making structure.

Visit **go.SolutionTree.com/schoolimprovement** for a free reproducible "Chapter Summarization Tool to Inspire Action" and use its prompts to refresh your ideas and reflections from what you read in this chapter

Meant for MoreMENTUM: Stories That Ignite Us

In Jordan, Minnesota, a rural community southwest of Minneapolis–St. Paul, diversity and equity consultants Sarah and Malik were approached by a group of exasperated students. These students were concerned with experiences they had witnessed at school, and they wanted to create a platform to share their observations with others. They wanted to build a bridge, hopeful that their efforts to share their observations would be an impetus for the healing was desperately demanded among and between students, staff, and their community as a whole.

This initial student cohort recruited other students to join equity leadership teams within the school community. The students agreed they did not want to form affinity groups (that is, a group of individuals who share a common identity or interest) but wanted to design integrated spaces for any student to collectively share in the discussion and the development of changes and actions needed. With the support of Sarah and Malik, the students utilized a Caring and Committed Conversation process (more background on this in chapter 3, page 110) to bring an intentional structure to the planning, implementation, and reflection on each topic.

By design, the students led a sixty- to ninety-minute conversation, beginning with a whole-group welcome, a review of the guidelines and agreements for the day, and an agreement of the assumed facts and working definitions for vocabulary being used. Then, students engaged in conversation about the topic with a small group of people at their table, utilizing story-starting question prompts as needed. Students continued developing their voice during the post-conversation as well. As the large group determined the truths from the day's conversation, the students and facilitators learned how to work with the words until the groups arrived at a truth that they could all agree on. It is here that the students learned where the group is most vulnerable; while it may be easier to accept words just to be done with the conversation on a given day, ending there exposes everyone to continued misunderstandings or misrepresentations of the key points. Sarah shares, "When people stop caring about words or give up on a process, it means they have given up hope. Or when people stop contributing at all because they don't want to share a voice if it appears that a decision has already been made. Words *do* matter. We believe in keeping hope alive." As educators, we have a responsibility to attend to the psychology of the words we choose and how they impact the truths we share.

Teachers who participated in the conversations at this school describe how the stories and discussions have brought about real changes in their classrooms. They also have improved or deepened their relationships with students. Students in the community built confidence and hope as they engaged in a process that invited, inspired, and resulted in relation and empowerment. Sarah reveals, "Students don't feel the pressure to change, but have the inspiration to change." She affirms that students say that these conversations promote a connection to their school and, most meaningfully, provide evidence of how their collective energy and voice can make positive changes in their community. (S. Miller, personal communication, February 15, 2023.)

"A key component of empowering voice is that we are—by design—creating spaces that allow learners to grow into who they want to be because they know how to productively advocate for their needs and display a tenacity to engage, even in moments where their voice is being diminished."

Listen, Learn, and Lead Process Outline

Current campus issue or idea needing resolution: Current adult-driven solution: Evidence that the adult-driven solution is ineffective:
Listen: What are my students saying? What are they not saying?
Learn: What do I know now after hearing what students had to say?
Lead: What actions can students take—as a cohort or in collaboration with adults—to move toward resolution?

Empathy Map

Write the person's name in the center box. That person can be you or another person, including a classmate or someone you are learning about in class. In the surrounding boxes, write what that person thinks, feels, does, and says.

	Thinks	
Says	**Person**	**Feels**
	Does	

Chapter 6

Nurturing Resilience

I met my friend, let's call her *Giselle*, during my first week in a new job with a new school district. Within five minutes of our first conversation, I was confident that I had found a work sister. As it turns out, she felt the same way! I soon found creative ways to weave my department with Giselle's (which was a natural fit, but past practice had forced everyone into silos), which enabled her human-centric ways of thinking to enhance our approaches toward solution orientations for projects within my department. The closer we grew, the more we noticed people in other departments and school sites were drawn to how we approached our work and leveraged the gifts and talents of the people within. We were gaining momentum around growth and achievement efforts for students in ways that were unprecedented—and in a relatively short amount of time. Giselle and I weren't doing anything special; we were simply bringing people *in* and activating their personal strengths and professional talents to reveal what was possible.

And it was beautiful! Until . . . it wasn't. Until we were told by a person in an authoritative position that our work was moving too fast because he didn't understand our approach and how it could be sustainable, even though it was already benefiting students and adults alike. Soon after, we were told to stop altogether.

Here's how Giselle describes the experience:

> I was fully committed to the work of the system for one and a half decades. In my relentless leadership pursuit for equity, social justice, and inclusion, I accepted that there would be tragedy and loss—my own—through demotion, reassignment, and misrepresentation. I had not anticipated the loss of my personal identity. There came a time when I could no longer unsee that which I had seen.
>
> I had allies in the work, but the allies were outnumbered by people taking action incongruent with the mission, others maintaining the status quo through conscious inaction, and still others operating in a state of unconsciousness or denial. I felt the horror, understood the wrongness, and the inevitable impact on our stakeholders' lives. Through the support of a small network of colleagues championing the work, women authentically empowering other women, and my husband, I showed up each day ready to do battle. I convinced myself each evening that I loved my job while simultaneously ranting about the inequities and systemic barriers that felt insurmountable. This led to questioning my own knowledge and skill and occasionally my beliefs. I would prep for difficult conversations, saturate myself in the words of empowered and affirming thought partners, and I would seek out others. And some days, I would fall into commiserating, gossiping, and judgment—yet excuse my behaviors because I wore my relentless commitment as a badge of honor. I believed that I was strong for enduring dehumanizing words and actions in service of the mission.
>
> But what I wanted was to be seen, heard, and valued! I wanted this for those that I served as well. Mentorship from a courageous, female leader helped me reframe my thinking and reclaim my power. She encouraged unapologetic leadership. I developed this capacity over time, but ultimately, freedom came to me when I decided I would leave, and I began to show up—unapologetically as me. (G. Rinland, personal communication, November 22, 2022)

Reflect on the questions in figure 6.1 before moving forward.

How do you connect with Giselle's story?

Think about a time when your known strengths could have been utilized but weren't. How did it feel? How would the outcome have been different if your gifts and talents had been accessed?

How do you think Giselle's story might connect with this chapter topic of *nurturing resilience*?

FIGURE 6.1: Story reflection.

In our profession, we are consistently being asked to do more with less, demonstrate vulnerability in the face of adversity, and display an endless supply of grit and perseverance. You may have heard colleagues reference the idea that every system is perfectly designed to achieve the results it gets. That begs the question: are our current feelings and emotions about our work connected to the design and infrastructure of the system in which we are working?

Consider this: If you feel exhausted, burned out, wiped, or dismayed, can you also say that your school or district functions with competing or changing priorities, offers limited collaboration or professional learning opportunities, shares inconsistent or untimely communication, or determines inequitable distribution of resources? And if you feel empowered, trusted, and valued within your school or district, is it because there has been dedicated time to building relationships across and between departments, you receive direct and timely communication from your peers and supervisors (including feedback and celebrations), and decision-making processes are student-focused around a tight mission, vision, and goals with clear and targeted priorities?

As you consider your current feelings about your job, your colleagues, and your level of hope about your abilities to transform student achievement, can you also see how the system in which you operate may be contributing to those feelings, for better or for worse? The focus of this chapter is nurturing resilience. But the real question is: Why should I (or my students) be asked by the system to work more and fight harder against setbacks, when that system shouldn't unrealistically demand so much of me in the first place?

What Do We Mean by *Nurturing Resilience*?

No matter how many years of life experience you have coming into this chapter, there may be at least one idea that all generations can share agreement on: life is predictably *un*predictable. In our classrooms, we may have the best-laid lesson plans but then the students show up with unexpected knowledge, questions, or wonderings. We think we know how a critical conversation is going to play out with a colleague when it suddenly veers off course, and feelings of dismay or unpreparedness take over. The same premise holds true in various moments throughout our personal lives, with some moments of unpredictability being more disruptive than others. Resilience is the attribute that helps us recover in such moments.

Janice Gair (2020), an emotional intelligence coach, cites three areas to build resilience: (1) commitment, (2) control, and (3) challenge. To align these three areas to the professional environment, consider the following.

1. **Commitment:** This means setting purposeful goals and breaking the achievement of that goal into manageable tasks. For example, planning a unit of study in advance of instruction can be an overwhelming task. Example tasks involved here include determining the instructional window during which essential learning targets or standards should be monitored and assessed, the best pedagogical strategies to ensure each student learns the material at the required level, and appropriate expression and representation in your instructional materials. Your ability to plan a discussion with colleagues, put dates on the calendar for your collaborative planning, and then determine shared or delegated responsibilities for the unit is an example of the commitment factor of resilience.
2. **Control:** This means securing our self-efficacy and the belief that we can succeed during hard or challenging times. In the classroom, this means that—despite reviewing your third-period class roster for life science and noticing that you have a range of readers from grade 2 to collegiate level, nine students who have an IEP, and twelve students who are learning English as a new language—you believe that you can (and will) move each of those students to high proficiency levels. You generate a list of the professional learning you need in order to support this particular class's diverse needs, as well as the inclusive or co-teaching strategies that will help you be most successful. You

demonstrate the control factor of resilience through belief in yourself *and* by knowing what to ask for in order to effectively do your job.

3. **Challenge:** This means reconsidering how a setback or difficult situation could actually be an opportunity to grow. In this case, "Instead of framing a stressor as something to be endured, or dreaded, we can change our perception to one that puts us in the driver's seat, and gives us a sense of empowerment" (Gair, 2020). An upcoming supervisor observation could be a possible moment for heightened anxiety. You started a new curriculum this year and this observation will focus on its effectiveness, specifically around how students are responding to your instruction. One way to reframe this stressor is by thinking, "What areas of my instruction or classroom engagement am I already proud of?" and "Which parts of implementation am I truly struggling with and could use some guidance to improve?" Then, be bold and get ahead of your stress by emailing the message in figure 6.2 to your supervisor before the observation. Your proactive reframe of the stressor models the challenge factor of resilience by naming your successes and your vulnerabilities directly, and then using them as focal points during an observation to help you grow.

I am looking forward to your observation next week. I have been proud of how I am currently implementing [*your point of pride*] within this curriculum. Could you notice these moments and see if you agree? I also am struggling with [*your struggle*] when it comes to implementation. Could you be on the lookout for when this happens, and give me specific feedback on how to improve?

FIGURE 6.2: An outline for a proactive reframe of a supervisor's upcoming observation.

At school, sometimes we would rather put our students in bubble wrap to protect them from the challenges, disruptions, and conflicts that naturally present themselves during social interactions or academic endeavors at school. This isn't possible. Every day, students demonstrate the need to develop resilience, in task completion, in friendships, in time management, and in decision making.

And yet, let us not forget that life events that trigger stress or dissonance, and hence activate the need for resilience, are on a vast and evolving continuum. While some of us would describe some of the following scenarios as certain calls to open our resilience toolkit, others might think, "Come on! What's the big deal about *that?*" The range of responses to various situations demands our observation and compassion. The examples offered next are part of a real, unnerving continuum of regulation for our students—and please, add to this list as you reflect on your own students and schools.

- Not getting to play with a certain piece of equipment at recess
- Receiving a grade 0.1 percent below the threshold you need to maintain your GPA
- Observing your teacher consistently implement different consequences for the same behavior between two students in your class
- Watching a close friend start choosing other relationships over spending time with you
- Learning that the person for whom you were developing romantic feelings for actually likes your best friend instead
- Getting picked last every time for teams in physical education class
- Wearing your brand-new outfit or sporting your new hairstyle or color to school and not having anyone notice

The factors that activate a student's stress or anxiety when faced with such situations are relative to the unique attributes and preparation of each learner. Research from the Center on the Developing Child (n.d.a) provides additional context:

> One way to understand the development of resilience is to visualize a balance scale or seesaw. Protective experiences and coping skills on one side counterbalance significant adversity on the other. Resilience is evident when a child's health and development tips toward positive outcomes—even when a heavy load of factors is stacked on the negative outcome side.

A growing body of research further strengthens the evidence from Harvard University that students who have at least one supportive, caring adult (parent or caregiver) in their life will be more likely to develop and access tools to adapt and counter the effects of adversity when necessary (Borba, 2021; Ginsburg & Jablow, 2020; Kaplowicz, 2021).

So how can we nurture the development of this competency in our students? First, consider that *Meant for More* classrooms nurture resilience when doing the following: (1) set clear expectations, (2) reveal what is possible, (3) prepare scaffolded opportunities for students to respond to challenges, and (4) model the pause and use language to lift, rather than level.

Set Clear Expectations

Students will meet our expectations of them, for better or for worse. If we believe that all students are capable of learning at high levels, we will be relentless in our partnership with students to make that happen. For example, the transition from a highly supervised, highly predictable elementary school schedule to a middle school schedule that includes navigating between different teachers' expectations, as well as their physical classrooms, every fifty minutes can be quite difficult for some students. Students who thrived in the consistency and familiarity of elementary school may now be floundering with their newfound independence in this environment. Students who know the expectations ahead of time and believe they can achieve them are more likely to take ownership of their learning, noticing how they can activate resilience skills (although they might not know that's what we call them) in order to meet the goal. Conversely, if we convey to students, even nonverbally, that we don't believe they are capable of meeting our expectations, many won't. Some of these students will work much harder to achieve those expectations in spite of our perception of their capabilities, and others will check out, act out, or drop out of school entirely (Dary, Pickeral, Shumer, & Williams, 2016; Flores & Brown, 2019; Yang et al., 2023). Making students aware of the requirements for their learning environment—and their expected behaviors within it—can support students' understanding of how to work toward that level of expectation.

Reveal What Is Possible

Overcoming students' fixed mindset about what they are capable of is at or near the top of the priority list of each educator. Self-esteem and confidence are not developed through inauthentic affirmations or empty, disconnected praise. Rather, research shows that people who are self-confident are not only more likely to bounce back after a setback, but they can do so quickly because of a strong belief in their ability to be successful (Sutton, 2019). People show resilience when they can fall down, get back up, brush themselves off, and figure out what to do next.

You may also notice the connection between resilience and growth mindset as we carry beliefs about what we are truly capable of. During a 2016 interview, Dweck explained:

> When students had more of a fixed mindset—the idea that abilities are carved in stone, that you have a certain amount and that's that—they saw challenges as risky. They could fail, and their basic abilities would be called into question. When they hit obstacles, setbacks, or criticism, this was just

> more proof that they didn't have the abilities that they cherished. In contrast, when students had more of a growth mindset, they held the view that talents and abilities could be developed and that challenges were the way to do it. Learning something new, something hard, sticking to things—that's how you get smarter. Setbacks and feedback weren't about your abilities, they were information you could use to help yourself learn. With a growth mindset, kids don't necessarily think that there's no such thing as talent or that everyone is the same, but they believe everyone can develop their abilities through hard work, strategies, and lots of help and mentoring from others.

When it comes to our mental and emotional health, having a fixed or growth mindset directly impacts our capacity to be resilient. *Resilience* is the ability to bounce back. Think of a skyscraper that can withstand the wind velocity of an intense storm, the salmon that swims upstream, or even the malleability of that fidget putty you've told your student to put away now for the third time. The ability to bounce back in our personal lives is pivotal, and as adults we must prevent ourselves from swooping to rescue students from the stressor—or, equally damaging, providing empty praise for effort without clarifying how the student's behavior resulted in specific praise.

When showing students what is possible, we want to be clear about how what they did (the action) enabled a particular outcome (the result) to occur. Adding celebration or acknowledgment for tasks well done or behaviors that helped improve circumstances honor the work of students and how their contributions positively impacted self or others. This practice begins opening the door for students to see something new or deeper within and reframes what they thought to be true about themselves.

Prepare Scaffolded Opportunities for Students to Respond to Challenges

While being stressed is not a preferred state, not all stress is bad. In fact, a certain level is referred to as positive stress and "is a normal and essential part of healthy development, characterized by brief increases in heart rate and mild elevations in hormone levels" (Center on the Developing Child, n.d.b). The first day of the new school year or having to speak in front of the class are examples of positive stress. Positive stress is essential to developing resilience, since most competence comes from experiencing the need to demonstrate it in response to an event or action.

How does resilience serve as an asset when students are faced with a challenge, disappointment, frustration, or heartbreak? We nurture this part of resilience by establishing scaffolds, or incremental levels of support that we remove as students' confidence in their independent ability grows (Gair, 2020; Sutton, 2019). In describing how he strives to connect with his medical patients, Robert Trevino (2019), shares, "Scaffolding when communicating is meeting the other person where they are in their understanding." We can apply this to our work with students when we first name the skills and attributes required to move forward and second, through the cultivation of a growth mindset and the determination of manageable benchmarks for success, appropriately teach students how mistakes are just problems in need of a solution. This often means explicit instruction on various coping tools (such as, what they are and how to use them) as well as how to select or create the right tool in the right moment to reconcile the situation.

Children respond more favorably when we tell them what they did right in a situation, before launching into our concerns. Kenneth R. Ginsberg and Martha Jablow (2020) suggest the following conversation tool for parents, which you can adapt for responding to students after listening to their stories, as a scaffolding opportunity:

1. "I noticed what you are doing right." (Share the positive things you want to affirm from what the student shared.)
2. "I am worried about you." (And here's why . . .)
3. "Can we address their problem?" (Let's talk about what happened if we keep going down this path.)

You can remove the formality of the process once students build confidence and demonstrate they are using the process without your prompting and support.

Model the Pause and Use Language to Lift, Rather than Level

Each of us can recall a time when our words were interpreted differently from our intention. Tone matters. And when it comes to how we communicate with students, we rely on our ability to exercise care and compassion to honor students and ourselves in those moments. If students are continuing to talk, despite your agreed-on callback cue, we can be quick to toss our care and rationale aside and holler, "Hey! That's enough, class!" And then we pause and reflect, "Oh *no*! Did I just say that out loud?" You pinch yourself, only to realize that yes, you just said that, and no, you can't take it back. And our students can't unhear the words we say either. It's quiet in the classroom now, but not for the right reasons. You may not have meant to, but you just leveled the room with your verbal bulldozer. What kind of language, then, would lift our students to display resilience (for self and each other) when faced with a difficult feeling, thought, or situation? Let's start by modeling the pause.

For example, I once observed a first-grade teacher while students were engaged in a center rotation activity. Students were totally engaged in a word- and sentence-making activity—as evidenced by heads buried around their word mats as well as their boisterous chatter. However, I noticed one group had caught the teacher's eye. As the teacher approached the student group, I saw their face noticeably relax as they crouched down next to the students, and began laughing themselves! They later told me that their first thought was to ask, from across the room, "Group four, what's going on?" Thinking better of the public comment, they chose to pause, in order to learn more about what was happening before reacting to their perspectives of the situation. They walked over and learned that students were laughing because they were adding sentences one by one to create a silly poem! The teacher beautifully affirmed the students' creative thinking and then reframed their expectations by asking which student wanted to be responsible for making sure the group's laughter didn't go above a level three. Rather than prohibiting students from laughing or feeling any sort of joy with the learning activity, they promoted the capacity for students to have fun while also navigating the volume engagement levels that would benefit the whole class.

How Do I Get Myself Ready?

There is much to be leveraged from the teacher-student connection. Showing students they are not alone in their feelings or reactions to something is important. We want students to understand that their problem is real and that they can handle it. As noted in the previous section, sometimes they need a scaffold of support. Consider these two ideas for your own preparation: (1) notice how resilience currently manifests in you, and (2) discover resilience in your professional practice.

Notice How Resilience Currently Manifests in You

The fulfilling impacts of displaying resilience cannot be understated. Without it, being able to move through moments of difficulty, troubling relationships, or the weight of student and staff trauma upon you can negatively contribute to your physical and mental wellness in significant ways. The Mayo Clinic (2022) indicates that resilience, such as positive thinking and self-talk, helps to protect us from the impacts of traumatic behaviors, like bullying or stress, as well as reduces the intensity of conditions such as anxiety and depression.

The good news is that we can cultivate resilient behaviors at any time throughout our lives (Mental Health First Aid, 2022). We can learn to armor ourselves against paralyzing or self-deprecating behaviors using what research describes as *protective factors* (Cooper, Flint-Taylor, & Pearn, 2013; Mayo Clinic Staff, 2022; Mental Health First Aid, 2022; Sutton, 2019). Although several lists of skills are available, they all recognize the following as essential characteristics of resilient people.

- **Social support network:** People need other people! If the COVID-19 pandemic didn't teach us that we are not wired to be alone or figure things out by ourselves, what will? Do you have one or two people you can truly rely on and who have your best interests at heart? It's important to assess who or what makes up your social core, since "those with strong social support networks are better equipped to bounce back from loss or disappointment" (Ackerman, 2017b). Strong social support networks include having secure, stable, enriching relationships with a small group, or engaging in activities in your community, which helps you stay connected with other people you can trust.
- **Confidence:** When we believe we can achieve our goals, we stay motivated to pursue them. And, when we meet our goals or overcome our challenges, we often get an extra boost of confidence because we just proved to ourselves that we could succeed even in the face of something difficult.
- **A sense of purpose:** Strive to do something every day that gives you a sense of purpose. This includes setting clear goals with reasonable targets so that you can celebrate your milestones. Those milestones are important, since, "it's key to set many small goals and celebrate successes. Once you reach those goals, set new ones. That way you're always advancing instead of feeling stuck" (Davis, n.d.).
- **Hope and optimism for the future:** Do you choose to see possibility in what lies ahead? (We dive deeper into this one later in the chapter on page 212.)

Additional attributes in highly resilient people include engagement in joyful activities or hobbies, physical movement, adaptability, coping mechanisms, displaying gratitude, and showing kindness (Mayo Clinic Staff, 2022). These elements have been utilized across the field to develop online scales and self-assessments that are easily accessible, such as the following.

- Resiliency Wheel at https://tinyurl.com/44cufjap

- Everyday Health Resilience Assessment at https://tinyurl.com/5yt4pyzs
- Scales with various lengths and resiliency focal points at https://positivepsychology.com/3-resilience-scales

Learning more about your own stamina and how you demonstrate resolve in response to unexpected or undesirable situations can play a role in determining how your tendencies may impact your classroom design and structure.

You might also want to consider this sampling of questions as you begin exploring your current levels of resilience (Mind Tools Content Team, n.d.).

- When given a new task, I am confident that I'll succeed.
- When one attempt fails, I learn from it and change my approach next time.
- When a task doesn't go to plan, it affects my self-belief.
- When I encounter a difficulty, I lose sight of my goal quickly.
- Sometimes, I question my commitment to my job.
- I have strategies in place for dealing with stress.
- I feel positive about the future.
- I have strong goals that are clear in my mind.

What are your reactions to these questions? I wonder if you found statements where you felt confidence in your response and other statements that gave you a bit of pause.

My confidence lies in statements like, "When given a new task, I am confident that I'll succeed" and "I have strong goals that are clear in my mind", but I struggle with, "I have strategies in place for dealing with stress" (Mind Tools Content Team, n.d.). While this statement is technically true—I do have some strategies to lean on—admittedly, I have trouble consistently demonstrating *productive* or *self-nurturing* strategies when it comes to responding to my sources of stress. (Anyone else with me on this one?) As a mother, caregiver, and a trusted confidant among my neighbors and friends, I don't always have something left in the tank for *me* after I've provided support to those I love and care about. An early mentor reminded me that just because I have availability in my calendar (or access to email after hours) doesn't mean that I am *accessible*. Since this was a personal place of vulnerability, I identified it as an area of growth for me, and I haven't looked back since.

What about you? Are your thoughts compromised because you want to be a rock for others to lean on, but also establish and maintain boundaries for how and when you are accessible to others? Consider the questions in figure 6.3 as a way to reflect on how resilience currently shows up in your thoughts and actions.

What does resilience mean to me?
When do I feel confident in my resilience and how do I feel when that happens?
When am I letting setbacks stall me from bouncing back?
When do I need to sit in a challenging or difficult moment for a while, before I try to pull myself up and out of it?
What social support network can I lean on, to help me carry the load when it gets too heavy?

FIGURE 6.3: Personal resilience reflection.

Visit ***go.SolutionTree.com/schoolimprovement*** *for a free reproducible version of this figure.*

Discover Resilience in Your Professional Practices

As you began to informally reflect on your own resilience, you may have noticed an area in figure 6.2 to explore more deeply. Let's shift our mindset into the professional realm for this next section.

For this part, we access the work of Harold S. Koplewicz, president of Child Mind Institute and author of *The Scaffold Effect: Raising Resilient, Self-Reliant, and Secure Kids in an Age of Anxiety*. Koplewicz (2021) leans into the *scaffolding* metaphor by detailing three pillars (in addition to five planks and ten strategies across his research to further stabilize the pillars) that serve as a foundation where the development of resilience can thrive: (1) structure, (2) support, and (3) encouragement. Review Koplewicz's (2021) pillars in more detail here.

- **Structure:**
  + Predictability in routines and procedures
  + Consistency in rules, consequences, and follow through
  + Environmental security and stability
- **Support:**
  + Affirmation of emotions and thoughts, and how to name those appropriately
  + Awareness of when to observe and when to intervene
  + Instruction that enables the learner to grow and develop
- **Encouragement:**
  + Feedback on what went well as well as what could be done differently to improve
  + Stamina for risk-taking and responding to failure
  + Serving as a role model of independence

The COVID-19 pandemic jolted educators into a situation that required adaptability, collaboration, and problem solving. As you reflect on that moment of transition for you, your team, and your school or district, how do you connect with the preceding pillars? Do you recall how the in-person school structure was significantly compromised because routines and procedures were no longer predictable? In addition, how we could enjoy fellowship and camaraderie with our peers completely changed. And yet, because we are a resilient cohort of people, we found ways to improve. For example, do you relate to the following behaviors?

- I modified my instructional practices and materials to meet the demands of a virtual learning environment.
- I successfully maintained relationships with my students.
- I learned something new that improved my ability to connect remotely with students and families.
- I realized how this challenge allowed me to engage in deeper, more purposeful collaboration with my colleagues about student learning.

If you said, "Hey, I did that" or even, "I started working on that" to at least one of these options, you showed resilience.

Now that you know the framework, if you will, for nurturing resilience, let's dive into some language that further enables your capacity to display it. As noted earlier in this chapter, tone matters in our use of language; being conscious of how things are being said, in addition to what is being said, as well as how we are connecting our words together to share a perspective or give advice can demonstrate our personal capacity to model resilience. (Be patient with yourself here, as this part takes some practice.)

Our language and our tone can either lift or deflate students' spirit. *Meant for More* classrooms aspire to prepare students with words and skills. Rather than jumping in and solving problems for students, consider using approaches that instill self-validation, self-redirection, self-affirmation, or try helping them reframe with language like, "I learned that didn't work as well as I thought it would, and now I know how to do better next time." We also want our students to know that *we* believe in them and that they can count on us for support, guidance, and celebration. As such, it is equally important to be aware of language *not* to use in order to avoid undermining students or diminishing their confidence or decision making (that includes sarcasm, shaming, doubting, and nagging). Furthermore, modeling our own coping strategies for navigating hardships or mishaps allows students to take notice and gain confidence in applying those same strategies to their own challenges and in their ability to make sound decisions.

How Do I Get My Team Ready?

As you make connections to your personal and professional practices, perhaps a situation will emerge that would benefit from discussion with your team or a trusted colleague. Numerous books, videos, blog posts, workshops, and other resources are available on how to have courageous conversations with your peers, nurture your heart into bravery, or renew your outlook on your life or profession; perhaps more exploration into those tools is necessary for your team. Books such as the following might help nurture your resilience like they do mine. (Remember, start on yourself before you start on your team.)

- Arianna Huffington's (2015) *Thrive: The Third Metric to Redefining Success and Creating a Life of Well-Being, Wisdom, and Wonder*
- Patrick Lencioni's (2012) *The Advantage: Why Organizational Health Trumps Everything Else in Business*
- Bob Goff's (2020) *Dream Big: Know What You Want, Why You Want It and What You're Going to Do About It*
- Kim Scott's (2017) *Radical Candor: How to Get What You Want By Saying What You Mean*

Speaking of teams, a critical point of awareness for your collaborative crew is the interplay between resilience and the other *Meant for More* attributes we have discussed. Amit Sood (2022), executive director of the Global Center for Resiliency and

Well-Being, explains how qualities such as patience, acceptance, and kindness actually serve as a boost to our resilience. For example, when we need to listen to someone or something we don't want to, a resilient person is able to demonstrate strength through their patience. In addition, when we accept the unpredictability of life and learn how to embrace that uncertainty, we demonstrate resilience through our acceptance of the things we cannot control. Furthermore, kindness is connected to resilience through our displays of compassion, particularly as we model forgiveness, are slow to place blame, and provide support when others are demonstrating difficulty.

As it pertains to students, resilience and self-worth (or self-love) are the result of raising student voice (which we deeply explored in the previous chapter), since, according a 2016 Quaglia Institute for School Voice and Aspirations study conducted in 239 schools across fourteen states, "student voice leads to an increased likelihood that students will experience self-worth, engagement, and purpose in school . . . [which, per Toshalis & Nakkula, 2012] can impact a student's level of effort and persistence, which is one of the most important factors that affect achievement" (p. 1–2). You can read more about student voice in chapter 5 (page 153).

The following sections offer three strategies: (1) learn which attributes affect and develop student resilience, (2) notice how research informs relevant themes for building resilience, and (3) make a plan for how to scaffold instruction to build resilience. These strategies will help your team keep the discussion centered around students in a productive and collaborative manner.

Learn Which Attributes Affect and Develop Student Resilience

Learning what attributes impact resilience will support our ability as educators to create a rewarding, uplifting, and sustainable social-emotional ecosystem within our schools. Educators want to be most efficient and effective with their time, so developing our understanding of *what* we seek and *how* to obtain it is critical. Kenneth Ginsburg and Marsha Jablow (2020) bring forward three critical themes for adults to leverage in the development of resilience in students: (1) students benefit from a sense of security in our unconditional care and support for them, (2) students will meet the expectations we communicate about them, and (3) students watch what we do more closely than they listen to what we say. Although the research intention was directed toward parental or guardian support, let's make the connection to the development of resilience within our students in the school environment.

Use table 6.1 to consider how resilience applies in the *Meant for More* classroom.

TABLE 6.1: Considerations When Developing Resilience in Students

Conditions (Ginsburg & Jablow, 2020)	Example Application in *Meant for More* Classrooms
Students benefit from a sense of security in our unconditional care and support for them.	When students display behaviors that are counterproductive to the learning environment, their own safety, or the safety of others, it is important to separate how we respond to the behavior itself from how we display our care and support for the student. We may disapprove of the behavior, but this does not mean we disapprove of the student themselves. Students should feel secure in knowing that the relationship is not jeopardized simply because of the behavior.
Students will meet the expectations we communicate about them.	For better or worse, students will rise or sink to the expectations we hold for them. We may say we believe "all students can learn," "we are ready to support each learner to reach this goal," or "we will do whatever it takes to help students demonstrate this behavior," but then we counter that statement when we accept work or behavior from students that does not align with those expectations. Helping students understand the goal and the pathway to achieving the goal is essential, but equally important is that learners get feedback along the way regarding actions that move them away from the goal and how to reconcile their trajectory to connect back to the expectations. Focus on the habits to be developed, not the achievements to be awarded.
Students watch what we do more closely than they listen to what we say.	We can (and want to be) consistent with policies and procedures to support stable learning environments for our students. However, if our reactions—whether verbal or nonverbal—suggest our inability to self-regulate our emotions in response to things we disapprove of or are frustrated by, students will notice that. If we ask students to use respectful tone and language, but then we publicly shame a student for a mistake, the misalignment is confusing. Students will naturally lean toward modeling what is observed, even though it may be counter to what was initially taught and expected.

The big idea here is that students will follow your example in the classroom. As you continue to develop your own capacity to demonstrate resilience, use the considerations above to inspire continued action.

Find Patterns in the Research to Help You

Fortunately, there is a vast body of research around the acquisition of resilience and a comprehensive acknowledgment of the various strategies and mindsets that assist in the development of this skill set (Borba, 2021; Dweck, 2015; Ginsburg & Jablow, 2020; Grant, 2017; Venet, 2021). Your team may find it overwhelming to sift through all the language, tips, tools, and guidance to best support *how* to begin.

While there is often validation from parental or collegial blogs, as well as opportunities for affirmation from social media posts, it is critical that your team's approach to developing resilience in *students* is grounded in more than anecdotal evidence. For the purposes of our work as educators, let's explore a few perspectives that are grounded in scientific research. My request is that you take some time to explore the three figures shared in this section. Annotate as you go, noticing ideas or strategies that would be beneficial for your team and your students.

Figure 6.3 (page 201) describes Ginsburg and Jablow's (2020) scaffolding planks, which align with the pillars of structure, support, and encouragement (Koplewicz, 2021; page 201) referenced earlier in this chapter. The reproducible "Interpreting the Scaffolding Planks for Adult Resilience" (page 220) has space for you to reflect on how you currently use—or could use—this scaffolding strategy with your students. Review the example connections for how to display those scaffolding planks in the classroom environment in figure 6.4. Jot notes in the margins as you read these strategies, to either affirm or make connections with past practices. You could also circle or highlight ideas for application in your own classroom.

Scaffolding Plank	Examples of How to Use This Plank in My Professional Practice
Patience Stay steady, even when you have to teach the same lesson over and over again.	*I proactively anticipate mistakes or misconceptions that students might display as they are learning. This not only prepares me to be patient with their needs, but also enables me to think about how I might respond before I'm actually in the moment. Because I have planned ahead, my frustration levels are lower, naturally creating more space for me to display steadiness through patience.*
Warmth Model empathy, affection, and kindness. Show your compassion, even when setting limits.	*I am intentional about greeting my students before each class period and being in the hallways during passing time. I display warmth by acknowledging each learner with a greeting, asking about their day, and perhaps even following up on what they told me they were excited about or dealing with the day before (grandpa is sick, baseball game tonight, and so on). When students respond unfavorably to a situation or event at school, I leverage kindness to redirect behaviors. If a student pushes another student because he took his pencil, I might affirm that it's OK to be mad, but it's not OK to get physical, and then I work alongside the student to figure out a different solution for next time. I empathize with the student, but also adhere to the safety boundaries established in our classroom.*

Awareness Notice your students' emotional and practical needs and motivations—as well as your own.	*I ask about their preferences regarding the design space as much as I can. This includes considerations for classroom lightning, individual or group work, music during work time, or which seating arrangements would be more conducive to our classroom goals around learning at high levels. I display awareness when I listen to students' perspectives (and this connects to empowering voice as well) and notice where our respective needs can be mutually beneficial for the greater good.*
Dispassion Stay calm, no matter how upset you are or how challenging your students' behavior can be.	*I have a hard time showing dispassion in situations when students are disengaged and not following the guidelines we created together in our classroom social contract. I've tried to ignore the behavior, but that doesn't work so well because the student just keeps escalating until I have no choice but to respond. I recently learned about a strategy that could help me stay calm.* *For example, one of my students is constantly talking with her neighbor when I'm giving instructions. Instead of getting annoyed, I could reclarify my expectations by privately saying: "Morgan, I appreciate that sometimes you already know what to do before I'm finished given directions to the whole class. Your independence is one of the things I like most about you! However, not every student understands things in the same way, and when you are talking you are preventing other students from hearing the directions and fully understanding what to do. Tomorrow, I want you to practice staying quiet during my directions so that your classmates feel just as confident about the task as you do. I also want you to be quiet so that in case I miss an important part of the directions, you can chime in to help me out. Can you agree to that plan?"*
Monitoring Keep close observation on your students and make sure your supports are providing benefit.	*I develop individual relationships with each of my learners, which helps me monitor their needs and behaviors well. For example, Tashana often arrives at school with a positive attitude and smile on her face. She still smiles at me today, but she isn't talking too much and certainly isn't her normal joyful self. I'll get our morning routine started, but then stop by her desk to remind her that that I'm happy she's here today. I don't pry. This check-in allows her to know that I know something's up and she'll talk to me about it if and when she's ready.*

Source: Adapted from Ginsburg & Jablow, 2020; Koplewicz, 2021, p. 12.

FIGURE 6.4: Interpreting the scaffolding planks for adult resilience.

As you are sitting with your reflections from figure 6.4, feel free to pause before moving into the next table on observations of character within our students. You might even consider journaling about these five planks as a place to gather strategies and evidence of your growth and development in these areas over the course of the school year.

As we shift from the themes for adult resilience, notice the seven character strengths outlined in table 6.2 that emerged from research by Borba (2021). These seven character traits are woven across three categories (parts) identified within the scope of teacher influence. First, *nurturing a caring heart* encompasses the character strengths of self-confidence and empathy. Second, the character strengths of self-control, integrity, and curiosity are nestled in the category of *developing qualities of a strong mind.* And finally, perseverance and optimism support students in *cultivating a determined will.* Borba further defines character strength in practice, highlighting conditions required for global preparedness, mental and emotional health, and high levels of academic readiness and performance. Such conditions can further develop students' capacity for resilience both inside and outside of the classroom. And here's the better news: each of these conditions is teachable.

As you review table 6.2, which character strengths do you connect with? Are there any strengths that have emerged as an unintended but ideal consequence of your compassionate and careful actions on your team or in your classroom?

TABLE 6.2: Interpreting the Seven Essential Character Strengths of Thrivers

Character Parts	Character Strength	Strength Defined
Nurture a caring heart	Self-Confidence	Students can recognize their strengths and accept their vulnerabilities, to then apply their knowledge to seek the best path forward.
	Empathy	Students can recognize and understand their own feelings and needs, as well as the feelings and needs of others, in order to develop positive, sustainable relationships with peers and adults.
Develop qualities of a strong mind	Self-Control	Students can think clearly and rationally, even when faced with challenging or stressful situations and respond with appropriate coping mechanisms.
	Integrity	Students can embrace values that develop a solid ethical and moral code of conduct to guide their lives.
	Curiosity	Students can be open to possibilities and alternate perspectives and seek new information, in order to be creatively inspired to realize their potential and achieve their dreams.

Cultivate a determined will	Perseverance	Students can recognize they have the emotional and mental fortitude to overcome mistakes and missteps and progress toward their goals.
	Optimism	Students can access tools within to respond to challenges, stay positive, and maintain hope and purpose in their lives.

Source: Borba, 2021, p. 16–17.

Additional supports include using the reproducible "Choosing From the Seven Essential Character Strengths of Thrivers" (page 221) to select one character strength from each part that you will intentionally grow in your learning environment and jot some quick notes in the margins about how you might get started. The reproducible "Interpreting the Seven Crucial Cs of Resilience" (page 223) offers its own reflective questions, alongside each of the components and their attributes, to promote a deeper level of thought around these principles.

There is a great deal of research for you to absorb from these past few pages. Take a breath before moving on to the last idea that supports team readiness. What did you notice about how the planks described in figure 6.4 (page 207) intersect with the character strengths in table 6.2? Pause at the end of the chapter and select one (or part of one) reflection tool to support your move from information to action.

Plan Scaffolded Instruction to Build Resilience

As noted earlier in this chapter, *scaffolds* are incremental levels of support that we remove as students' confidence in their independent ability grows (Gair, 2020; Sutton, 2019). Late author, philosopher, and lecturer Charles B. Handy (1989) claims, "The best learning happens in real life with real problems and real people and not in classrooms" (p. 45). Although Handy is accoladed for his contributions to the fields of organizational theory and management, we have classrooms across the globe that have busted through this now antiquated stand-alone view of what classrooms can and cannot do. Aside from the phenomenal access to information, which effortlessly connects us to real people solving real problems that impact our real lives, let us also remember that everything happening in our school—and I mean *everything*—is real and raw for each student. *Meant for More* classrooms take ownership of that mental and emotional reality for students by creating conditions where they can falter, juggle, steady, disagree, build consensus, and then do it all over again. They are becoming braver and stronger with each moment of practice.

If your team isn't sure how to embed a real-world problem of practice (climate change, social injustice, or natural resource access, for instance), that's OK. You can look back into chapter 5 (page 153) for examples, specifically around democratic classrooms. Just have team members start with the people inside their classroom and create moments for students to work together, collaborate, troubleshoot, and resolve the learning activities planned for them. Students cannot build resilience by staying silent all day long. They cannot build resilience by staying in their comfort zone. And they definitely cannot build resilience if we don't give them an opportunity to fail, so they can learn how to recover.

For example, one strategy is to cascade your communication to students who are learning a new task. This could look like providing a bite-sized chunk of information, then allowing students to work independently or with a partner to digest the information before practicing that skill in their learning. As students tackle the first layer of a task, then you offer the next bite-sized chunk of information. This cascade creates powerful systems of scaffolded communication, which can help students better manage and access the information needed to meet the learning expectations.

How Do I Get My Students Ready?

As you continue this work to prepare a resilient-rich environment for students, you may notice something a bit startling. Students have been more ready for this type of environment than you realized. Gholdy Muhammed (2020), scholar and author of *Cultivating Genius*, proclaims:

> Educators need to move toward cultivating the genius that already lies within students and teachers. History from Black communities tells that us educators don't need to empower youth or give them brilliance or genius. Instead, the power and genius is already within them. (p. 13)

Muhammed's teaching reminds us of another opportunity to *design* learning spaces that allow students to leverage the gifts and talents they bring to our classrooms, rather than wondering or hoping that students will do that on their own (by *chance*).

Students will engage with two vastly different types of adults at school: (1) diminishers, who marginalize others by "draining [their] intelligence, energy, and capability" and (2) multipliers, "who use their intelligence to amplify the smarts and capabilities of the people around them" (Wiseman, 2017). I hope the research and samples provided thus far in the chapter are securing your belief that students can learn resilience, with your guidance as their teacher, principal, or other trusted adult at school. The following three strategies could aid you in becoming a multiplier for your students, supporting them to further construct their resilience:

(1) help students see where they are in control, (2) encourage mindful risk taking and modeling learning from mistakes, and (3) teach students to set bold goals.

Help Students See Where They Are in Control

When facing a moment of difficulty or adversity, it can be tough for students to step away from the issue and think about how to center themselves. In these moments, we want to pause and have students first articulate what is happening right now. Fortunately there is growing evidence that we can, in fact, teach resilience because we already have the capacity within us. ReachOut Australia (2023), an organization focused on improving mental health and well-being for young people, shares, "We are all innately resilient, but fear, insecurity and doubt can take over in moments of stress or anxiety. These responses can affect our ability to draw on our resilience just when we need it most."

Teaching students how to recognize what is happening in the present can be a productive strategy when helping them regain control and see multiple pathways. When working with students, I always start with two questions: (1) What happens if we keep going down this path? and (2) What happens if we choose another way? You can even draw this out on a piece of paper with students and have them talk through possibilities for success as well as potential for missteps as you document their ideas. The more you model it visually for students, the faster they can adapt that strategy to an internal mental processing exercise as well.

The element of uncontrollable life experiences sometimes force us into developing resilience due to the nature of our environments. Students, for example, may come from abusive homes, lack basic food and shelter needs, have violent or unsafe neighborhoods, been witness to (or are experiencing their own) mental health crises, or have suffered a new medical diagnosis that threatens the stability of their core family unit. These life experiences manifest in students from all ethnic and socioeconomic backgrounds and encompass all gender identities. Any of these scenarios could be manifesting for our peers and colleagues as well.

We must take care to remember that not all children or adults are ready for the same kind of nurturing at the same times. Christina Torres (2019), an eighth-grade English teacher, shares a specific perspective regarding her own students:

> So many of [them] are already processing hurt, trauma, and shame in deep, intense ways that not a lot of us understand. To push them into conversations where they have to name and work through their shame

> and potential trauma in ways that fail to fully honor those stories is very dangerous ground to tread on.

This sentiment also links back to chapter 3 (page 108) on fostering connection through restorative practices. As such, resilience must be intentionally nurtured and cultivated in each of us, educator and student alike, so that we can access the right tools for coping successfully at the required times.

Encourage Mindful Risk Taking and Model Learning From Mistakes

Is your classroom safe enough for students to raise their hand, share a *wrong* answer, and have their response attempt and effort be *accepted* by both the teacher and other students? Whether it's a simple mistake, or you truly didn't understand how to do something, messing up in front of your peers is never easy. *Meant for More* classrooms are embedded with learning moments where mistakes are truly viewed as opportunities to grow and learn and opportunities to take appropriate risks are abundant (Borba, 2021; Safir, 2017). This approach is successful because we actually provide students with the time and space to unlearn, relearn, and try again.

However, that doesn't mean students implicitly know this is our goal when we challenge them. Student fears over challenge and failure are results of their past experiences, leaving them with a mindset that projects an indifference to the struggles of learning. Our students should not believe that they are incapable of learning something just because they didn't get it right (or even close) on the first attempt. Helping them name their disappointments and take ownership of those feelings allows them to figure out what went wrong and to try again. Continue to praise students' attentiveness, effort, and perseverance to a task, even when it is in their second, third, or even thirteenth attempt.

I once worked with a science teacher who taught with a *rough-draft mindset*, establishing a way of being in his classroom that encouraged eraser marks and feedback from peers to better improve the work before it was submitted. This sharing of thinking with peers also invited opportunities for risk taking; the person sharing their work was vulnerable to their peers noting errors or misconceptions in their thinking, and the person reviewing the work was learning how to provide both constructive and complimentary feedback in a manner than connected to the work itself instead of the person who produced the work. This opportunity created a rhythm of productivity and focus for students, nurturing student confidence and safety in the classroom.

Teach Them to Set Bold Goals

Students who display resilience more readily than others exhibit a personal belief that they are capable of making good decisions in the first place. Stixrud and Johnson (2018) teach us how to help students by reminding them that they want to live a life that works, is satisfying, and brings them joy.

Resilience represents your capacity to adapt when stressful or unexpected situations arise (Mayo Clinic Staff, 2022). People generally don't *choose* a lifestyle laden with complexity, chaos, or stress. But they can choose how to work around or through it by believing that they have the capacity to change their circumstance and know they are truly the only ones who can. Our students can also develop that sense of efficacy and learn that they are capable by setting bold personal goals.

Many teachers are familiar with the SMART goal-setting framework (Conzemius & O'Neill, 2014) described here.

- **Strategic and specific:** These are associated with set priorities and avoid vagueness.
- **Measurable:** These allow metrics.
- **Achievable:** It has to be within your control and attainable with current resources.
- **Results oriented:** Particular outcomes are indicated.
- **Time bound:** A specific amount of time is given.

Despite being familiar with the framework, we may not often use it with students. This can be helpful, but be mindful that it can sometimes be confusing to students. Instead, when we focus on teaching students to set *bold* goals, two specific things can happen: (1) students can demonstrate self-awareness by selecting an area that would benefit from improvement, and (2) students can feel the stretch and discomfort of working through whatever has been blocking them from achieving their goal in the first place.

This type of goal setting moves from

I will get a better grade next trimester

to

I will use an improved note-taking strategy to more clearly organize my thoughts. I will study two more hours per week and see my teacher for help before school every Wednesday with the content I'm still having trouble with so I can improve my overall performance on the final exam by half a letter grade.

Naturally, once students achieve the goal—or even make progress—celebrate this accomplishment with them. Show students the direct connection between their intentional efforts to name a problem, set a goal, make a plan, and then follow through toward success.

Elementary students might also benefit from some sample sentence frames, such as *I can build resilience inside myself when I* ________________________________. *This means I am (or I can)* ________________________________. Another example is, *I saw someone else being resilient when they did or said* ________________________________. *One way I can show resilience is by* ________________________________.

What Infrastructure Do I Need to Make It Happen?

Nurturing resilience is not an individual endeavor, nor is it a straight line from point A to point B. You've already begun building the infrastructure. I suggest two things to consider as you move forward: (1) use and enjoy your personal days and (2) hold tight to hope.

Use and Enjoy Your Personal Days

Although you have great passion for the work you do daily, taking a short time away from work can improve your health. According to the American Institute of Stress (n.d.), "40% of workers reported their job was very or extremely stressful, 29% of workers felt quite a bit or extremely stressed at work, and 25% view their jobs as the number one stressor in their lives." Oh goodness, that sounds terrible! And it's definitely not an example of the *Meant for More* mindset and lifestyle. This sounds like burnout, which the Mayo Clinic describes as "a special type of work-related stress—a state of physical or emotional exhaustion that also involves a sense of reduced accomplishment and loss of personal identity" (Mayo Clinic Staff, 2021).

Continued review of the research reveals the following statistics.

- Employee health and well-being improve even during short vacations (de Bloom, Geurts, & Kompier, 2012; Mayo Clinic Staff, 2021; York, 2021).
- In 2017, about half of U.S. employees used only about half (54 percent) of their paid time off in the preceding twelve months. The following year, a reported 768 million days of paid time off went unused (York, 2021).

- A National Education Association survey reveals that 90 percent of its members report feeling seriously burned out, with "67% [reporting it being a] very serious" issue; over 50 percent "of members plan to leave education sooner than planned" (Jotkoff, 2022).

How do we keep ourselves from burnout? Take a break. As in, an actual, legitimate, self-fulfilling break (which is *very* different from taking a break from your day job in order to catch up on work!) For example, you could book a trip you've been wanting to take, since a "vacation can help you feel rested, refreshed, resilient, and prepared to handle whatever comes when you return" (Reilly, 2022). Or enjoy a staycation. Spend time engaging in a hobby you've been neglecting. Do nothing. Whatever you choose to do *with the time you've earned* is up to you. It's a beautiful chance to recharge, rejuvenate, and refresh your body and mind to reclaim that amazing version of *you.*

When I was a district director, I was called into the Human Resources department and asked to explain why I had already used six of my ten contracted personal days. While I was still perplexed by the question, I was asked if I was planning to use the remaining four before June. What became clear in that moment was that my health and well-being were of little concern to my employer. Personal days—although granted in the contract—were viewed with the sentiment "How could anyone take a personal day when there is so much work to do?" In reality, I used my personal days exactly for their designed purpose—to rest, refresh, and recharge.

Clearly, I was in a culture that misaligned with my values, since using paid time off was viewed as a deficit to the organization instead of as a healthy empowerment that promoted productivity and positivity among its employees. If you find yourself in a culture like this, clarify for yourself whether change in this environment is possible. Is this really where you want to be? Figure out your answers, which unfortunately, might mean leaving that school or district. Resilience represents your capacity to adapt to stressful or unexpected situations (Mayo Clinic Staff, 2022), but being resilient does not equal a willingness to accept unhealthy projections or expectations that demoralize and debilitate you as a human. Renew your belief that you are meant for more by nurturing what you need most.

Hold Tight to Hope

As previously noted, although education is an incredibly rewarding profession, being a teacher or administrator is not for the faint of heart. For each amazing moment of glory and inspiration we have with our students, it seems like there is a countering stressor waiting in the wings. Funding streams, resource allocations, standardized testing, increased security, and mounting familial and community pressures can pull joy out of our profession and make our situations feel hopeless. The COVID-19 pandemic and the resulting trauma have only served to further exacerbate an already strained workplace.

Educators suffer tremendously under this trauma if there are no safeguards to protect against it. Researchers Laurie Anne Pearlman and Paula S. Mac Ian (1995) coined the term *vicarious trauma* to indicate the residual feelings and emotions that are present from indirect exposure to (hearing and seeing) another person's traumatic experiences. It was first identified by Charles Figley (1982) as *the cost of caring* and has also been known as *compassion fatigue* (Pearlman & Saakvitne, 1995) and *secondary trauma* (Schepers & Young, 2021). We work in an environment that can include highly stressful situations and work with many children who are traumatized outside our schools. Being privy to that trauma makes educators vulnerable to secondary trauma, which can show up with symptoms similar to those for depression: appetite changes, numbness or helplessness, proneness for being startled, and trouble concentrating, among others (Administration for Children and Families, n.d.).

Immediate responses for educators include knowing where the counseling office is in case you are having a mental health emergency or, if you have an employee assistance program, seeking out your benefits and keeping the hotline on hand. Using these resources can not only assist you, but also ensure they stay available and accessible to others. And, moving forward, there are some actions we can take in order to break away from hopelessness.

While having hope itself is not a strategy, it does take practice to develop. John Parsi (as cited in Shrikant, 2021), executive director at Arizona State University's Center for the Advanced Study and Practice of Hope, shares how having hope may prove more difficult and complex than one might think, since "hope requires a person to take responsibility for their wants and desires and take action in working towards them. Optimistic people see the glass as half full, but hopeful people ask how they can fill the glass full."

As such, let's determine how we can hold tight to hope in our classroom and schools. Whether you're new to education or an experienced teaching veteran, "your belief in yourself as an educator plays a fundamental role in your day-to-day motivation and job satisfaction" (Eva, 2022). The strategies of finding inspiration from other educators you look up to and setting goals are opportunities to keep hope alive, burning brightly in your classrooms and across your school communities (Eva, 2022).

We truly have so much to be hopeful for in the moments, years, and careers ahead. But if you're stuck or not yet convinced, start with the most promising hope I know.

You can hold tight to hope because *you* continue to choose this profession.

You can hold tight to hope because *you* show up for students and *you* show up for your peers.

And, you can hold tight to hope because *you are not the only one.*

Whether we intend to be or not, each educator, regardless of role, is a beacon of hope for another person. And the rest of us can hold tight to hope because we know that you know you're not done just yet. There is still one more student, one more colleague, one more someone who absolutely *needs you*. Reflect on that for a while before you move on. Who needs *you*? Who do you need to keep serving as your inspiration? Figure 6.5 offers reflective questions and space for you to record ideas.

Reflective Question	Responses That Inspire Hope
In what ways do you believe in yourself as an educator, or how do you know that others believe in you?	
In whom do you find inspiration to continue this profession? Who connects with you as a source of inspiration?	
What goals do you have yet to achieve? How do you provide support and guidance for someone else to achieve their goals?	
Who is the student who absolutely needs you right now?	
Who is the adult who absolutely needs you?	

FIGURE 6.5: Questions and Ideas for holding tight to hope.

*Visit **go.SolutionTree.com/schoolimprovement** for a free reproducible version of this figure.*

Visit **go.SolutionTree.com/schoolimprovement** for a free reproducible "Chapter Summarization Tool to Inspire Action" and use its prompts to refresh your ideas and reflections from what you read in this chapter.

Meant for MoreMENTUM: Stories to Ignite Us

Megan Rains is a middle school algebra teacher at Texas High School in Texarkana, Texas. Her class rosters primarily include students who have low academic achievement in mathematics or have previously failed a mathematics course. By the numbers, 85 percent of the students she serves are economically disadvantaged, and the majority come with fractured or fragmented stability in their home environments. Most of her students' parents are currently or have been incarcerated and many continue to be unemployed. Her students describe priorities other than education, given their pre-eminent need for survival.

Megan is clear on what content she needs to implore her students to learn, and is keenly aware that very little can be learned without a reliable and personal relationship between her and each of her students. She asserts, "The biggest goal I have for myself is to ensure that my students know that their DNA does not have to be their destiny. They are capable of breaking the mold. They are capable of overcoming any obstacles they encounter. I want them to learn *that* life skill most of all."

Many of her students are in and out of in-school suspension as a result of indifferent relationships with some teachers. She has to advocate on behalf of her students to other adults, while also ensuring that her students learn how to navigate things or people they don't like or moments when they are feeling frustrated, disrespected, or incapable. She offers the advice of being relevant, being real, and being relatable. She continues, "Don't accept the pressure to push content 100 percent of the time. Take time to talk about life. When you notice a dysregulated cohort of students walking into the room, check in with them. Incorporate easier content days when they make sense. Adjust your teaching, but don't adjust your expectations. As students see you demonstrating flexibility when you see what they need, they will grace you with that respect in return. I promise, you'll catch up on the content. But it's much harder to catch up on a student."

Megan's academic data speak for themselves. In the short time Megan's students are in her course, 78 percent of her students in 2021–22 passed their algebra end-of-course exam, and, for those who didn't pass, 61 percent passed on the course retest in December 2022.

Sometimes, students learn in spite of us. Megan's students are learning ***because of*** her. Her ***Meant for More*** classroom demands high expectations of herself, with the flexibility to notice what she needs to nurture (M. Rains, personal communication, January 25, 2023).

"Whether we intend to be or not, each educator, regardless of role, is a beacon of hope for another person."

Interpreting the Scaffolding Pillars for Adult Resilience

Scaffolding Pillar	How This Pillar Connects to My Personal or Professional Practices
Structure Predictability, consistency, and stability	
Support Affirmation and instruction	
Encouragement Feedback, stamina, and modeling	

Source: Adapted from Ginsburg, K. R., & Jablow, M. M. (2020). Building resilience in children and teens: Giving kids roots and wings (4th ed., pp. 10–12). *Elk Grove Village, IL: American Academy of Pediatrics.*

Choosing From the Seven Essential Character Strengths of Thrivers

Select one character strength from each part that you will intentionally grow in your learning environment. In the right column, write ideas about how you might get started.

Character Strength	How I Can Begin Growing This Character Strength
Nurture a caring heart.	
Self-Confidence: Students can recognize their strengths and accept their vulnerabilities, to then apply their knowledge to seek the best path forward.	
Empathy: Students can recognize and understand their own feelings and needs, as well as the feelings and needs of others, in order to develop positive, sustainable relationships with peers and adults.	
Develop qualities of a strong mind.	
Self-Control: Students can think clearly and rationally, even when faced with challenging or stressful situations and respond with appropriate coping mechanisms.	

Integrity: Students can embrace values that develop a solid ethical and moral code of conduct to guide their lives.	
Curiosity: Students can be open to possibilities and alternate perspectives and seek new information, in order to be creatively inspired to realize their potential and achieve their dreams.	
Cultivate a determined will.	
Perseverance: Students can recognize they have the emotional and mental fortitude to overcome mistakes and missteps and progress toward their goals.	
Optimism: Students can access tools within to respond to challenges, stay positive, and maintain hope and purpose in their lives.	

Source: Adapted from Borba, M. (2021). Thrivers: The surprising reason why some kids struggle and others shine. *New York: G. P. Putnam's Sons.*

Interpreting the Seven Crucial Cs of Resilience

Crucial Component	**Competence**
Observable Attributes	Trusts own judgment Has the skills and tools to make effective choices in the face of adversity

Reflection questions about competence:

Do I notice and affirm what my students are doing well, or am I more inclined to give feedback on mistakes?

Do I communicate in a manner than emboldens students or does my language cast doubt?

Do I help my students see their strengths within, without comparison to other students?

Do I create safe spaces for mistakes that show students they can handle themselves and recover when things go sideways?

Crucial Component	**Confidence**
Observable Attributes	Displays a belief in one's own ability Gained by demonstrating competence Shows stability to cope with challenges

Reflection questions about confidence:

Do I catch my students doing the right thing, and give them positive affirmation in the moment?

Do I have reasonably high expectations and give space for my students to show me what they are capable of?

Do I give feedback that shows mistakes are part of the journey rather than moments to be ashamed?

Crucial Component	**Connection**
Observable Attributes	Has positive, secure relationships within their family, people at school, or within their community. Increases their sense of safety by belonging to something outside themselves

Reflection questions about connection:

Do my students know how much I care about them as *people*, and they are more than just names on a roster?

Do I create moments that foster development of relationships between students?

Do my students know what to do when problems arise in their friendships?

Crucial Component	**Character**
Observable Attributes	Distinguishes between fundamental right and wrong Grounded in their self-confidence and know their own value

Reflection questions about character:

Do my students understand how their words and actions impact others?

Do I help my students see themselves as caring, kind, compassionate people?

Do I model the value of community in my classroom?

Do I hold students accountable for my expectations or do I accept less from them?

Crucial Component	**Contribution**
Observable Attributes	Understands how the world is better because they are a part of it Engages in actions and behaviors that improve their relationships and community

Reflection questions about contribution:

Are my students aware of the diverse environments in which people live?

Do my students see themselves as helpers?

Do my students see me as a role model and example of contributing for the greater good?

Crucial Component	**Coping**
Observable Attributes	Possesses a variety of strategies to navigate unexpected or disappointing scenarios Understands how to access strategies of support to work through worry, sadness, or stress

Reflection questions about coping:

Do my students recognize the difference between a real crisis and a perceived emergency?

Do I consistently model strategies and language that teaches students how to cope?

Do I protect my students from challenges, or do I provide support for students as those challenges arise so they can strengthen their confidence and learn to rely on their own tools?

Crucial Component	**Control**
Observable Attributes	Recognizes how actions directly connect to consequences, whether positive or negative Understands how to take actions that will replicate or reconcile situations as necessary Demonstrates an awareness of their responsibility in how they choose to respond to whatever happens

Reflection questions about control:

Do my students understand that our rules and structures are intended to provide safety?

Do my students understand the balance between being responsible for their own actions and the knowledge that other things that happen (divorce or illness, for example) are outside their control?

Do I affirm my students' positive choices with giving them more responsibility and increased access to opportunities or privileges?

Source: Adapted from Ginsburg, K. R., & Jablow, M. M. (2020). Building resilience in children and teens: Giving kids roots and wings (4th ed., pp. 42–47). *Elk Grove Village, IL: American Academy of Pediatrics.*

Interpreting the Scaffolding Planks for Adult Resilience

Scaffolding Plank	How do I currently use—or in what ways could I use—this plank in my personal or professional practices?
Patience Stay steady, even when you have to teach the same lesson, over and over again.	
Warmth Model empathy, affection, and kindness. Show your compassion, even when setting limits.	
Awareness Notice your students' emotional and practical needs and motivations—as well as your own.	
Dispassion Stay calm, no matter how upset you are or how challenging your students' behavior can be.	
Monitoring Keep close observation on your students and make sure your supports are providing benefit.	

Source: Adapted from Ginsburg, K. R., & Jablow, M. M. (2020). Building resilience in children and teens: Giving kids roots and wings (4th ed.). *Elk Grove Village, IL: American Academy of Pediatrics; Koplewicz, H. S. (2021).* The scaffold effect: Raising resilient, self-reliant, and secure kids in an age of anxiety. *New York: Harmony Books.*

Chapter 7

Giving Grace

Leon was a secondary principal who believed he was capable of great leadership. In fact, his colleagues all believed in him too. He was personable, charismatic, approachable, and visionary. Leon was able to establish strong relationships with staff, students, and families and exercised fairness, honesty, and discipline in his work. In his quest to become a great leader, he created a vision board complete with goals, powerful and motivating quotes, and a description of what his version of success would look like. He verbalized those goals to others and made checklists for things to read and learn more about to enhance his ability to be a great leader. His staff felt inspired by his enthusiasm and passion for this journey. Leon charted a course and was prepared to begin his first year as a principal.

Yet it wasn't too long before he, inevitably, was presented with a challenge regarding a teacher's practices. Students, parents, and colleagues alike had made him aware of a teacher who used marginalizing language to some of her students. Unfortunately, this had been going on for years, but none of the past leaders had addressed it. This continued avoidance not only hurt students, but also created tension among the teachers on the team. Leon gave the staff hope. They believed he would address the issue with clear expectations about how to move forward, with high levels of support for this individual to modify her behavior and preserve the school's vision and values.

Things went awry, however, during the inquiry to determine what happened. Instead of staying aligned with his vision for being a great leader—which included courageous integrity and tenacious pursuit of equitable learning environments for each student—Leon decided to move the students who were directly targeted by the teacher to another classroom and did not engage the teacher in question with corrective instruction of her own. Although Leon's thoughts and words were aligned in service to the mission of the school community, his actions were not. In fact, it was his inaction to a clear injustice that created a barrier of mistrust and disrespect between him and the rest of the staff, as well as some families who were privy to the anecdotal details of the situation. The school community was fractured, and wondered how they would move forward from there. One of their leaders had convinced them that he was invested in the community and the students' well-being, but when it came down to it, he took the path of least resistance.

Reflect on the questions in figure 7.1 before moving forward.

Think about a moment when you were troubled by an action or decision that you or another person made, similar to the narrative outlined in the previous story. How did you react?
What did you choose to give yourself or that individual. Was it grace or something else?
Why did you choose that?

How would extending grace have helped you or that individual? Is there anything you would do differently now, looking back, to inform how to respond to a similar situation in the future?

FIGURE 7.1: Story reflection.

Reflecting on one's personal experiences with forgiveness serves as a reminder that we already possess the courage and integrity required for extending grace to others, especially our students. Let's explore the connection between forgiveness, acceptance, and grace in order to create this next attribute in our *Meant for More* learning environment.

What Do We Mean by *Giving Grace*?

Positive psychologists define *grace* as "the gift of acceptance given unconditionally and voluntarily to an undeserving person by an unobligated giver" (Emmons, Hill, Barrett, & Kapic, 2017, p. 277). We can reframe this definition into actions or emotions, such as: living in balance, practicing forgiveness, being kind to self and others, and displaying respect for and consideration toward others. Research indicates that believing in and experiencing grace is related to "positive mental health outcomes" and relationship health. It is similar to gratitude in that grace actively helps counter guilt, shame, and hopelessness (Hodge et al., 2020), which students and teachers can leverage as a reminder that each individual in the school community has intrinsic value and is worthy of forgiveness and, by extension, grace. Such grace allows relationships to strengthen between and among members of the classroom and school community, increases happiness and emotional regulation, and perhaps most notably in the school setting, improves student growth and achievement (Greater Good in Education, n.d.).

Within our learning spaces, grace is easy to understand but far more difficult to employ. As teachers, we are wired to do things correctly and to do them with high quality. This can make it difficult for us to extend ourselves some grace when things don't go accordingly to plan. We are willing to give others grace yet can have a harder time receiving it. So, what would grace look like in the learning environment? The following four sections review some simple actions that will enhance the grace you give to yourself and others: (1) practice patience; (2) show gratitude; (3) harmonize your thoughts, words, and actions; and (4) whisper joy.

Practice Patience

One of the first ways we can learn about grace (before we can effectively practice and give it) is to notice opportunities at school in which you find yourself needing to practice patience. No matter how long you've been in education, you've experienced a time with a student, parent, or colleague in which you started to get irritated, annoyed, or even upset and, as such, your patience began to wane. For example, when is the last time you heard yourself telling a colleague or student, "How many times have I asked you to *X*?" Was it yesterday? Ten minutes ago? Please insert an empathic hug here. I *feel* you. Working with students (and adults) can be a constant exercise in deep breaths and meditations. As you have probably noticed, the question *How many times . . . ?* does nothing on its own to correct the behavior. In these moments, it's vital that you make an intentional *choice* to start with patience.

Instead of the initial reaction, consider the impact of grace-empowered phrases like, "I see you are having trouble with ________________________. How can you fix it?" or "Double check the space around you. Do you notice anything else you need to do before leaving the classroom?" I know such moments are often not as simple as I make them sound here, but as I've stressed throughout this book, we need to deliberately design how our learning spaces look, sound, and feel. In a *Meant for More* classroom that means catching others in a safety net of compassion and grace when they struggle. Maybe the safety net looks like an anchor chart with phrases or sentence stems that model patience through mindful language, such as "It's now time to ________________________", "Please wait for me to help you," or "I am asking you to stop." Or the safety net could sound like a class discussion on behaviors that frustrate or bother other students in class. You could create and post a list of student-generated pet peeves for everyone to see on the classroom wall since the visual reminder may thwart those types of behaviors from occurring (Kriegel, n.d.). In a *Meant for More* classroom, you could further this idea by generating responsive, humanizing language for students to use with each other. This could redirect the annoying or distracting behavior or pose statements or questions about the undesirable behavior.

The language we model in front of our colleagues and students has tremendous influence over our ability to give grace to others, and ultimately, to ourselves as well.

Show Gratitude

Why is gratitude so important? Researchers explain that "grace is closely related to gratitude" (Hodge et al., 2020). But how? In *Soul! Fulfilling the Promise of Your*

Professional Life as a Teacher and Leader, colleague and friend Tim Kanold (2021) writes, "Gratitude, I believe, allows for the extension of grace" (p. 225). When we show gratitude, it promotes our ability to consider others' feelings and display empathy, along with reducing anxiety and depression (Smith, 2021). Gratitude also fits in with taking a *both/and* approach, as we discussed in chapter 4 (page 122), in that "Gratitude doesn't negate pain. It's a 'both and' not an 'either or' practice. You can be both hurting AND grateful" (Smith, 2021). It teaches us to honor what other people are thinking and why someone else might want to treat you (or a situation) with such kindness. Sometimes our students just need to know that we are proud of them and that we care about them, no matter what. When I feel gratitude *for* others, I can accept grace *from* others.

One way we can show gratitude is through a strategy discussed in chapter 6 (page 197) about pausing and using language that lifts (rather than *levels*). In fact, international speaker and appreciation expert Christopher Littlefield (2020) encourages this practice, honoring how, when we find ourselves focused solely on what's going wrong, we can lean into a routine of practicing gratitude: "If we want to trigger gratitude in ourselves, we need to intentionally shift our focus to that which we are grateful for."

Littlefield (2020) encourages us to act on that shift in focus by reflecting on one or two of the following questions:

- What have I gotten to learn recently that has helped me grow?
- What opportunities do I currently have that I am grateful for?
- What physical abilities do I have but take for granted?
- What did I see today or over the last month that was beautiful?
- Who at work am I happy to see each day and why?
- Who is a person that I don't speak to often, but, if I lost them tomorrow, it would be devastating?
- What am I better at today than I was a year ago?
- What material object do I use every day that I am thankful for having?
- What has someone done for me recently that I am grateful for?
- What are the three things I am grateful for right now?"

By reflecting on any of these questions, and either writing the answers or discussing them with a friend or trusted family member, we are building a habit of showing gratitude. Going even further, know that there is value in starting a journal, writing a letter, or visiting someone directly as methods for intentionally showing gratitude (Millacci, 2023). Writing or speaking your gratitude aloud enables your brain to better habitualize this practice and embed it into your daily life (Millacci, 2023).

The following list has more concrete examples of these research-based strategies for showing gratitude (Ackerman, 2017a, 2017b; Băbău, 2022; DeSteno, 2018; Gheen, n.d.; Littlefield, 2020; Millacci, 2023).

- **Gratitude journal:** A running log—daily, weekly, or monthly—that chronicles things that have gone well or brought you joy; consider life experiences, events, or circumstances (graduations, promotions, wealth, or health) as well as simple, everyday moments that might normally go unnoticed by others but were special to you (a gorgeously colored sunset, the young child holding the door open for a stranger, or an unexpected encounter with an old friend)
- **Gratitude letter:** A text message, handwritten letter, thank-you note or other form of written communication that lets other people know how and why you appreciate them
- **Gratitude visit:** A visit—over FaceTime or at someone's kitchen table—in which you can directly communicate your appreciation for another human being, including specifically telling them how their words, thoughts, or actions have positively impacted you

Research indicates that, "people assigned to engage in simple interventions to feel and express gratitude show enhanced feelings of social connection and relationship satisfaction over time" (DeSteno, 2018). In addition, these methods for intentionally displaying gratitude look back to an attribute first explored in the introduction of this book: confirming that our desired attributes, behaviors, and environments happen *by design*, rather than by chance.

Harmonize Your Thoughts, Words, and Actions

Speaking of things that happen by design, such is true with securing alignment in our personal and professional lives. When I suggest harmonizing the components of thoughts, words, and actions, I am not talking about general work-life balance. Although managing how you spend your personal and professional time and energy is a necessary and ongoing exercise in patience and grace itself, achieving a state of harmonious balance is an evolving component for leading with grace in the *Meant for More* classroom.

There are many perspectives among the stakeholders in a school community, and yet it remains essential that a school district be vigilant in its alignment between the actual work and the intended purposes outlined in its respective missions and visions. In the continued aftershocks of the COVID-19 pandemic, as well as continued episodes of racial, social, and political unrest across the globe, we have seen how disruptive a single voice can be to upholding equitable access to academic, emotional, and physical resources a school community can offer. We are rewriting policies and procedures and protocols without fully understanding both the history of how we arrived at this juncture and the implications of swift, reactive decisions. Career coach and leadership trainer Angela Meyburg (2022) states that "while we cannot control others, we can control ourselves by developing a greater level of self-awareness, finding our why, and doing our best not to defer from our inner compass."

Think back to the story of Leon, which introduced this chapter. Fortunately, Leon came to realize how his inaction was out of alignment with his visions of being a great leader. Stepping away from the issue, he could see how it did not connect with what he learned and who he wanted to be. Not just as a leader, but as a person. He thought about resigning. He questioned his ability to be a great leader. He started using self-deprecating language of his own and doubted his ability to restore his school community to the place of trust, loyalty, and integrity that it once was. But, as great leaders do (and with some encouragement from people closest to him), he decided to ask for help to repair what had been broken. Leon asked for forgiveness from his colleagues, who agreed to extend him grace. The teacher in question publicly acknowledged how her words were creating an unhealthy environment and she, too, asked for help from her peers to reclaim trust and safety for those in her community.

How does heightened awareness of the impact of our actions make room for grace?

> Self-forgiveness requires striking a balance between taking responsibility and maintaining a positive sense of self. When you successfully find this equilibrium, you reach self-forgiveness. When we do something bad, wrong, or against our values, we may be greeted with painful, negative emotions such as shame, guilt, resentment, or anger. We may also have negative thoughts about ourselves, such as, "It's all my fault" or "I'm a terrible person." Self-forgiveness does not mean we skip the step of feeling bad; it simply means that we work through these feelings of self-resentment and then relieve ourselves of them once they've served their purpose. (Woodyatt, Worthington, Wenzel, & Griffin as cited in Brown, 2021)

We all make mistakes. And we each deserve an opportunity to get back on track, learn from our missteps, and move *forward*. Sackstein (2017) recognizes the values in the moments, stating, "As we begin to forgive ourselves for our digressions and/or missteps, we can embrace our humanness and offer real advice and modeling for how to behave when being human gets in the way of doing what is best."

The idea of giving oneself grace sounds great in theory but you know just how tricky it is to do, especially if some part of you doesn't believe you are worthy of receiving it. But you are. As was the leader featured in the introductory story to this chapter. Brené Brown (2019) shares, "Our work is to get to the place where we like ourselves and are concerned when we judge ourselves too harshly or allow others to silence us. The wilderness demands this level of self-love and self-respect" (p. 150).

Consider the ways you speak to and about yourself. Would you use those same words when talking to someone else? Would you be proud to reveal your self-talk with a friend or family member? What about to a student or your own child? If you find yourself, thinking, "Whoa. I would never speak [act, think] that way to or about another human being," perhaps it's time to reflect on your personal levels of alignment and harmony. Most urgently, show yourself some grace by being tender to who you see in the mirror. Work toward manifesting such a mindset. This would enable you to confidently use language out loud and inspire gracious and grateful action, which will ultimately allow you to model that kind of self-love and self-acceptance for your own students as well.

Whisper Joy

Ingrid Fetell Lee (2021) researched and wrote a book about joy—*Joyful: The Surprising Power of Ordinary Things to Create Extraordinary Happiness*—and she had this to say about the topic in an interview: "Joyful moments may be fleeting, but they're not necessarily a passive force. You can actively weave them into your day, into your life, and tune into them all around you."

I have an idea that I imagine will come to fruition after this manuscript goes to print (and I have a little bit more time on my hands). I want to start a Just Joy Project. I envision it to be a blog post, a social media feed, an organization, whatever—but its sole purpose is to spread joy and make others happy. I often thought that when I retire, I would deliver flowers, read books to children, play the piano in a hospital foyer—anything that would bring people comfort and make them smile. In the meantime, however, I have been intentional about the ways in which I whisper joy to others around me.

Can we always so easily choose between living life in pain or in joy? No question, we must be equipped to navigate between both. And some days, let's be honest, it's really hard to choose anything. I know it's not always as easy as, "Just choose joy today!" But it is a place to start. In *Meant for More* classrooms, I encourage you to be a joy whisperer. Notice the joyful things you see that make you smile, and then show and tell people about them. Colleagues or students, even if they're hesitant to show it, will welcome the chance to be part of your ripple of joy.

How can we cultivate joy in our classrooms and teach students to acknowledge what makes them truly happy? Rather than be sidetracked by a fleeting moment of pleasure, students can learn how to recognize what authors James Baraz and Michele Lilyanna (2016) call *authentic happiness*. Curiously enough, two practices that promote authentic happiness are (1) practicing gratitude (discussed earlier in this chapter on page 232) and (2) building resilience, the Meant for More attribute featured in chapter 6 (page 189). Baraz and Lilyanna (2016) further advocate for research-based practices, such as teaching students to practice mindfulness and showing compassion. Not only have these practices proven to decrease stress and increase happiness, but caring for others is essential for establishing one's own emotional and social health and well-being.

The *whisper* part of this section is an intentional play on words. You can shout about joy or be loudly passionate in your acknowledgment of authentically happy moments in your classroom. The idea is for *Meant for More* teachers to learn how to layer joy into classroom practices throughout the day. We whisper to students—directly or indirectly—about where to see joy, so that they may then learn to see it for and within themselves.

How Do I Get Myself Ready?

Every journey starts with a first step, and this is the moment you've been working toward. Giving oneself grace is perhaps the most vulnerable of any of the attributes we have learned about thus far. The following three sections talk about how to: (1) speak to yourself with kindness, (2) draft a permissions mantra, and (3) schedule time for yourself on the calendar as ways to bring more grace into your personal practice.

Speak to Yourself With Kindness

As crazy as it sounds, I had to learn how to speak to myself with kindness. As in, I had to actually teach myself what self-love was (and was not) and how to be kind to the person I saw in the mirror each morning. I needed to more intentionally monitor my self-talk. Research qualifies *self-talk* as the internal narrative or dialogue you have about yourself; think of it as the constant stream of thought running through your head (Mayo Clinic Staff, 2022; Mead, 2019; Waters, 2021). The practice "is generally thought to be a mix of conscious and unconscious beliefs and biases that we hold about ourselves and the world generally" (Mead, 2019). The more positive this stream is, the more proficient you will be at speaking to yourself with kindness and giving yourself grace when life doesn't go according to plan. This gift of grace to yourself "means making the choice to interact with the world—and yourself—with goodwill and kindness" (Integris Health, 2023).

Images in the world can lift us up or drag us down. Social media posts can take us into a dark place of unproductive comparison and self-loathing, or they can be an exercise in practicing how we are tender with ourselves as live our lives. Interrupting yourself when *mental rumination* (repeatedly "replaying negative thoughts") takes control can reduce stress and have other long-lasting health benefits (Waters, 2021). For example, researchers at the Mayo Clinic (2022) continue to study the link between positive thinking and improved mental and physical health:

- Increased life span
- Lower rates of depression
- Lower levels of distress and pain
- Greater resistance to illnesses
- Better psychological and physical well-being
- Better cardiovascular health and reduced risk of death from cardiovascular disease and stroke
- Reduced risk of death from cancer
- Reduced risk of death from respiratory conditions
- Reduced risk of death from infections
- Better coping skills during hardships and times of stress

I have words of kindness tucked away in all sorts of places; notes from friends that I use as bookmarks, magnets on the fridge, or self-affirming words in my home. But, most importantly, I have also been given the gift of a daughter. And images and thoughts of her catch me when I start speaking about myself in ways that contradict how I'm teaching her to talk to herself.

Author and former clinical psychologist Alice Boyes (2021) identifies three examples of what compassionate self-talk can look like in the real world: (1) a gentle, encouraging nudge, (2) a tenacious challenge of your beliefs, or (3) a reframe of a personal trait or tendency. Use table 7.1 to see how compassionate self-talk might look or sound in the classroom.

TABLE 7.1: Compassionate Self-Talk Examples

Characteristic of Compassionate Self-Talk	Initial Thought	Reframed, *Meant for More* Thought
A gentle, encouraging nudge	"I have so much work today and not enough time to do it. I can't figure out how to get started because I'm too overwhelmed."	"There is a lot of work I want to do in order to be best prepared for my students. I don't have all day. I think I can do [specific task] quickly, so I'm going to manage my time and start there."
A tenacious challenge of your beliefs	"I can't believe I forgot to organize the parent permission form for the field trip. I am always forgetting things. I am a terrible teammate."	"I've had a busy week, and it's natural for people to forget things when they are moving too fast. I am usually very organized, and I know how much my teammates appreciate that quality in me."
A reframe of a personal trait or tendency	"My principal emailed me that she will observe me tomorrow during third period. I don't have a schedule observation until next month. Am I doing something wrong? Did one of my students complain about yesterday's lesson?"	"I am a thoughtful teacher. I take great pride in planning my lessons to ensure that each of my students is learning at high levels. Maybe my principal wants to observe my teaching in order to get ideas and strategies to help someone else in the building. I'm not going to worry about any of this until I am told there is a problem."

There is only one of me. And there is only one of you. Isn't that reason enough to be tender with ourselves and choose to think, speak, and live in a manner that promotes self-affirmation and kindness?

Draft a Permissions Mantra

Practicing self-love and kindness could evolve into crafting a mantra of permission for yourself. A *mantra* is a word or a phrase that is repeated and generally expresses a strong emotion or belief. Mantras "are short phrases or words a person chants or repeats to themselves, often while meditating, cultivating mindfulness, or breathing deeply" (Villines, 2022b). Remember *The Little Engine That Could*? The engine's mantra was "I think I can, I think I can, I think I can" (Piper, 1930, p. 27). Mine evolves, but at the time of this writing it sounds something like *I am enough as I am*. That's it. It works for me. What's yours? Revisit it until you feel it *inside* of you.

Whatever the case, remember that you are human, which means your life is a continual cadence of laughter, tears, successes, shortcomings, joys, and trials. It's easy to lose sight of the fact that you are truly the only person responsible for your life. What we are willing to accept from ourselves and from others determines how we choose to live our life—out loud, in the shadows, or somewhere in between. Here's a hard truth I realized about fifteen years into my career (better late than never!): my busyness was a shield from slowing down long enough to face the cataclysmic expectations of things I was "supposed to be." I slowed down by beginning from a place of grace: grace from being my own worst enemy, from apologizing for my good work, from not taking chances, from not standing up to inequities or injustices, and grace regarding my own fear of what might happen if I did the things I knew I was capable of. I had to grant myself permission to not be all the things to all the people all of the time. I needed to give myself the same grace I was offering others.

This work of giving oneself "permission" is incredibly personal. Mantras "ease an anxious mind, focus a person's attention on positive messages, or induce a meditative state" (Villines, 2022b), including the permission you want to grant yourself and allow for a calming, restorative impact. Figure out what *you* need and—if it's necessary right now—stop chasing someone else's version of what success looks like for you and start by defining what permissions you will grant yourself.

Schedule Time for Yourself on the Calendar

Given all of the demands placed on our time—whether self-imposed or how others communicate that they need you—it is important to adhere to the boundaries and permissions you granted yourself in your mantra in the preceding section. You can and should give yourself this grace. Always. And when I say always, I actually mean *always*. Self-grace is important to your well-being and impacts your ability to give others grace (Moiseeva, Gantseva, & Lyamina, 2020; Wepfer, Allen, Brauchli, Jenny, & Bauer, 2018). Maybe you're an early riser who tends to be most productive in the morning. Could you declutter your brain by engaging in some self-care before launching into the day's work? You may wake up throughout the night with instant to-do lists dominating your thoughts. To manage these thoughts and allow them to pass, try what I do; keep sticky notes and a pen by the bed so that when you wake up with such thoughts in the middle of the night, you have a place to record them until *after* you have prioritized your rest.

Having these sorts of self-care life hacks at your disposal is priceless. As another example, you could schedule for yourself one or two "Self-Care Saturdays" each month with dedicated time to spend outside or engage with a hobby or other interest. I'm a fan of hiking and enjoy quality time with Mother Nature to recharge my battery. It's not unusual for me to be backing out of my driveway at 6:00 a.m. on a Saturday morning, chasing a sunrise somewhere as a graceful way to kick off a glorious weekend. I have a standing weekday appointment in my calendar, from 5:15–6:15 a.m., titled Self-Care. Assign a unique color to that calendar for activities you deem to be self-care. The different color will catch your eye as you look through your schedule and get you excited for those moments. Plus, putting self-care time in your calendar makes it feel like a commitment. A promise to yourself. Just be mindful that this is *self-care* time. If it starts to feel like an obligation that brings more stress than it takes away, it's time for a different approach or to give yourself a different kind of break. Rather than going for a hike, sometimes I choose more time to rest as a different kind of self-care to start my day.

When it comes to recharging your personal energy batteries, recognizing where your needs are on any given day is more important than adhering to a rigid structure. I'm a coffee person in the morning, but I found that if I go downstairs to brew a cup after my 5:15 a.m. alarm, I would get distracted with other tasks not in alignment with my self-care appointment. As such, I splurged on a small coffeemaker for my bedroom, and I keep it on the same table as my reading material (which, in that space, is about something other than my profession). For me, this financial investment was worth the assurance that my morning time could stay protected for what I need it to be.

What are some ways that you might bring a similar sense of calm, routine, stillness, or joy to your world when you need it most? When it comes to building in healthy time for you into your daily routines, let your creativity flow. In addition to my hiking time or that morning cup of coffee, I often engage in some meditation (when my mind needs to calm after my morning reflections), pick up a book to read for enjoyment, or—my personal favorite—turn to a page in my coloring book and get busy. In the mornings, my alarm chimes a second time when I need to wrap up whatever I was doing for self-care and start other preparations for the day.

As you enter your more "productive" routines for the day, think about other ways and quick visual cues to remind yourself of the need for grace. The final part of my morning routine is entering my bathroom and reviewing the five post-it notes I have hanging on the mirror. They never move. I'm sure there is a lot of dust underneath them, but I accept that! Each of the five sticky notes represents another *S* to my self-care.

- **Sleep** (Quality over quantity)
- **Sweat** (Taking care of my body and health)
- **Skin** (Loving what I see in the mirror)
- **Soul** (Feeding my heart and mind in positive and productive ways)
- **Smile** (Do it big and bold, many times a day)

As you consider these examples, ask yourself: What does the phrase *self-care* mean to you? When will you schedule this type of time for yourself? Can you commit to ten minutes of self-care to start and put it on your calendar? Consider the best time of day for you to truly focus on yourself, without interruption or distraction. Maybe that ten minutes is sitting in your car, centering yourself for the day ahead before entering the school building? Whatever it is, whenever it is, make it happen. Then lather, rinse, repeat. You may quickly find that your self-care time expands beyond those initial ten minutes. My self-care time started there, eventually grew to an hour, and my world has been better for it. Notice the positive consequences that result from nurturing this priority for yourself.

How Do I Get My Team Ready?

How many times have you seen your teammates roll their eyes when the wellness initiative comes around, usually at the start of the new year? The intentions are pure and good (and we *should* engage in that form of physical or mental self-care), but sometimes it's hard to make this stuff stick or work well in a team context. Instead, I recommend you and your colleagues establish a routine to focus on taking care of each other so that you can take care of the students you are blessed to serve—whatever that means for you and for your teammates. For some initial guidance, review the following three strategies: (1) talk to each other, (2) hold each other to a high standard, and (3) forgive each other. See if one connects for you and your team or if you are inspired to create something new.

Talk to Each Other

Has a colleague ever done something that bothered you, and you didn't address that person, and then—all of a sudden—*everything they did* became worthy of five-alarm status and you felt like a volcano about to erupt? Well, you aren't alone. It can be challenging to have difficult conversations with your colleagues. But it's important to notice those little things that start to compromise or unravel the integrity of your team infrastructure and talk about them before they blow up and make a huge mess of the trust, credibility, relations, and effectiveness you have nurtured previously. When we can do the hard work of having courageous conversations early on, it empowers our team and honors the people within it to keep everyone's best interest at heart. As teammates, we don't always have to be best friends, but we are better together when we can encourage and support the well-being of those people we work alongside each day.

Author Tina H. Boogren is a champion for educator wellness. Her ladder in figure 7.2 is an interpretation of Abraham Maslow's (1943) hierarchy of needs. In that hierarchy, a person has basic needs (at the bottom) and must have them met before they can start meeting the need on the next rung up. As you read up the ladder, honestly assess whether you have the conditions on your team to make these conversations possible.

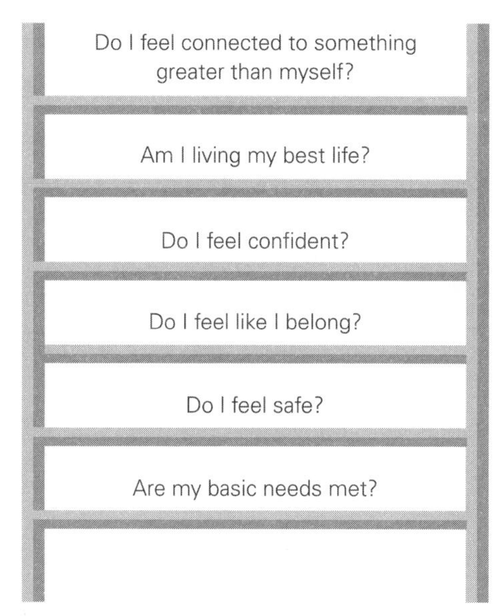

Source: Boogren, 2018, p. 19. Adapted from Maslow, 1943.

FIGURE 7.2: Ladder of needs.

Select one question each week to address as a team—for five minutes or fifty—and get to know each other as people, not just teammates. Do you each have what you need to be the best versions possible of yourself at school? Notice each other, so that you can nurture the needs of the team together. Until you talk to each other about taking care of yourselves, you won't be able to best take care of the students.

Hold Each Other to a High Standard

Author Lisa Delpit (2013) invites us to become warm demanders for our students. *Warm demanders,* she describes, are educators who "expect a great deal of their students, convince them of their own brilliance, and help them to reach their potential in a disciplined and structured environment" (Delpit, 2013, p. 77). *Meant for More* classrooms activate student hope and possibility by designing a learning environment that enables the manifestation of such bold displays of self-awareness and self-efficacy from students themselves. Students may be more prepared to give themselves grace if they are aware of the expectations, have a system of support when navigating opportunities that involve risk, and have also experienced moments where their failures have resulted in productive responses.

However, students are not the only ones who need that nurturing layer of support. This guidance applies to your team as well. In fact, "warm demanders are instructional leaders (coaches, principals, assistant principals) who expect a great deal of their colleagues, convince them of their own capacity to improve, and support them with a range of resources and coaching moves" (Safir, 2019). In their book, *Street Data: A Next-Generation Model for Equity, Pedagogy, and School Transformation,* authors Shane Safir and Jamila Dugan (2021) suggest four key principles for becoming a warm demander.

1. Building trust
2. Believing in the impossible (Do you believe every educator on your campus is able to improve and grow, and if not, are you prepared to coach them up?)
3. Teaching self-discipline (Because I trust and respect you, I'm going to have high expectations for you as well.)
4. Embracing failure (What is your next move, or what goals are you setting for yourself and your practice?)

Review the permissions mantra excerpt from the preceding section (page 239) and create your own set of statements of grace as a team. For example, *We will support each other through thick and thin* or *We agree to progress, not perfection* are helpful, encouraging, grace-giving phrases that hold you accountable for the work while honoring that you are also *human.*

Forgive Each Other

As you have realized, there are definitely times in your professional practice where you need to ask for forgiveness. In a classroom, it may mean:

> giving students second (and third, and fourth) chances. It means making the effort to remember students may carry a burden unknown to me, and thus my giving them the benefit of kindness. It's making the choice to be in a good mood every day. (McComb, 2021)

Connecting to the idea of holding each other to a high standard in the previous section, forgiving each other is a *choice* we have to make. We can fall victim to what is known as the *fundamental attribution error*, which explains our tendency to connect other people's actions to their innate character or personality, while attributing one's own actions to external, situational factors outside of their control (Healy, 2017; Lee, 1977; Safir & Dugan, 2021). For example, when your teammate shows up late for a meeting, you might roll your eyes or think, "Would it hurt him to set an alarm clock in the morning?" but when you show up late to a meeting, it was because there was an accident on the freeway and you had to take a detour that was fifteen minutes out of your way. When you believe your teammate's lateness is clearly a result of an internal character flaw, while your own tardiness was completely someone else's fault, you are demonstrating fundamental attribution error. The point is that assuming positive intent from our teammate is more aligned to showing grace.

What are the most common times of year when you and your teammates need to show forgiveness the most? When do things begin to go sideways? If you anticipate that, you make a plan to resolve it. For example, you know that the beginning of the year is busy and you'll need to lend each other a hand on occasion because someone is inevitably going to forget *something*. Another idea is to end team meetings with a mindful reflection of what you are grateful for. Schedule lunch together once a month, or talk to your principal about staying fifteen minutes past contract one night to leave fifteen minutes early on Friday. Little moments that bring joy should not be underestimated; they can lead to mountains of grace.

How Do I Get My Students Ready?

The Collaborative for Academic, Social, and Emotional Learning (CASEL) has pioneered the development of social and emotional learning (SEL) in schools and communities across the country, and I want to intentionally highlight their research and framework here in our final approach in *Meant for More* classrooms. CASEL's (2020) SEL framework identifies core competencies that help humans "develop healthy identities, manage emotions and achieve personal and collective goals, feel and show empathy for others, establish and maintain supportive relationships, and make responsible and caring decisions." We can link our work in chapter 2

(embracing authenticity, page 49) to developing healthy identities; chapter 3 (fostering connection, page 83) to displaying empathy and building healthy relationships, chapters 5 (empowering voice, page 153), and 6 (nurturing resilience, page 189) to emotional regulation, goal setting, and decision making. The marriage of those competencies with the attributes of *Meant for More* classrooms can equip our students with the self-confidence, self-awareness, and self-love necessary to honor themselves with the gift of grace throughout their schooling experience.

The three strategies are discussed in the following sections: (1) check the facts, (2) promote affirmation and gratitude, and (3) try the "name it, teach it, live it" method—are offered as considerations in your instructional and relational approach with students.

Check the Facts

How many times have you heard your students say things like, "I *never* get picked first for the kickball game at recess," "I am *always* sitting on the buddy bench, waiting for a friend to come play with me," or "I got a bad score again, just like *every other* time." This language is debilitating for students, and it stops any chance for hope and optimism in its tracks. Instead, ask your students to check the facts on their comments. Check the Facts is a behavior therapy strategy that can regulate an emotional response because it encourages a person to slow down and think through what is actually happening (based on facts) before determining how to respond. A strategy such as this can encourage you to "think before you react on your emotions. It allows you to step back, assess the situation, and determine if what you're feeling is appropriate given the context" (Zeman, 2019).

Consider the following example (Mead, 2019), which demonstrates a potential socialization scenario in schools that could benefit from a check-the-facts approach: When having to speak to someone new, negative self-talk might sound like "They'll think I'm weird and they won't want to talk to me." Positive self-talk might sound like "I'm interesting and this person seems interesting too. Maybe I'll make a new friend." In another scenario, one of your students might be upset because she texted a friend about a personal problem, and the friend hasn't responded yet. Your student is now catastrophizing, wondering why her friend is ignoring her, thinking, "She's probably judging me. Doesn't she understand how important this is?" In this situation, the Check the Facts strategy could involve a series of questions that sound something like the following.

- What do I know about my relationship with my friend?

- Does what I know about my relationship with my friend align with my belief that she is ignoring me?
- Has anything in our relationship changed that would contribute to my friend's lack of response?
- Does my emotional response still seem appropriate?
- What can I say or think instead that better aligns with how I know my friend normally acts or responds?

This kind of fact-check discussion can help this particular student consider that something else must be going on, because her friend would never knowingly ignore something this urgent. And, not long after, your student learns that her friend accidentally dropped her phone over the balcony in the gym while watching the basketball game last night, and it shattered into several pieces. Her friend wasn't ignoring her; rather, she didn't even have access to her phone to see the text in the first place.

Instead of negating someone's feelings with a "Oh no, that's not true," model with something like "Tell me more" or "What makes you say that?" Often, students will reset and become more connected to what actually happened in the moment, instead of overgeneralizing during a dysregulated emotional response.

Promote Affirmation and Gratitude

Before asking students to show grace toward themselves, it may be easier for students to express that kindness and gratitude toward someone else. A gratitude wall or glow board are spaces in your classroom where students can spotlight another student's positive words or actions that made their classroom or school a better, kinder place. Showing gratitude toward others can, in turn, help us appreciate the good in ourselves (Smith, 2021).

How do we teach it? And, honestly, when do we even have time to navigate this type of instruction in the classroom? Encouragingly enough, our days are rich with opportunities to practice self-love and show affirmation and gratitude toward others. Remember, *Meant for More* classrooms are human-centric spaces in which all people—adults and students alike—can further develop self-efficacy and integrity through authentic, inclusive learning spaces. Here are a few more strategies that can serve as a blank canvas (meaning, use them as they are or morph them into something that works best for you) for your efforts with your students.

- **Early childhood and lower elementary school:** During morning meeting, students partner up and do a Count to Five exercise in joy and gratitude, naming five things, people, or experiences that made

them happy or grateful during the week. They can use their fingers to count each one and either name all five at once or take turns with their happy thoughts until each friend gets to five.

- **Elementary school:** A strategy similar to that is known as *gratitude breathing*. Borba (2021) shares that during gratitude breathing, you take "a deep breath, count 'one' as you exhale, and think of something you're grateful for" (p. 98). Students ideally keep breathing, counting, exhaling, and affirming their gratitude until they reach five. Since science has proven that slowed breathing can actually change our physiology, which allows our minds to reduce negativity and allow positive feelings to manifest more quickly, this is a powerful self-regulation strategy that can further empower our students (André, 2019; Harvard Health Publishing, 2020; Heath, 2022).
- **Secondary school:** Many schools have adapted their master schedules to include an advisory or homeroom time, and it may focus on social-emotional regulation or executive functioning work habits. Such a class period might benefit from the Notice, Think, Feel, Do strategy described here (Hussong, 2020).

    1. *Notice* what you have in your life or has come into your life, no matter how small.
    2. *Think* about why you have received this gift, who played a role in making it possible and why they did so.
    3. *Feel* the positive emotions that come with receiving from others and connecting them to the real gift—the kindness, generosity, or love that someone else has shown you.
    4. *Do* something to express your appreciation.

This strategy could be formalized on paper or discussed among partners or small groups within the classroom. This mindful practice certainly promotes an attitude of gratitude, along with an inspired action for student expression.

Try Name It, Teach It, Live It

As we promote that attitude of gratitude in our classrooms, we can shift from simply *identifying when or how* we should show grace to *living with* and openly *giving* grace as human beings. Let's walk through a Name It, Teach It, Live It framework to mobilize our teaching and learning experiences for giving grace in the classroom environment.

NAME IT

The first element in this framework is Name It, because hopefully students gain confidence using language that specifically identifies the nature of what happened; ideally, that leads to them feeling more hopeful and optimistic about taking whatever next step is necessary. The act of giving grace in a learning environment is rooted in a spirit of hope. Erkens and colleagues (2017) further define *hope* as a "feeling of reasonable confidence in one's ability to control the circumstances of any desirable or predicted outcome" (p. 17). However, it can be difficult for students to feel hopeful about their abilities if they have never experienced success within the learning environment. It matters that students have opportunities for success at school so they have an anchor to retrieve when they need to model their own spirit of hopefulness and optimism. Borba (2021) shares that "optimistic kids view challenges and obstacles as temporary and *able to be* overcome, and so they are more likely to succeed" (p. 227).

Can you think of language to use with your learners that oozes hope and optimism? Can you create conditions in your classroom by which students can make a mistake and recover? Can you help students see that their response to a situation that goes sideways is a *choice*? We can and should talk openly with students about the imbalances life presents outside of school. Our students are inundated with messages on the news and social media that elevate fear, stress, and trauma to create a gloom-and-doom, nothing-will-ever-be-happy mindset. Remind students they will practice being able to let go; review these considerations as you support students when they name (and then reframe) the challenge presented in order to return to grace to oneself.

- **Reframe conditional language:** Words like *never, no one,* and *always* marginalize students' feelings of hope and possibilities because they describe the situation as an either/or. Ask yourself if the situation can be a both/and.
- **Model optimistic thinking:** Surround your students with words of hope for the future, spoken with a tone of possibility. When students hear the language of affirmation, even when mistakes and missteps are made, their ability to rebound from these setbacks increases and they learn how to boost their own confidence by mirroring that type of language in their own self-talk.

TEACH IT

After helping students connect with their internal sense of hope and possibility, it is time to provide both context and explicit instruction on how to self-regulate or activate that spirit in times of need. For example, conduct a field trip around your campus to show students where the counseling office is, or invite after-school club mentors into your class to talk with students about the various opportunities for student alliances (racial, gender, environmental, and so on). Focusing on breathing is another way to self-regulate. One research-based strategy to help younger students learn how to regulate their own emotions is asking them to HALT—stop and consider whether they are *h*ungry, *a*ngry, *l*onely, or *t*ired before reacting (Earle-Dennis, 2021).

For me, teaching about grace connects most brightly to the self-management competency discussed in the opening of this section, which CASEL (2020) further defines as the "ability to manage one's emotions, thoughts, and behaviors effectively in different situations and to achieve goals and aspirations." Creativity expert, author, and educational psychology professor Ron Beghetto (2018) suggests the following framework for helping students engage in discussions and reflections regarding any moments of failure, which allows them to accept, learn from, and move forward toward authenticity after such intentional self-examination.

You can ask students to consider a favorite moment of failure, and then using simple yet effective question stems to prompt discussion—and, simultaneously, build trust through this shared risk-taking moment in the classroom (Beghetto, 2018):

- What happened when you failed?
- How did you feel when it happened?
- What did you learn from that situation?
- What did you learn from yourself?
- Why is this failure your favorite?

Remember also the physical and mental disconnect between stress and the ability to give oneself grace (Ginsburg & Jablow, 2020). For example, even when there are no real emergencies, our students' emotions can make their bodies act like there is a huge crisis. Since the brain regulates both emotions and stress, our students' bodies will react to their brain's thoughts. As such, even a small dose of constant stress can trick their bodies, making it work harder to prepare for a crisis that doesn't really exist (Ginsburg & Jablow, 2020). We can help students learn to distinguish between a mild stress, such as preparing for an oral presentation, and an emergency, such as evacuating the building due to a fire.

Navigating stress, practicing patience, and managing personal emotions are central to one's ability to administer self-grace, and as such, provides further advocacy for this type of direct, supportive instruction at school.

LIVE IT

Now it's time to walk your talk! Think about how you could create a classroom that normalizes asking for help. Students cannot learn these skills in isolation and then not be provided an opportunity to further develop those muscles in the learning environment. Include pause moments within your day for students to engage in journaling and reflection as embedded parts of advisory or morning meeting. Model breathing techniques or ways of slowing down when you feel yourself becoming frustrated with a student or a situation. As you level the playing field by removing positional authority from the infrastructure of your classroom, students will see that even when things go sideways, recovery—through the gift of grace—is possible.

Another consideration is to provide moments that author and leadership expert John Maxwell (2011) describes as *failing forward*: "I believe it's nearly impossible for any person to believe he or she is a failure and move forward at the same time." He describes this phenomenon of failing forward as a perseverance through feelings of setback through seven specific actions (Maxwell, 2011).

1. Reject rejection.
2. Don't point fingers.
3. See failure as temporary.
4. Set realistic expectations.
5. Focus on strengths.
6. Vary approaches to achievement.
7. Bounce back.

How could Maxwell's seven actions weave into our collective commitments or classroom values? My wheels are already spinning; perhaps yours are too. For example, rejecting rejection feels linked to authenticity and inclusion, discussed in chapter 2 (page 49). The idea of bouncing back connects well to nurturing resilience, discussed in chapter 6 (page 189), along with seeing failure as temporary. Additionally, Erkens and colleagues (2017) connect well with the concept of focusing on strengths as they assert the notion of productive failure; situations in which students can feel confident in risk taking within the learning space because their teacher is going to honor both their strengths (students can think, *What was good about my*

work or behavior, even though it wasn't what my teacher wanted?) and their next steps (students can think, *Even though I might not be too close to the target yet, I see what my first next step is, and that motivates me to keep trying.*)

What Infrastructure Do I Need to Make It Happen?

You. That's what is needed. Just *you*. Real talk here: You need no money, no resources, no support from your team or principal, no fancy banners, newsletter, or bulletin boards. Of course, those things are valuable and enrich the learning community you are trying to create in your school or classroom. But they aren't required. Your students simply need *you* to be one of their biggest advocates and be their beacon of hope, and that starts with ensuring you provide for your own self-care: shelter, enough sleep, healthy food, and socialization. That is the basis of self-care. With a healthy and balanced self, you are better positioned to help students see what they may not yet see in themselves. Show them how to look within for their power and their strength. You are an important ally in their pathway to believing they are, indeed, meant for more.

Visit **go.SolutionTree.com/schoolimprovement** for a free reproducible "Chapter Summarization Tool to Inspire Action" and use its prompts to refresh your ideas and reflections from what you read in this chapter.

"We all make mistakes. And we each deserve an opportunity to get back on track, learn from our missteps, and move forward."

Epilogue

Until We Meet Again

It is with profound gratitude that I welcome you to this moment. I am honored to have walked alongside you in this *Meant for More* journey. I look forward to hearing from each of you—all the successes and missteps and joys and wonderings and learnings and everything in between. Connect with me at meantformorementum.com or via social media @meantformorementum. I do hope that we can stay connected.

As I mentioned in the introduction, this book has been on my heart for a while. Yet it almost didn't get written. The COVID-19 pandemic presented all sorts of opportunities for distraction; concern for the present, uncertainty of the future, general angst and wondering in all the moments that connected one day to the next. I found my intellectual and emotional tanks empty. When it came to this book, I just couldn't think straight. I knew the magnitude of this conversation and was so eager to let the words pour out of me onto the pages. But I just *couldn't.* I found myself wondering, "What's wrong with me? Why can't I just get my thoughts on paper?" I began a downward spiral into the abyss of imposter syndrome; I mean, who was *I* to define and describe a *Meant for More* learning space? Would I miss something? Would people identify with what I wanted to offer?

I chose to walk away from the manuscript for nearly a year as I worked through these moments of self-doubt. (Yes, the *very same* self-doubts I just attempted to teach you to overcome and self-reflections I asked you to boldly walk into.) It was my sweet daughter Kennedy who ultimately helped me regain my confidence to share these ideas, research, and guidance, and tell these stories about moments of possibility for what our classrooms are capable of becoming for students and adults. Even though she is only thirteen years old as of this writing, she is a trusted source of perspective and gives me strength and wisdom every day. This book, in so many ways, is written for her, too.

But what I learned through the fear, the pressure, and the normalized unpredictability of my life during that time is actually what propelled this book forward. It represents a language and tone that is authentically me, fierce in my poignancy, yet vulnerable in opening my heart and mind to potentially intense personal criticism. But I just *knew* I had to find a way to let these words flow. This manuscript is not perfect. Far from it! The journey is ongoing as we all seek to continuously improve. But I know you, the reader, are best positioned to chart your course from where this book leaves off.

I leave you with a gift from my friend and colleague Nancy Redman. Nancy was an angel on Earth; truly a gift from above. She and I worked together during my first years of teaching, and we formed a special bond. She later gifted me with a copy of *Wisdom From the World According to Mister Rogers: Important Things to Remember* (Rogers, 2006), and this mini book of beautiful words and phrases has sat on my desk every day since 2007. There is one quote in particular that I'd like to share with you, as I believe it sings the pure and genuine spirit of this manuscript:

> You don't ever have to do anything sensational for people to love you. When I say, 'It's you I like," I'm talking about that part of you that knows life is far more than anything you can ever see or hear or touch . . . that deep part of you that allows you to stand for those things without which

> humankind cannot survive: *love* that conquers hate, *peace* that rises triumphant over war, and *justice* that proves more powerful than greed . . . So in all your life, I wish you the strength and the grace to make those choices which will allow you and your neighbor to become the best of whoever you are. (Rogers, 2006, p. 94–95)

What you are looking for is out there and ready for the taking. So go and get it! Live these next chapters of your life big and bold and bright, unapologetic in your fervor, and equipped with the genuine knowledge that you are indeed meant for more. Consider the following prompts as you close the pages of this book and open your heart and mind to the *Meant for More* way of being.

- What chapters made the most sense to you?
- Which chapters were easiest to respond to, and which were more difficult?
- Which chapters have you excited but may be challenging to implement or to create visible impact so far?
- What could your classroom look like if you did everything discussed in this book?
- How will you know that you have built it?
- What is your next step in this *Meant for More* journey?

Be in touch, my friend. The world is waiting for you to unleash all the *more* that is still inside of you.

In tenacious grace,

References and Resources

Ackerman, C. E. (2017a). *Gratitude journal: 66 templates and ideas for daily journaling.* Accessed at https://positivepsychology.com/gratitude-journal on July 6, 2023.

Ackerman, C. E. (2017b). *How to measure resilience with these 8 scales.* Accessed at https://positivepsychology.com/3-resilience-scales on August 6, 2023.

Ackerman, C. E. (2018). *What is self-acceptance? 25 exercises + definition & quotes.* Accessed at https://positivepsychology.com/self-acceptance on September 1, 2023.

Adams, J. M. (2017). *For teachers, it's not just what you say, it's how you say it.* Accessed at https://edsource.org/2017/for-teachers-its-not-just-what-you-say-its-how-you-say-it on March 5, 2023.

Administration for Children and Families. (n.d.). *Secondary traumatic stress.* Accessed at www.acf.hhs.gov/trauma-toolkit/secondary-traumatic-stress on May 4, 2023.

Aguilar, E. (2016). *When we listen to students.* Accessed at www.edutopia.org/blog /when-we-listen-students-elena-aguilar on July 10, 2023.

Alabama Code Title 16. Education § 16-40A-2(c)(8). (2022).

Alexander, M. (2012). *The New Jim Crow: Mass incarceration in the age of colorblindness.* New York: The New Press.

Alexander, M. (2020). *The New Jim Crow: Mass incarceration in the age of colorblindness.* 10th anniversary edition. New York: The New Press.

American Association of University Women. (2020). *Early gender bias.* Accessed at www .aauw.org/issues/education/gender-bias on April 6, 2023.

American Institute of Stress. (n.d.). *Workplace stress.* Accessed at www.stress.org /workplace-stress on October 17, 2023.

Amorim Neto, R. do C., Golz, N., Polega, M., & Stewart, D. (2022). The impact of curiosity on teacher–student relationships. *Journal of Education, 202*(1), 15–25. Accessed at https://doi.org/10.1177/0022057420943184 on June 19, 2023.

André, C. (2019). *Proper breathing brings better health.* Accessed at www.scientific american.com/article/proper-breathing-brings-better-health on July 10, 2023.

Arango, T., Bogel-Burroughs, N., Burch, A. D. S., Cramer, M., Eligon, J., Fernandez, M., et al. (2022, July 29). How George Floyd died, and what happened next. *The New York Times.* Accessed at www.nytimes.com/article/george-floyd .html on April 2, 2023.

ASCD. (2004). *The power of student voice.* Accessed at www.ascd.org/el/articles /the-power-of-student-voice on March 5, 2023.

Aungst, G. (2016). *5 ways to activate curiosity in the classroom.* Accessed at https://corwin-connect.com/2016/12/5-ways-activate-curiosity-classroom on June 19, 2023.

Băbău, S. R. (2022). *The iceberg of gratitude and how to make the most out of everyday little things.* Accessed at https://medium.com/thank-you-notes/the-iceberg -of-gratitude-c83f79f86b99 on July 6, 2023.

Bailey, S. M., & Campbell, P. B. (1999, February 9). *The gender wars in education.* Accessed at www.campbell-kibler.com/Gender_Wars.htm on March 5, 2023.

Bakkegard, D. (2023). *Nurturing changemakers with an ELA project.* Accessed at www .edutopia.org/article/teach-students-changemakers on June 16, 2023.

Baraz, J., & Lilyanna, M. (2016). *Awakening joy in kids: A hands-on guide for grown-ups to nourish themselves and raise mindful, happy children*. Berkeley, CA: Parallax Press.

Beghetto, R. (2018). *Taking beautiful risks in education*. Accessed at www.ascd.org/el/articles/taking-beautiful-risks-in-education on July 6, 2023.

BetterHelp Editorial Team. (2023). *How to get people to accept me for who I am*. Accessed at www.betterhelp.com/advice/how-to/how-to-get-people-to-accept-me-for-who-i-am on March 5, 2023.

Biddle, C., Brown, L. M., & Tappan, M. (2022). *Letting student voice lead the way*. Accessed at www.ascd.org/el/articles/letting-student-voice-lead-the-way on March 5, 2023.

Birt, J. (2023). *Humility in the workplace and the benefits it brings*. Accessed at www.indeed.com/career-advice/career-development/humility-in-the-workplace on August 30, 2023.

Bishop, R. S. (2015). *Mirrors, windows, and sliding glass doors*. Accessed at https://scenicregional.org/wp-content/uploads/2017/08/Mirrors-Windows-and-Sliding-Glass-Doors.pdf on April 25, 2023.

Blad, E. (2015). *Student insights guiding districts on policy and practice*. Accessed at www.edweek.org/leadership/student-insights-guiding-districts-on-policy-and-practice/2015/06 on May 31, 2023.

Blad, E. (2018). *Watch: The power of student voice to shape schools and engage kids*. Accessed at www.edweek.org/leadership/watch-the-power-of-student-voice-to-shape-schools-and-engage-kids/2018/06 on March 5, 2023.

Blain, T. (2022). *Why is it important to stay humble?* Accessed at www.verywellmind.com/why-is-it-important-to-be-humble-5223266

Blodget, A. (2022). *When it comes to school culture, words aren't enough*. Accessed at www.ascd.org/el/articles/when-it-comes-to-school-culture-words-arent-enough on July 10, 2023.

Boogren, T. H. (2018). *Take time for you: Self-care action plans for educators*. Bloomington, IN: Solution Tree Press.

Borba, M. (2021). *Thrivers: The surprising reason why some kids struggle and others shine*. New York: G. P. Putnam's Sons.

Boudreau, E. (2020, November 24). *A curious mind: How educators and parents can guide children's natural curiosity—in the classroom and at home*. Accessed at www.gse.harvard.edu/news/uk/20/11/curious-mind on June 12, 2023.

Bowen, J. (2021). *Why is it important for students to feel a sense of belonging at school?* "Students choose to be in environments that make them feel a sense of fit," says associate professor DeLeon Gray. Accessed at https://ced.ncsu.edu/news/2021/10/21/why-is-it-important-for-students-to-feel-a-sense-of-belonging-at-school-students-choose-to-be-in-environments-that-make-them-feel-a-sense-of-fit-says-associate-professor-deleon-gra on November 4, 2023.

Bowman, K. D. (2020, August 4). *Strategies for countering unconscious bias in the classroom.* Accessed at www.nafsa.org/ie-magazine/2020/8/4/strategies-countering-unconscious-bias-classroom on July 10, 2023.

Boyd, N. (2018). *Five simple ways to boost social capital in schools.* Accessed at www.nassp.org/2018/08/09/five-simple-ways-to-boost-social-capital-in-schools on March 5, 2023.

Boyes, A. (2021). *Be kinder to yourself.* Accessed at https://hbr.org/2021/01/be-kinder-to-yourself on July 10, 2023.

Bradberry, T. (2016). *This is what passionate people do differently.* Accessed at www.weforum.org/agenda/2016/07/this-is-what-passionate-people-do-differently on June 16, 2023.

Brando, E. (2021). *Wilma Mankiller.* Accessed at www.womenshistory.org/education-resources/biographies/wilma-mankiller on July 10, 2023.

Brassard, D. (2022). *The pandemic's impact on students may have long-lasting effects.* Accessed at www.cpacanada.ca/en/news/pivot-magazine/pandemic-impact on May 18, 2023.

Brea-Spahn, M. R. (2021 6). *BLLING: Learning as belonging.* Accessed at https://leader.pubs.asha.org/do/10.1044/leader.AE.26012021.36/full on June 5, 2023.

Breuer, C., Hüffmeier, J., Hibben, F., & Hertel, G. (2020). Trust in teams: A taxonomy of perceived trustworthiness factors and risk-taking behaviors in face-to-face and virtual teams. *Human Relations, 73*(1), 3–34. Accessed at https://doi.org/10.1177/0018726718818721 on May 5, 2023.

Brennen, A., & Kahloon, S. (2021). *Beyond prom planning: Engaging students voice and shifting power in Kentucky to improve academic achievement and education equity.* Accessed at www.sir.advancedleadership.harvard.edu/articles/beyond-prom-planning-engaging-student-voice on June 5, 2023.

Britannica Education. (2016, March 2). *The value of inquiry.* Accessed at https://britannicaeducation.com/blog/the-value-of-inquiry on April 30, 2023.

Brooks, P. (2022, June 2). *9 ways to spark curious thinking in young children* [Blog post]. Accessed at https://blog.brookespublishing.com/9-ways-to-spark-curious-thinking-in-young-children on June 10, 2023.

Brown, B. (2010). *The gifts of imperfection: Let go of who you think you're supposed to be and embrace who you are.* Center City, MN: Hazelden Publishing.

Brown, B. (2015). *Daring greatly: How the courage to be vulnerable transforms the way we live, love, parent, and lead.* New York: Avery.

Brown, H. (2021). *Fostering self-forgiveness: 25 powerful techniques and books.* Accessed at https://positivepsychology.com/self-forgiveness on August 6, 2023.

Brown, P. (2023, April 7). *Exploring before explaining sparks learning.* Accessed at www.edutopia.org/article/explore-before-explain-in-elementary-science on June 16, 2023.

Brown, T. (2010). *The power of positive relationships.* Accessed at www.amle.org/the-power-of-positive-relationships on March 5, 2023.

Brykman, K, & Raver, J. (2021). *Why employees hesitate to speak up at work—and how to encourage them.* Accessed at https://theconversation.com/why-employees-hesitate-to-speak-up-at-work-and-how-to-encourage-them-15435 on June 2, 2023.

Buck, M. (2020, October 22). *The power of "both-and" thinking: Embracing apparent conditions can enhance healing* [Blog post]. Accessed at www.psychologytoday.com/us/blog/unleashing-the-potential/202010/the-power-both-and-thinking on May 18, 2023.

Burns, M. (2018). *Strategies to promote inquiry in your classroom.* Accessed at https://classtechtips.com/2018/10/02/promote-inquiry-in-your-classroom/#:~:text=The%20more%20voice%20and%20choice,having%20more%20agency%20over%20learning. On August 31, 2023.

Camera, L. (2018). *Black teachers improve outcomes for black students.* Accessed at www.usnews.com/news/education-news/articles/2018–11–23/black-teachers-improve-outcomes-for-black-students on March 5, 2023.

Camera, L. (2022). *New federal achievement data shows grim trajectory for country's 9-year-olds.* Accessed at www.usnews.com/news/education-news/articles/2022-09-01/new-federal-achievement-data-shows-grim-trajectory-for-countrys-9-year-olds on May 18, 2023.

Campbell, E. (2015). *Six surprising benefits of curiosity.* Accessed at https://greatergood.berkeley.edu/article/item/six_surprising_benefits_of_curiosity on July 3, 2023.

Carrington, J. (2020, May 26). *Connection before direction* [Blog post]. Accessed at www.drjodycarrington.com/connection-before-direction/#:~:text=To%20me%2C%20so%20much%20of,before%20you%20try%20and%20teach. On September 1, 2023.

Carroll, L. (2009). *Alice's adventures in Wonderland and through the looking glass.* London: Penguin Classics. (Original work published 1865.)

The Center for American Progress. (2019). *What to make of declining enrollment in teacher preparation programs.* Accessed at www.americanprogress.org/article/make-declining-enrollment-teacher-preparation-programs on May 13, 2023.

Center on the Developing Child. (n.d.a). *Resilience.* Accessed at https://pediatrics.developingchild.harvard.edu/concept/resilience on April 30, 2023.

Center on the Developing Child. (n.d.b). *Toxic stress.* Accessed at https://developingchild.harvard.edu/science/key-concepts/toxic-stress on May 3, 2023.

Cherry, K. (2022). *5 reasons emotions are important.* Accessed at www.verywellmind.com/the-purpose-of-emotions-2795181 on July 3, 2023.

Chowdhury, M. R. (2019). *Emotional regulation: 6 key skills to regulate emotions.* Accessed at https://positivepsychology.com/emotion-regulation on August 31, 2023.

Cimpian, J. (2018, April 23). *How our education system undermines gender equity, and why culture change—not policy—may be the solution* [Blog post]. Accessed at www.brookings.edu/blog/brown-center-chalkboard/2018/04/23/how-our-education-system-undermines-gender-equity on March 5, 2023.

Clark, D. (2021, December 16). *Google's '20% rule' shows exactly how much time you should spend learning new skills—and why it works.* Accessed at www.cnbc.com/2021/12/16/google-20-percent-rule-shows-exactly-how-much-time-you-should-spend-learning-new-skills.html#:~:text=Enter%3A%20Google's%20%E2%80%9C20%25%20time,wrote%20in%20their%20IPO%20letter on March 5, 2023.

The Coherence Lab Fellowship. (n.d.). *Addressing fragmentation in public education.* Accessed at https://education-first.com/wp-content/uploads/2018/06/Addressing-Fragmentation-in-Public-Education-CLF_Final.pdf on March 5, 2023.

Collaborative for Academic, Social, and Emotional Learning. (n.d.). *What is the CASEL framework?* Accessed at https://casel.org/fundamentals-of-sel/what-is-the-casel-framework on November 30, 2022.

Collaborative for Academic, Social, and Emotional Learning. (2020). *CASEL's SEL framework*. Accessed at https://casel.org/casel-sel-framework-11-2020 on September 1, 2023.

Collaborative for Academic, Social, and Emotional Learning. (2022). *Student SEL data reflection protocol*. Accessed at https://schoolguide.casel.org/resource/student-sel-data-reflection-protocol on July 10, 2023.

Collins, C. (2021). *Toolkit: The foundations of restorative justice*. Accessed at www.learningforjustice.org/magazine/spring-2021/toolkit-the-foundations-of-restorative-justice on March 5, 2023.

Conner, J. O., Ebby-Rosin, R., & Brown, A. S. (2015). Introduction to student voice in American education policy. *Teachers College Record, 117*(13), 1–18.

Conzemius, A. E., & O'Neill, J. (2014). *The handbook for SMART school teams: Revitalizing best practices for collaboration*. Bloomington, IN: Solution Tree Press.

Cooper, C., Flint-Taylor, J., & Pearn, M. (2013). *Building resilience for success: A resource for managers and organizations*. London: Palgrave Macmillan.

Cooper, K., Haney, B., Krieg, A., & Brownell, S. (2017). What's in a name? The importance of students perceiving that an instructor knows their names in a high-enrollment biology classroom. *CBE Life Sciences Education, 16*(1), 1–13. Accessed at https://doi.org/10.1187/cbe.16-08-0265 on July 3, 2023.

Corliss, J. (2021, February 22). *Want to feel more connected? Practice empathy* [Blog post]. Accessed at www.health.harvard.edu/blog/want-to-feel-more-connected-practice-empathy-2021022221992 on March 5, 2023.

Cuncic, A. (2022, November 9). *What is active listening?* Accessed at www.verywellmind.com/what-is-active-listening-3024343 on March 5, 2023.

Curley, P. (2021, April 14). *Decision making in the classroom* [Blog post]. Accessed at www.thesocialemotionalteacher.com/decision-making-in-the-classroom on June 2, 2023.

Darling-Hammond, L., & Oakes, J. (2019). *Preparing teachers for deeper learning*. Cambridge, MA: Harvard Education Press.

Dary, T., Pickeral, T., Shumer, R., & Williams, A. (2016). *Weaving student engagement into the core practices of schools: A National Dropout Prevention Center/Network position paper*. Clemson, SC: National Dropout Prevention Center/Network. Accessed at https://dropoutprevention.org/wp-content/uploads/2016/09/student-engagement-2016-09.pdf on July 2, 2023.

Davis, T. (n.d.). *What does resilience mean? Definition, qualities, and examples.* Accessed at www.berkeleywellbeing.com/what-does-resilience-mean.html on August 28, 2023.

de Bloom, J., Geurts, S. A. E., & Kompier, M. A. J. (2012). Effects of short vacations, vacation activities and experiences on employee health and well-being. *Stress and Health*, *28*(4), 305–318.

Defuria, C. (n.d.). *Solving the student engagement crisis.* Accessed at www.ednewsdaily.com/solving-the-student-engagement-crisis/#:~:text=While%20engagement%20is%20strong%20at,a%20third%20of%20high%20school on August 31, 2023.

Delahunty, M., & Chiu, C. L. (2021). Exploring the overrepresentation of Black male students in special education: Causes and recommendations. *Journal of Gender and Power*, *14*(2), 9–21. Accessed at https://doi.org/10.2478/jgp-2020-0011 on July 3, 2023.

Delpit, L. (2013). *Multiplication is for White people: Raising expectations for other people's children*. New York: The New Press.

Denby, S. (2023). *What a new graduate needs to be successful*. Accessed at www.youscience.com/the-impact-of-profile-of-a-graduate on August 31, 2023.

DeSteno, D. (2018). *How to cultivate gratitude, compassion, and pride on your team.* Accessed at https://hbr.org/2018/02/how-to-cultivate-gratitude-compassion-and-pride-on-your-team on July 6, 2023.

Di Michele Lalor, A. (2022). *Feedback that empowers students*. Accessed at www.edutopia.org/article/feedback-empowers-students on September 1, 2023.

DiAngelo. R. (2020). *White fragility: Why it's so hard for white people to talk about racism.* Boston: Beacon Press.

Dow, G., & Kozlowski, K. (2020). *The creative brain*. Accessed at www.ascd.org/el/articles/the-creative-brain on June 16, 2023.

Dweck, C. (2015, September 22). Carol Dweck revisits the "growth mindset." *EdWeek*. Accessed at www.edweek.org/leadership/opinion-carol-dweck-revisits-the-growth-mindset/2015/09 on March 31, 2023.

Dweck, C. S. (2016). *Mindset: The new psychology of success* (2nd ed.). New York: Ballantine Books.

Earle-Dennis, C. (2021, January 6). *Emotional self-management: 8 tips for educators to self-regulate and co-regulate emotions and behaviors* [Blog post]. Accessed at www.learningsciences.com/blog/emotional-self-management-self-regulation-co-regulation on July 2, 2023.

EdWeek Research Center. (2020, September 25). *Anti-racist teaching: What educators really think.* Accessed at www.edweek.org/leadership/anti-racist-teaching-what-educators-really-think/2020/09 on March 5, 2023.

Editors of Goop. (2018). *Forget happiness—pursue joy.* Accessed at https://goop.com/wellness/mindfulness/forget-happiness-pursue-joy on July 2, 2023.

Edutopia. (2019, October 3). *Social contracts foster community in the classroom* [Video file]. Accessed at www.youtube.com/watch?v=OjzweCyJIok&t=3s on May 3, 2023.

Eich, D. (2022). *Innovation skills for the future: Insights from research reports.* Accessed at www.innovationtraining.org/innovation-skills-for-the-future on June 22, 2023.

Ellis, A. (1977). Rational-emotive therapy: Research data that supports the clinical and personality hypotheses of RET and other modes of cognitive-behavior therapy. *The Counseling Psychologist, 7*(1), 2–42. Accessed at https://doi.org/10.1177/001100007700700102 on July 3, 2023.

Ellis, C., Holston, S., Drake, G., Putman, H., Swisher, A., & Peske, H. (2023). *Teacher prep review: Strengthening elementary reading instruction.* Accessed at www.nctq.org/dmsView/Teacher_Prep_Review_Strengthening_Elementary_Reading_Instruction on September 1, 2023.

Elmer, J. (2022). *Why are feelings important?* Accessed at https://psychcentral.com/lib/why-are-feelings-important on July 3, 2023.

Emmons, R. A., Hill, P. C., Barrett, J. L., & Kapic, K. M. (2017). Psychological and theological reflections on grace and its relevance for science and practice. *Psychology of Religion and Spirituality, 9*(3), 276–284. Accessed at https://doi.org/10.1037/rel0000136 on July 3, 2023.

Epstein, S. (2021, February 23). *What is both/and thinking: How two words can change our outlook and your relationship with yourself* [Blog post]. Accessed at www.psychologytoday.com/us/blog/between-the-generations/202102/what-is-bothand-thinking on May 18, 2023.

Erkens, C., Schimmer, T., & Dimich, N. (2018). *Instructional agility: Responding to assessment with real-time decisions.* Bloomington, IN: Solution Tree Press.

Erkens, C., Schimmer, T., & Dimich, N. (2019). *Growing tomorrow's citizens in today's classrooms: Assessing seven critical competencies.* Bloomington, IN: Solution Tree Press.

Eva, A. (2018). *How to cultivate curiosity in your classroom.* Accessed at https://greatergood.berkeley.edu/article/item/how_to_cultivate_curiosity_in_your_classroom on March 5, 2023.

Eva, A. (2022). *Three ways to feel more hopeful as an educator.* Accessed at https://greatergood.berkeley.edu/article/item/three_ways_to_feel_more_hopeful_as_an_educator on July 10, 2023.

Field, S., & Hoffman, A. (1994). Development of a model for self-determination. *Career Development and Transition for Exceptional Individuals, 17*(2). Accessed at https://doi.org/10.1177/088572889401700205 on July 3, 2023.

Figley, C. R. (1982). *Traumatization and comfort: Close relationships may be hazardous to your health* [Keynote presentation]. Families and Close Relationships: Individuals in Social Interaction Conference. Lubbock, TX: Texas Tech University.

Finley, T. (2017). *Making sure your praise is effective.* Accessed at www.edutopia.org/article/making-sure-your-praise-effective on June 16, 2023.

Fleming, N. (2020). *6 exercises to get to know your students better—and increase their engagement.* Accessed at www.edutopia.org/article/6-exercises-get-know-your-students-better-and-increase-their-engagement on August 30, 2023.

Flores, M. E., & Brown, C. G. (2019). An examination of student disengagement and reengagement from an alternative high school. *School Leadership Review, 14*(1). Accessed at https://scholarworks.sfasu.edu/slr/vol14/iss1/5 on June 1, 2023.

Fontein, D. (May 23, 2022). *7 ways to promote student voice in the classroom* [Blog post]. Accessed at https://thoughtexchange.com/blog/student-voice-in-the-classroom on March 5, 2023.

Forbes Coaches Council. (2020, October 8). *14 masterful ways to foster curious and innovative teams* [Blog post]. Accessed at www.forbes.com/sites/forbescoachescouncil/2020/10/08/14-ways-to-foster-curious-and-innovative-teams/?sh=4dccec7a33e8 on June 20, 2023.

Forristall, J. (2018). *Authenticity is a choice.* Accessed at https://umbrellaproject.co/category/authenticity/page/2/#:~:text=Authenticity%20is%20the%20ability%20to,someone%20else%20to%20impress%20others. on August 30, 2023.

Freire, P. (1970). *Pedagogy of the oppressed.* Great Britain: Penguin Random House.

Fueurstein, R., Fueurstein, R. S., Falik, L., & Yaacov, R. (2006). *Creating and enhancing cognitive modifiability: The Feuerstein Instrumental Enrichment Program, Part 1 Theoretical and conceptual foundations, Part 2, Practical applications of the Feuerstein Instrumental Enrichment Program.* Jerusalem: ICELP Publications.

Gair, J. (2020, February 18). *The 3 Cs of resilient leadership: Challenges, control, and commitment.* Accessed at www.linkedin.com/pulse/3-cs-resilient-leadership-challenge-control-janice on July 3, 2023.

Gallagher, E. K., Dever, B. V., Hochbein, C., & DuPaul, G. J. (2019). *Teacher caring as a protective factor: The effects of behavioral/emotional risk and teacher caring on office disciplinary referrals in middle school.* Accessed at https://link.springer.com/article/10.1007/s12310-019-09318-0 on July 2, 2023.

Garcia, R. (2023). *American Library Association reports record number of demands to censor library books and materials in 2022.* Accessed at www.ala.org/news/press-releases/2023/03/record-book-bans-2022 on September 1, 2023.

Garmston, R. J., & Wellman, B. M. (2016). *The adaptive school: A sourcebook for developing collaborative groups* (3rd ed.). Lanham, MD: Rowman and Littlefield.

Gaskell, A. (2021). *Why people don't always speak up at work.* Accessed at www.forbes.com/sites/adigaskell/2021/03/23/why-people-dont-always-speak-up-at-work/?sh=44338ac42934 on June 2, 2023.

Gates Foundation. (2017). *Teachers know best: Teachers' views on professional development.* https://usprogram.gatesfoundation.org/news-and-insights/articles/teachers-know-best-teachers-views-on-professional-development on August 28, 2023.

Gates, Z. (2018). *A study of the protective factors that foster resilience in teachers* [Published dissertation]. University of Southern Mississippi. Accessed at https://aquila.usm.edu/dissertations/1540 on July 3, 2023.

Gehlbach, H., Brinkworth, M. E., & Harris, A. (2011). *Social motivation in the secondary classroom: Assessing teacher-student relationships from both perspectives.* Paper presented at the American Educational Research Association, New Orleans. Accessed at https://files.eric.ed.gov/fulltext/ED525284.pdf on May 3, 2023.

Gheen, M. (n.d.). *Shifting teacher language to communicate effectively and respectfully.* Accessed at www.crslearn.org/publication/embracing-change/shifting-teacher-language-to-communicate-effectively-and-respectfully on July 6, 2023.

Ginsburg, K. R., & Jablow, M. M. (2020). *Building resilience in children and teens: Giving kids roots and wings* (4th ed.). Elk Grove Village, IL: American Academy of Pediatrics.

Global Partnership for Education. (n.d.). *Education data highlights.* Accessed at www.globalpartnership.org/results/education-data-highlights on May 18, 2023.

Goff, B. (2020). *Dream big: Know what you want, why you want it and what you're going to do about it.* Nashville, TN: Nelson Books.

Goleman, D. (2020). *Emotional intelligence: Why it can matter more than IQ* (25th anniversary ed.). New York: Bantam.

Gonser, S. (2020). *If you can't love every student, try finding common ground.* Accessed at www.edutopia.org/article/if-you-cant-love-every-student-try-finding-common-ground on July 10, 2023.

Gonzalez, J. (2021, November 26). *Teachers are being silenced. What can be done about it?* [Blog post]. Accessed at www.cultofpedagogy.com/silenced on June 2, 2023.

Gottman, J. (1999). *The marriage clinic: A scientifically based marital therapy.* New York: W. W. Norton & Co.

Grant, A. [@AdamMGrant]. (2021, November 22). *A sign of intellect is the ability to change your mind in the face of new facts. A mark of . . .* [Tweet]. Twitter. Accessed at https://twitter.com/AdamMGrant/status/1462789874000486415?ref_src=twsrc%5Egoogle%7Ctwcamp%5Eserp%7Ctwgr%5Etweet on March 5, 2023.

Grant, A. (2017). *Kids, would you please start fighting?* Accessed at www.nytimes.com/2017/11/04/opinion/sunday/kids-would-you-please-start-fighting.html?_r=0 on March 5, 2023.

Gray, J. P. (2013). It's a gray area: Einstein's brilliant thoughts pertinent to today's woes. *Los Angeles Times.* Accessed at www.latimes.com/socal/daily-pilot/opinion/tn-dpt-me-0602-gray-20130531-story.html#:~:text=Einstein%20modestly%20said%2C%20%E2%80%9CIt's%20not,he%20is%20probably%20still%20correct on August 4, 2023.

Greater Good in Education. (n.d.). *Forgiveness for students.* Accessed at https://ggie.berkeley.edu/student-well-being/forgiveness-for-students/#tab__2 on July 6, 2023.

Greenberg, J., McKee, A., & Walsh, K. (2013). *NCTQ teacher prep review: Executive summary.* Accessed at www.nctq.org/dmsView/Teacher_Prep_Review_executive_summary on April 6, 2023.

Greguska, E. (2018, October 19). *Science of hope practices to flourish at university, changes the perceptions about at-risk children.* Accessed at https://research.asu.edu/science-hope-more-wishful-thinking on July 3, 2023.

Gross, T. (2017). *A 'forgotten history' of how the U. S. government segregated America.* Accessed at www.npr.org/2017/05/03/526655831/a-forgotten-history-of-how-the-u-s-government-segregated-america on March 5, 2023.

Hamilton, J. (2017). *Feedback vs blame.* Accessed at https://medium.com/@jmh0437/feedback-vs-blame-cd3f93761d01 on July 10, 2023.

Hammond, Z. (2015). *Culturally responsive teaching and the brain: Promoting authentic engagement and rigor among culturally and linguistically diverse students.* Thousand Oaks, CA: Corwin.

Handy, C. B. (1989). *The age of unreason: Reflections of a reluctant capitalist.* Boston: Harvard Business School Press.

Harvard Graduate School of Education. (n.d.). *How to build empathy and strengthen your school community.* Accessed at https://mcc.gse.harvard.edu/resources-for-educators/how-build-empathy-strengthen-school-community on August 30, 2023.

Harvard Graduate School of Education. (2023). *Relationship mapping strategy.* Accessed at https://mcc.gse.harvard.edu/resources-for-educators/relationship-mapping-strategy on September 1, 2023.

Harvard Health Publishing. (2020, July 6). *Relaxation techniques: Breath control helps quell errant stress response.* Accessed at www.health.harvard.edu/mind-and-mood/relaxation-techniques-breath-control-helps-quell-errant-stress-response on July 10, 2023.

Healy, P. (2017, June 8). *The fundamental attribution error: What it is and how to avoid it* [Blog post]. Accessed at https://online.hbs.edu/blog/post/the-fundamental-attribution-error on July 10, 2023.

Heath, N. (2022, November 24). *3 ways your breath can help you cultivate gratitude today* [Blog post]. Accessed on https://resbiotic.com/a/blog/3-ways-your-breath-can-help-you-cultivate-gratitude-today on July 10, 2023.

Heick, T. (2017). *Eight strategies to help students ask great questions.* Accessed at www.teachthought.com/critical-thinking/strategies-to-help-students on June 22, 2023.

Heick, T. (2021). *10 strategies to promote curiosity in learning.* Accessed at www.teachthought.com/learning/curiosity-in-learning on May 30, 2023.

Henderson, N., & Milstein, M. (2003). *Resiliency in schools: Making it happen for students and educators.* Thousand Oaks, CA: Corwin Press.

Henebery, B. (2021). *How COVID-19 continues to affect Australian schools.* Accessed at www.theeducatoronline.com/k12/news/how-covid19-continues-to-affect-australian-schools/277439 on May 18, 2023.

Hodge, A. S., Hook, J. N., Davis, D. E., Van Tongeren, D. R., Bufford, R. K., Bassett, R. L., et al. (2020). Experiencing grace: A review of the empirical literature. *Journal of Positive Psychology, 17*(3), 375–388. Accessed at https://doi.org/ 10.1080/17439760.2020.1858943 on July 3, 2023.

Hodges, T. (2018). *School engagement is more than just talk.* Accessed at www.gallup.com/education/244022/school-engagement-talk.aspx on June 16, 2023.

Holquist, S. (2019, December 20). *Uplifting student voices: Effective practices for incorporating student experiences into decision making* [Blog post]. Accessed at https://ies.ed.gov/ncee/edlabs/regions/pacific/blogs/blog19_consider-student-voices.asp on June 2, 2023.

Horsager, D. (2012). *The trust edge: How top leaders gain faster results, deeper relationships, and a stronger bottom line.* New York: Free Press.

HRC Foundation. (n.d.). *Schools in transition: A guide for supporting transgender students in K–12 schools.* Accessed at www.hrc.org/resources/schools-in-transition-a-guide-for-supporting-transgender-students-in-k-12-s on April 2, 2023.

Huffington, A. (2015). *Thrive: The third metric to redefining success and creating a life of well-being, wisdom, and wonder.* New York: Harmony Books.

Hughes, J. M., Oliveira, J., & Bickford, C. (n.d.). *The power of storytelling to facilitate human connection and learning.* Accessed at https://sites.bu.edu/impact/previous-issues/impact-summer-2022/the-power-of-storytelling on April 11, 2023.

Hussong, A. (2020, November 24). *How to practice gratitude? Notice. Think. Feel. Do.* Accessed at www.unc.edu/discover/how-to-practice-gratitude-notice-think-feel-do on March 5, 2023.

Indeed Editorial Team. (2023). *14 ways to be your authentic self in the workplace.* Accessed at https://au.indeed.com/career-advice/career-development/ways-to-be-your-authentic-self on July 10, 2023.

Integris Health. (2023). *What does giving yourself grace mean?* Accessed at https://integrisok.com/resources/on-your-health/2023/march/what-does-giving-yourself-grace-mean on July 10, 2023.

International Institute for Restorative Practices. (2015). *International Institute for Restorative Practices self-study report.* Accessed at www.iirp.edu/images/pdf/Self-Study_Report_2015.pdf on June 30, 2023.

Jackson, Y. (2011). *The pedagogy of confidence: Inspiring high intellectual performance in urban schools.* New York: Teachers College Press.

Jobs, B. (n.d.). *Disrupting the culture of silence in schools.* Accessed at www.college.columbia.edu/cct/latest/lions-den/disrupting-culture-silence-schools-brendon-jobs-05 on June 2, 2023.

Johnson, E. (2019). *Leadership: Why humility is the top trait for success.* Accessed at https://teamzy.com/leadership-why-humility-is-the-top-trait-for-success on July 10, 2023.

Johnson, Z. D., & LaBelle, S. (2017). An examination of teacher authenticity in the college classroom. *Communication Education, 66*(4), 423–439.

Jotkoff, E. (2022). *NEA survey: Massive staff shortages in schools leading to educator burnout; alarming number of educators indicating they plan to leave profession.* Accessed at www.nea.org/about-nea/media-center/press-releases/nea-survey-massive-staff-shortages-schools-leading-educator on May 5, 2023.

Jung, L. A. (2023). *Seen, heard, and valued: Universal Design for Learning and beyond.* Thousand Oaks, CA: Corwin.

Kanold, T. (2021). *Soul!: Fulfilling the promise of your professional life as a teacher and leader.* Bloomington, IN: Solution Tree Press.

Kaplowitz, H. S. (2021). *The scaffold effect: Raising resilient, self-reliant and secure kids in an age of anxiety.* New York: Harmony Books.

Keats, E. J. (1962). *A snowy day.* New York: Viking Press.

Kendi, I. X. (2019). *How to be an anti-racist.* New York: Random House.

Kenton, W. (2022). *What is social capital? Definition, types, and examples.* Accessed at www.investopedia.com/terms/s/socialcapital.asp on April 27, 2023.

Kervan, L. (2023). *The power of a 45-second investment in relationship building.* Accessed at www.edutopia.org/article/building-relationships-students-first-week on July 10, 2023.

King, W., Hughto, J. M. W., & Operario, D. (2021). *Transgender stigma: A critical scoping review of definitions, domains, and measures used in empirical research.* Accessed at www.ncbi.nlm.nih.gov/pmc/articles/PMC7442603 on May 1, 2023.

Koplewicz, H. S. (2021). *The scaffold effect: Raising resilient, self-reliant, and secure kids in an age of anxiety.* New York: Harmony Books.

Kriegel, O. (n.d.). *Having patience as a teacher: How to cope with inevitable pet peeves.* Accessed at www.wgu.edu/heyteach/article/having-patience-teacher-how-cope-inevitable-pet-peeves1711.html on July 6, 2023.

Kris, D. F. (2020). *Breathing exercises to help calm young children.* Accessed at www.pbs.org/parents/thrive/breathing-exercises-to-help-calm-young-children on June 29, 2023.

Lahey, J. (2015). *When success leads to failure.* Accessed at www.theatlantic.com/education/archive/2015/08/when-success-leads-to-failure/400925 on September 1, 2023.

Lambersky, J. (2016). Understanding the human side of school leadership: Principals' impact on teachers' morale, self-efficacy, stress, and commitment. *Leadership and Policy in Schools, 15*(4), 379–405. Accessed at https://doi.org/10.1080/15700763.2016.1181188 on July 3, 2023.

Lane, H. M., Morello-Frosch, R., Marshall, J. D., & Apte, J. S. (2022, March 9). Historic redlining is associated with present-day air pollution disparities in U.S. cities. *Environmental Science and Technology Letters, 9*(4), 345–350. Accessed at https://doi.org/10.1021/acs.estlett.1c01012 on July 3, 2023.

Latumahina, D. (2023). *4 reasons why curiosity is important and how to develop it.* Accessed at www.lifehack.org/articles/productivity/4-reasons-why-curiosity-is-important-and-how-to-develop-it.html on September 1, 2023.

Lau, Y. (2020). Nine tips for leading with grace and compassion. Accessed at www.forbes.com/sites/forbeshumanresourcescouncil/2020/12/07/nine-tips-for-leading-with-grace-and-compassion/?sh=48b2e99b898e on July 10, 2023.

Learning for Justice. (n.d.) *Fishbowl.* Accessed at www.learningforjustice.org/classroom-resources/teaching-strategies/community-inquiry/fishbowl on June 2, 2023.

Lebow, H., & Casabianca, S. S. (2022). *Do you know how to manage your emotions and why it matters?* Accessed at https://psychcentral.com/health/emotional-regulation on July 3, 2023.

Lee, R. (1977). The intuitive psychologist and his shortcomings: Distortions in the attribution process. *Advances in Experimental Social Psychology, 10*, 173–220.

Lee, A. M. I. (n.d.). *What is self-advocacy*? Accessed at www.understood.org/en/articles/the-importance-of-self-advocacy on March 5, 2023.

Lee, I. F. (2021). *Joyful: The surprising power of ordinary things to create extraordinary happiness*. New York: Little, Brown Spark.

The Lego Foundation. (2022, October). *How play can support children's mental health*. Accessed at https://learningthroughplay.com/how-we-play/world-mental-health-day-how-play-can-support-children-s-mental-health on March 5, 2023.

Lencioni, P. (2012). *The advantage: Why organizational health trumps everything else in business*. San Francisco: Jossey-Bass.

L'Engle, M. (1962). *A wrinkle in time*. New York: Ariel Books.

Lewis, J. (2012). *Across that bridge: A vision for change and the future of America*. New York: Hachette Books.

Lightner, L. (2021, October 10). *25 racist microaggressions heard in IEP meetings*. Accessed at https://adayinourshoes.com/racist-microaggression-iep on March 5, 2023.

Little, G. F. (2022). *Centering students for literacy engagement: Student voice, choice, and identity*. Accessed at https://cpet.tc.columbia.edu/news-press/centering-students-for-literacy-engagement-student-voice-choice-and-identity on July 3, 2023.

Littlefield, C. (2020). *Use gratitude to counter stress and uncertainty*. Accessed at https://hbr.org/2020/10/use-gratitude-to-counter-stress-and-uncertainty on July 6, 2023.

Mahboubi, P., & Higazy, A. (2022). *Lives put on hold: The impact of the COVID-19 pandemic on Canada's youth*. Accessed at www.cdhowe.org/sites/default/files/2022-07/Commentary_624_R4.pdf on May 18, 2023.

Making Caring Common Project. (2021). *Relationship mapping strategy*. Accessed at https://mcc.gse.harvard.edu/resources-for-educators/relationship-mapping-strategy on March 5, 2023.

Making Caring Common Project. (2022). *How to build empathy and strengthen your social community*. Accessed at https://mcc.gse.harvard.edu/resources-for-educators/how-build-empathy-strengthen-school-community on March 5, 2023.

Making Caring Common Project. (2023). *Strategies and lesson plans: Relationships mapping grades 6–12.* Accessed at https://static1.squarespace.com/static/5b7c56e255b02c683659fe43/t/642ae8c8872b55150304e75a/1680533705092/Relationship+Mapping+_+Strategy+and+Lesson+Plans+2022-23.pdf on July 10, 2023.

Malala Fund. (2023). *Girl programme.* Accessed at https://malala.org/girl-programme on May 18, 2023.

Mamorsky, J. (n.d.). *The importance of understanding your emotions* [Blog post]. Accessed at https://mytherapynyc.com/understanding-emotions on July 3, 2023.

Mardell, B., Wilson, D., Ryan, J., Ertel, K., Krechevsky, M., & Baker, M. (2016). *Toward a pedagogy of play: A Project Zero working paper.* Accessed at www.pz.harvard.edu/sites/default/files/Towards%20a%20Pedagogy%20of%20Play.pdf on March 5, 2023.

Marschall, C. (2021). *The power of a democratic classroom.* Accessed at www.edutopia.org/article/power-democratic-classroom on August 16, 2023.

Marschall, C., & Crawford, E. (2022). *Worldwise learning: A teacher's guide to shaping a just, sustainable future.* Thousand Oaks, CA: Corwin.

Marsh, C. (2019, November 1). *Honoring the global indigenous roots of restorative justice: Potential restorative approach for child welfare.* Accessed at https://cssp.org/2019/11/honoring-the-global-indigenous-roots-of-restorative-justice on July 10, 2023.

Masalimova, A. R., Khvatova, M. A., Chikileva, L. S., Zvyagintseva, E. P, Stepanova, V. V., & Melnik, M. V. (2022). Distance learning in higher education during Covid-19. *Frontiers in Education.* Accessed at www.frontiersin.org/articles/10.3389/feduc.2022.822958/full#B30 on May 3, 2023.

Maslow, A. H. (1943). A theory of human motivation. *Psychological Review, 50*(4), 370–396. Accessed at https://doi.org/10.1037/h0054346 on July 3, 2023.

Masters, S., & Barth, J. (2022). *Do gender conformity pressure and occupational knowledge influence stereotypical occupation preferences in middle childhood?* Accessed at www.frontiersin.org/articles/10.3389/feduc.2021.780815/full on May 15, 2023.

Maxwell, J. C. (2011, June 11). *Failing forward* [Blog post]. Accessed at www.johnmaxwell.com/blog/failing-forward on March 5, 2023.

Mayes, E., Finneran, R., & Black, R. (2019). The challenges of student voice in primary schools: Students 'having a voice' and 'speaking for' others. *Australian Journal of Education, 63*(2), 157–172.

Mayo Clinic Staff. (2021). *Job burnout: How to spot it and take action.* Accessed at www.mayoclinic.org/healthy-lifestyle/adult-health/in-depth/burnout/art-20046642 on June 5, 2023.

Mayo Clinic Staff. (2022). *Positive thinking: Stop negative self-talk to reduce stress.* Accessed at www.mayoclinic.org/healthy-lifestyle/stress-management/in-depth/positive-thinking/art-20043950 on July 10, 2023.

McComb, S. (2021, August 5). *Teaching with grace, learning with dignity* [Blog post]. Accessed at www.teachingchannel.com/k12-hub/blog/teaching-with-grace/#:~:text=In%20my%20classroom%2C%20grace%20means,a%20good%20mood%20every%20day on July 10, 2023.

McDowell, M. (2022). *Cultivating curiosity among older students.* Accessed at www.edutopia.org/article/cultivating-curiosity-among-older-students on June 22, 2023.

McNair, J. (2021). *How to avoid overidentifying black male students for special education.* Accessed at www.edutopia.org/article/how-avoid-overidentifying-black-male-students-special-education on May 15, 2023.

Mead, E. (2019). *What is positive self-talk?* Accessed at https://positivepsychology.com/positive-self-talk on July 10, 2023.

Meyburg, A. (2022). *The importance of seeking alignment with self and others at work.* Accessed at www.linkedin.com/pulse/importance-seeking-alignment-self-others-work-meyburg-acc-cpc- on July 10, 2023.

Michigan Medicine—University of Michigan. (2018). Study explores link between curiosity and school achievement: Promoting curiosity may be a valuable approach to foster early academic achievement, particularly for children in poverty, a new analysis finds. *ScienceDaily*. Accessed at www.sciencedaily.com/releases/2018/04/180430075616.htm on June 12, 2023.

Milbrand, L. (2023). *The 14 coolest things invented by kids.* Accessed at www.rd.com/list/things-kids-invented on June 16, 2023.

Miles, M. (2022, March 14). *Why is authenticity at work so hard? 5 ways to be more authentic* [Blog post]. Accessed at www.betterup.com/blog/authenticity-at-work on July 10, 2023.

Millacci, T. S. (2023). *What is gratitude and why is it so important?* Accessed at https://positivepsychology.com/gratitude-appreciation on July 6, 2023.

Milner, H. R. (2011). *Five easy ways to connect with students.* Accessed at www.hepg.org/hel-home/issues/27_1/helarticle/five-easy-ways-to-connect-with-students_492 on March 5, 2023.

Mind Tools Content Team. (n.d.). *Empathy at work: Developing skills to understand other people.* Accessed at www.mindtools.com/agz0gft/empathy-at-work on April 2, 2023.

Mitra, D. L. (2014). *Student voice in school reform: Building youth-adult partnerships that strengthen schools and empower youth.* New York: SUNY Press.

Moiseeva, N., Gantseva, E., & Lyamina, L. (2020). The phenomenon of psychological boundaries. In I. Murzina (Ed.), Humanistic Practice in Education in a Postmodern Age, vol 93. *European Proceedings of Social and Behavioural Sciences* (pp. 715–725). Accessed at https://doi.org/10.15405/epsbs.2020.11.73 on July 2, 2023.

Monsen, J. J., Ewing, D. L., & Kwoka, M. (2014). Teachers' attitudes towards inclusion, perceived adequacy of support and classroom learning environment. *Learning Environments Research, 17*(1), 113–126. Accessed at https://doi.org/10.1007/s10984-013-9144-8 on July 3, 2023.

Morin, A. (n.d.a). *4 tips for helping middle-schoolers learn to speak for themselves.* Accessed at www.understood.org/en/articles/4-tips-for-helping-your-middle-schooler-learn-to-self-advocate on June 16, 2023.

Morin, A. (n.d.b). *6 tips for helping your high-schooler learn to self-advocate.* Accessed at www.understood.org/articles/6-tips-for-helping-your-high-schooler-learn-to-self-advocate on June 16, 2023.

Movement Advancement Project. (2022, April 8). *LGBTQ equality maps update.* Accessed at www.lgbtmap.org/equality-maps on March 5, 2023.

Mulvahill, E. (2016). *8 fun ways to help your students collaborate in the classroom.* Accessed at www.weareteachers.com/8-fun-ways-to-help-your-students-collaborate-in-the-classroom on March 5, 2023.

Muhammad, A. (2015). *Overcoming the achievement gap trap: Liberating mindsets to effect change.* Bloomington, IN: Solution Tree Press.

Muhammad, A., & Cruz, L. (2019). *Time for change: 4 essential skills for transformational school and district leaders.* Bloomington, IN: Solution Tree Press.

Muhammad, G. (2020). *Cultivating genius: An equity framework for culturally and historically responsive literacy.* New York: Scholastic.

Murdoch, Y., Hyejung, L., & Kang, A. (2018). Learning students' given names benefits EMI classes. *English in Education, 52*(3), 225–247. Accessed at https://doi.org/10.1080/04250494.2018.1509673 on July 3, 2023.

Murthy, V. (2023). *Our epidemic of loneliness and isolation: The U.S. Surgeon General's advisory on the healing effects of social connection and community.* Accessed at www.hhs.gov/sites/default/files/surgeon-general-social-connection-advisory.pdf on August 31, 2023.

National Center for Education Statistics. (2022). *Scores decline in NAEP reading at grades 4 and 8 compared to 2019.* Accessed at www.nationsreportcard.gov/highlights/reading/2022 on May 18, 2023.

National Center for Learning Disabilities. (2020). *Significant disproportionality in special education.* Accessed at www.ncld.org/sigdispro on May 15, 2023.

National Center for Transgender Equality. (2021). *Understanding non-binary people: How to be respectful and supportive.* Accessed at https://transequality.org/issues/resources/understanding-nonbinary-people-how-to-be-respectful-and-supportive on April 2, 2023.

National Center of Safe Supportive Learning Environments. (n.d.). *Emotional safety.* Accessed at https://safesupportivelearning.ed.gov/topic-research/safety/emotional-safety on August 31, 2023.

National Council on Teacher Quality. (n.d.). Teacher prep review: Strengthening elementary reading instruction. Accessed at www.nctq.org/review/home on July 3, 2023.

National Education Association. (2022). *4 ways to increase educator voice, respect, and professional autonomy.* Accessed at www.nea.org/resource-library/4-ways-increase-educator-voice-respect-and-professional-autonomy on July 2, 2023.

National Institute of Mental Health. (2022). *Study furthers understanding of disparities in school discipline.* Accessed at www.nimh.nih.gov/news/science-news/2022/study-furthers-understanding-of-disparities-in-school-discipline on July 2, 2023.

National Math and Science Initiative. (2021, September 2). *The importance of post-COVID teacher professional development* [Blog post]. Accessed at www.nms.org/Resources/Newsroom/Blog/2020-(1)/September/The-Importance-of-Post-COVID-Teacher-Professional.aspx on June 29, 2023.

National Urban Alliance. (n.d.). *What we advocate.* Accessed at www.nuatc.org/our-work/what-we-advocate on April 1, 2023.

New South Wales Government—Education. (n.d.). *Student wellbeing.* Accessed at https://education.nsw.gov.au/student-wellbeing/student-voices/student-voice-and-leadership on September 1, 2023.

Nishioka, V. (2019). *Positive and caring relationships with teachers are critical to student success.* Accessed at https://educationnorthwest.org/insights/positive-and-caring-relationships-teachers-are-critical-student-success on May 3, 2023.

Novak, K. (2022). *UDL now!* [3rd ed.]. Wakefield, MA: CAST.

O'Brien, M., Leiman, T., & Duffy, J. (2014). The power of naming: The multifaceted value of learning students' names. *QUT Law Review, 14*(1), 114–128. Accessed at https://doi.org/10.5204/qutlr.v14i1.544 on July 3, 2023.

O'Brien-Richardson, P. (2019). *4 self-care strategies to support students: Why well-being matters in the classroom.* Accessed at https://hbsp.harvard.edu/inspiring-minds/4-self-care-strategies-to-support-students on March 5, 2023.

O'Rourke, S. (2022). *10 simple student voice strategies.* Accessed at www.ringcentral.com/us/en/blog/10-simple-student-voice-strategies on May 31, 2023.

Orr, A., Baum, J., Brown, J., Gill, E., Kahn, E., & Salem, A. (2015). *Schools in transition: A guide for supporting transgender students in K–12 schools.* Accessed at www.aclu.org/wp-content/uploads/legal-documents/schools.in_.transition.2015.pdf on August 28, 2023.

Owens, J. (2023). *Educator bias and organizational climates, together, produce racially disparate school discipline.* Accessed at www.brookings.edu/blog/brown-center-chalkboard/2023/04/25/educator-biases-and-organizational-climates-together-produce-racially-disparate-school-discipline on May 14, 2023.

Parker, T. (n.d.). *6 steps to mindfully deal with difficult emotions* [Blog post]. Accessed at www.gottman.com/blog/6stepstomindfullydealwithdifficultemotions on June 29, 2023.

Parliamentarians for Global Action. (n.d.). *How to respond to myths about LGBTI people.* Accessed at www.pgaction.org/inclusion/myths-and-reality.html on May 1, 2023.

PDK International. (2022). *The 54th annual PDK poll: Local public school ratings rise, even as the teaching profession loses ground.* Accessed at https://pdkpoll.org/2022-pdk-poll-results on May 1, 2023.

Pearlman, L. A., & Mac Ian, P. S. (1995). Vicarious traumatization: An empirical study of the effects of trauma work on trauma therapists. *Professional Psychology: Research and Practice, 26*(6), 558–565. Accessed at https://doi.org/10.1037/0735-7028.26.6.558 on July 3, 2023.

Pearlman, L. A., & Saakvitne, K. W. (1995). Treating therapists with vicarious traumatization and secondary traumatic stress disorders. In C. R. Figley (Ed.), *Compassion fatigue: Coping with secondary traumatic stress disorder in those who treat the traumatized* (pp. 150–177). Oxfordshire, England: Brunner/Mazel.

Pemberton, C. (2015). *Resilience: A practical guide for coaches.* Maidenhead, Berkshire, UK: Open University Press.

Pew Research Center. (2016). *The state of American jobs.* Accessed at www.pewsocialtrends.org/2016/10/06/the-state-of-american-jobs on June 22, 2023.

Pew Research Center. (2019). *The global divide on homosexuality persists.* Accessed at www.pewresearch.org/global/2020/06/25/global-divide-on-homosexuality-persists on April 10, 2023.

Phi Delta Kappan. (2018, September). *Teaching: Respect but dwindling appeal.* Accessed at https://pdkpoll.org/wp-content/uploads/2020/05/pdkpoll50_2018.pdf on June 29, 2023.

Phi Delta Kappan. (2020). *Public school priorities in a political year.* Accessed at https://pdkpoll.org/wp-content/uploads/2020/08/Poll52-2020_PollSupplement.pdf on June 29, 2023.

Piper, W. (1930). *The little engine that could.* New York: Grosset & Dunlap.

Pitler, H. (2017, August 7). *6 questions to ask your students on day one* [Blog post]. Accessed at www.ascd.org/blogs/six-questions-to-ask-your-students-on-day-one on July 3, 2023.

Playworks. (2021). *The science of joy and play.* Accessed at www.playworks.org/new-england/2021/12/07/the-science-of-joy-and-play on July 2, 2023.

Polite, L. L. (2020). *Teachers' perceptions of the role that school administrators play in their job satisfaction* [Dissertation, Walden University]. Accessed at https://scholarworks.waldenu.edu/cgi/viewcontent.cgi?article=11069&context=dissertations on May 4, 2023.

Poorvu Center for Teaching and Learning. (n.d.a). *Inclusive teaching strategies.* Accessed at https://poorvucenter.yale.edu/InclusiveTeachingStrategies on March 5, 2023.

Poorvu Center for Teaching and Learning. (n.d.b). *Learning student names and pronouns.* Accessed at https://poorvucenter.yale.edu/LearningStudentNames#:~:text=Use%20of%20student%20names%20has,with%20a%20course%20(Cooper%20et. on May 3, 2023.

Portman, J., Trisa Bui, T., & Ogaz, J. (n.d.). *Microaggressions in the classroom*. Accessed at https://adayinourshoes.com/wp-content/uploads/Micro-Aggressions-In-Classroom.pdf on March 5, 2023.

Potter, G. (2013, June 25). *The history of policing in the United States, part 1* [Blog post]. Accessed at https://ekuonline.eku.edu/blog/police-studies/the-history-of-policing-in-the-united-states-part-1 on April 2, 2023.

Pough, N. O. (2021). *A flaw in the foundation*. Accessed at www.learningforjustice.org/magazine/spring-2021/a-flaw-in-the-foundation on April 2, 2023.

Prentiss, S. (2021). *Speech anxiety in the communication classroom during the COVID-19 pandemic: Supporting student success*. Accessed at www.frontiersin.org/articles/10.3389/fcomm.2021.642109/full on May 4, 2023.

Price, C. (2021). *The power of fun: How to feel alive again*. New York: The Dial Press.

Price-Mitchell, M. (2021). *Curiosity is a core predictor of academic performance*. Accessed at www.rootsofaction.com/curiosity-academic-performance on August 31, 2023.

Price-Mitchell, M. (2023). *Skeptic or cynic? How to model positive skepticism to children*. Accessed at www.rootsofaction.com/skeptic on September 1, 2023.

Project Implicit. (n.d.). *Welcome to Project Implicit!* Accessed at www.projectimplicit.net on April 28, 2023.

Project Zero. (2016). *Toward a pedagogy of play*. Accessed at https://pz.harvard.edu/resources/toward-a-pedagogy-of-play on May 4, 2023.

Prothero, A. (2020, October 13). *The essential traits of a positive school climate*. Accessed at www.edweek.org/leadership/the-essential-traits-of-a-positive-school-climate/2020/10 on July 10, 2023.

Quaglia, R., Fox, K., Lande, L., & Young, D. (2020). *The power of voice in schools: Listening, learning, and leading together*. Alexandria, VA: ASCD.

Quaglia Institute for School Voice and Aspirations. (n.d.). *Why student voice matters*. Accessed at https://surveys.quagliainstitute.org on July 3, 2023.

Quaglia Institute for School Voice and Aspirations. (2016). *School voice report 2016*. Accessed at https://quagliainstitute.org/dmsView/School_Voice_Report_2016 on April 25, 2023.

Quaglia Institute for School and Voice Aspirations. (2020). *Voice definition: A school voice brief*. Accessed at https://quagliainstitute.org/dmsView/Voice_Definition_4_29_20 on April 7, 2023.

Rademacher, T. (2015, March 22). *When we talk about students . . .* [Blog post]. Accessed at https://misterrad.tumblr.com/post/114334406332/when-we-talk-about-students on June 2, 2023.

ReachOut Australia (2023). *What is resilience?* Accessed at https://schools.au.reachout.com/articles/what-is-resilience on September 1, 2023.

Reeves, D. B. (2006). *Leading to change/How do you change school culture?* Accessed at www.ascd.org/el/articles/how-do-you-change-school-culture on July 3, 2023.

Reilly, C. (2022). *The importance of vacation in the workplace.* Accessed at www.forbes.com/sites/colleenreilly/2022/07/12/the-importance-of-vacation-in-the-workplace/?sh=4aec826d71ec on June 5, 2023.

Renzulli, J. S. (1999). What is this thing called giftedness, and how do we develop it? A twenty-five year perspective. *Journal for the Education of the Gifted, 23*(1), 3–54. Accessed at https://doi.org/10.1177/016235329902300102 on July 3, 2023.

Reyes, V. (n.d.). *The beginning of biases.* Accessed at www.aauw.org/issues/education on March 5, 2023.

Rich, E. (2020, September 23). *Dismantling systemic racism in schools: 8 big ideas.* Accessed at www.edweek.org/leadership/dismantling-systemic-racism-in-schools-8-big-ideas/2020/09 on March 5, 2023.

Rogers, F. (2006). *Wisdom from the world according to Mister Rogers: Important things to remember.* Rye Brook, NY: Peter Pauper Press.

Rothstein, R. (2017). *The color of law: A forgotten history of how our government segregated America.* New York: Liveright Publishing Corporation.

Ryan, R. M., & Deci, E. L. (2018). *Self-determination theory: Basic psychological needs in motivation, development, and wellness.* New York: Guilford Press.

Sabol, T. J., Kessler, C. L., Rogers, L. O., Petitclerc, A., Silver, J., Briggs-Gowan, M., et al. (2021). A window into racial and socioeconomic status disparities in preschool disciplinary action using developmental methodology. *Annals of the New York Academy of Sciences, 1508*(1), 123–136. Accessed at https://doi.org/10.1111/nyas.14687 on July 3, 2023.

Sackstein, S. (2017). *Teachers, forgive thyself or burn out quickly.* Accessed at www.edweek.org/teaching-learning/opinion-teachers-forgive-thyself-or-burn-out-quickly/2017/05 on July 10, 2023.

Safir, S. (2017). *The listening leader: Creating the conditions for equitable school transformation.* San Francisco: Jossey-Bass.

Safir, S. (2019). *Becoming a warm demander.* Accessed at www.ascd.org/el/articles/becoming-a-warm-demander on March 5, 2023.

Safir, S. (2023). *Cultivating a pedagogy of student voice.* Accessed at www.ascd.org/el/articles/cultivating-a-pedagogy-of-student-voice on September 1, 2023.

Safir, S., & Dugan, J. (2021). *Street data: A next-generation model for equity, pedagogy, and school transformation.* Thousand Oaks, California: Corwin Press.

Sanchez, C. (2013, June 18). *Study: Teacher prep programs get failing marks.* Accessed at www.npr.org/2013/06/18/192765776/study-teacher-prep-programs-get-failing-marks on March 5, 2023.

Sands, B. (2017, November). *How open should you be with your students about your personal life?* [Blog post]. Accessed at https://study.com/blog/how-open-should-you-be-with-your-students-about-your-personal-life.html on July 10, 2023.

Sasmita, A. O., Kuruvilla, J., & Ling, A. P. K. (2018). Harnessing neuroplasticity: modern approaches and clinical future. *International Journal of Neuroscience, 128*(11), 1061–1077. Accessed at https://doi.org/10.1080/00207454.2018.1466781 on July 3, 2023.

Schepers, O. C., & Young, K. S. (2021). Mitigating secondary traumatic stress in preservice educators: A pilot study on the role of trauma-informed practice seminars. *Psychology in the Schools, 59*(2), 316–333. Accessed at https://doi.org/10.1002/pits.22610 on July 3, 2023.

Schreiner, K., & Falardeau, C. (2020). *Parenting to support self-advocacy in your child.* Accessed at www.foothillsacademy.org/community/articles/support-self-advocacy on June 16, 2023.

Scott, K. (2019). *Radical candor: How to get what you want by saying what you mean* [Fully revised and updated ed.]. New York: Pan Books.

Seltzer, L. F. (2008, September 10). *The path to unconditional self-acceptance* [Blog post]. Accessed at www.psychologytoday.com/us/blog/evolution-the-self/200809/the-path-unconditional-self-acceptance on March 5, 2023.

Shafer, L. (2017). *Giving students a voice: Five ways to welcome student input and bolster your school's success.* Accessed at www.gse.harvard.edu/news/uk/16/08/giving-students-voice on May 19, 2023.

Shapiro, A. (2020). *"Interrupting the systems": Robin DiAngelo on "White fragility" and anti-racism.* Accessed at www.npr.org/2020/06/17/879136931/interrupt-the-systems-robin-diangelo-on-white-fragility-and-anti-racism on March 5, 2023.

Sheldon, K., Jose, P., Kashdan, T., & Aaron, J. (2015). Personality, effective goal-striving, and enhanced well-being. *Personality and Social Psychology Bulleting, 41*(4). Accessed at www.researchgate.net/publication/272840340_Personality_Effective_Goal-Striving_and_Enhanced_Well-Being on June 12, 2023.

Shrikant, M. (2021). *The science of hope: More than wishful thinking*. Accessed at https://research.asu.edu/science-hope-more-wishful-thinking on July 3, 2023.

Singer, B., & Mogensen, J. (2021). *Getting students to self-advocacy—step by step*. Accessed at https://leader.pubs.asha.org/do/10.1044/leader.FTR1.26082021.32/full on June 5, 2023.

Small, I. (2019). *The unexpected leader: Exploring the real nature of values, authenticity, and moral purpose in education*. Carmarthen, UK: Independent Thinking Press.

Small, I. (2022, January 31). *Inclusive classrooms: Disrupting power dynamics* [Blog post]. Accessed at https://educationblog.oup.com/secondary/inclusive-classrooms-disrupting-power-dynamics on May 5, 2023.

Smith, A. J. (2021, November 8). *Gratitude: A mental health game-changer* [Blog post]. Accessed at https://adaa.org/learn-from-us/from-the-experts/blog-posts/consumer/gratitude-mental-health-game-changer on July 2, 2023.

Smith, B., Dalen, J., Wiggins, K., Tooley, E., Christopher, P., & Bernard, J. (2008). The brief resilience scale: Assessing the ability to bounce back. *International Journal of Behavioral Medicine, 15*(3), 194–200. Accessed at https://doi.org/10.1080/10705500802222972 on July 3, 2023.

Snelling, J. (2018, December 24). *8 ways to empower student voice in your classroom*. Accessed at www.iste.org/explore/In-the-classroom/8-ways-to-empower-student-voice-in-your-classroom on March 5, 2023.

Soffel, J. (2016). *Ten 21st-century skills every student needs*. Accessed at www.weforum.org/agenda/2016/03/21st-century-skills-future-jobs-students on June 22, 2023.

Sood, A. (2022). *9 essential skills that make you resilient*. Accessed at www.everydayhealth.com/wellness/resilience/essential-skills-that-make-you-resilient on May 29, 2023.

Sotomayor, S. (2019). *Just ask! Be different, be brave, be you*. New York: Philomel Books.

South Carolina Code of Laws. Section 59-35-5: Comprehensive Health Education Act. (1988).

Sparks, S. (2023). *Here's how to give feedback that students will actually use*. Accessed at www.edweek.org/teaching-learning/heres-how-to-give-feedback-that-students-will-actually-use/2023/04 on July 10, 2023.

St. John, K., & Briel, L. (2017). *Student voice: A growing movement within education that benefits students and teachers.* Accessed at https://centerontransition.org/publications/download.cfm?id=61 on April 25, 2023.

Stanley, T. (2021). *Go big or go home: Encouraging risk-taking in the classroom.* Accessed at https://creativityandeducation.com/go-big-or-go-home-encouraging-risk-taking-in-the-classroom on May 31, 2023.

Stenger, M. (2014, December 2017). *Why curiosity enhances learning* [Blog post]. Accessed at www.edutopia.org/blog/why-curiosity-enhances-learning-marianne-stenger on June 23, 2023.

Stixrud, W., & Johnson, N. (2018). *The self-driven child: The science and sense of giving your kids more control over their lives.* New York: Viking Penguin.

Stroman, R. (2019). *The value of humility: The doorway to opportunity.* Accessed at www.linkedin.com/pulse/value-humility-doorway-opportunity-randy-stroman on August 2, 2023.

Stuart, D. (2015, April 7). *How humility makes us better, saner teachers.* Accessed at https://davestuartjr.com/sanity-humility on July 10, 2023.

Sudderth, A. (n.d.). *How active listening in the classroom develops empathy.* Accessed at https://xqsuperschool.org/uncategorized/why-active-listening-in-the-classroom-develops-empathy-and-why-we-need-this on July 10, 2023.

Sue, D. W., & Spanierman, L. (2020). *Microaggressions in everyday life* (2nd ed.). Hoboken, NJ: Wiley.

Sutton, J. (2019). *What is resilience, and why is it important to bounce back?* Accessed at https://positivepsychology.com/what-is-resilience on September 1, 2023.

Talbot, C. (2021). *Incorporating student voice in the classroom.* Accessed at www.ecis.org/student-voice-in-the-classroom on September 1, 2023.

TED Talks. (2014, November 10). *The power of ummmm . . . Kath Murdoch* [Video file]. Accessed at https://youtu.be/LFt15Ig64Yg on July 2, 2023.

Terada, Y., & Merrill, S. (2020). The research on life-changing teaching. *Edutopia.* Accessed at www.edutopia.org/article/research-life-changing-teaching on June 29, 2023.

Torres, C. (2019). On shame and "daring classrooms": We need to fix systems, not kids. *EdWeek.* Accessed at www.edweek.org/education/opinion-on-shame-and-daring-classrooms-we-need-to-fix-systems-not-kids/2019/08#:~:text=So%20many%20of%20our%20students,dangerous%20ground%20to%20tread%20on. On September 1, 2023.

Toshalis, E., & Nakkula, M. (2012). *Motivation, engagement, and student voice.* Accessed at www.howyouthlearn.org/pdf/Motivation%20Engagement%20Student%20Voice_0.pdf on April 25, 2023.

Trevino, R. (2019). *Art of scaffolding conversations.* Accessed at https://closler.org/connecting-with-patients/the-art-of-scaffolding-conversations on September 1, 2023.

Truss, J. (2022). *My students (of color) aren't ready for PBL: 6 examples of implicit bias.* Accessed at https://trussleadership.com/pbl_hood on June 19, 2023.

Trust Edge Leadership Institute. (2022). *2022 Trust Outlook Global Research Study.* Accessed at https://trustedge.com/wp-content/uploads/2022/04/2022-Trust-Outlook.pdf on July 10, 2023.

Turner, C., Khrais, R., Lloyd, T., Olgin, A., Isensee, L., et al. (2016). *Why America's schools have a money problem.* Accessed at www.npr.org/2016/04/18/474256366/why-americas-schools-have-a-money-problem on March 5, 2023.

Turner, T. P. (2017). *Belonging: Remembering ourselves home.* Salt Spring Island, BC: Her Own Room Press.

The Umbrella Project. (n.d.). *The Umbrella Project: Authenticity.* Accessed at https://umbrellaproject.co/wp-content/uploads/2019/12/Handout_Authenticity.pdf on October 9, 2023.

UN Women. (2022, June 22). *UN women reveals concerning regression in attitudes towards gender roles during pandemic in new study* [Press release]. Accessed at www.unwomen.org/en/news-stories/press-release/2022/06/un-women-reveals-concerning-regression-in-attitudes-towards-gender-roles-during-pandemic-in-new-study on April 2, 2023.

United Nations Human Rights Office of the High Commissioner. (1989). *Convention on the rights of the child.* Accessed at www.ohchr.org/en/instruments-mechanisms/instruments/convention-rights-child#:~:text=Article%2012,-1.&text=States%20Parties%20shall%20assure%20to,and%20maturity%20of%20the%20child on June 2, 2023.

United Nations Human Rights Office of the High Commissioner. (2020). *Gender stereotyping: OHCHR and women's human rights and gender equality.* Accessed at www.ohchr.org/en/women/gender-stereotyping on May 15, 2023.

University of California Berkley. (n.d.). *Youth Participatory Action Research (YPAR).* Accessed at https://i4y.berkeley.edu/initiatives-projects-partnerships/youth-participatory-action-research-ypar on August 5, 2023.

University of North Carolina. (n.d.). *Microaggressions.* Accessed at https://portal.ed.unc.edu/resources/microaggressions on June 28, 2023.

Utley, J., & Klebahn, P. (2023). *5 ways to boost creativity on your team.* Accessed at https://hbr.org/2023/03/5-ways-to-boost-creativity-on-your-team?registration=success on June 22, 2023.

Valenzuela, J. (2021). *How a simple visual tool can help teachers connect with students.* Accessed at www.edutopia.org/article/how-simple-visual-tool-can-help-teachers-connect-students on June 2, 2023.

Venet, A. S. (2021). *What I wish my teacher knew about "what I wish my teacher knew."* Accessed at https://unconditionallearning.org/tag/trauma-informed-teaching on March 5, 2023.

Villines, Z. (2022a). *People pleaser: What it means and how to stop.* Accessed at www.medicalnewstoday.com/articles/people-pleaser on June 2, 2023.

Villines, Z. (2022b). *What to know about mantras for anxiety.* Accessed at www.medicalnewstoday.com/articles/mantras-for-anxiety on July 10, 2023.

von Stumm, S., Hell, B., & Chamorro-Premuzic, T. (2011). The hungry mind: Intellectual curiosity is the third pillar of academic performance. *Perspectives on Psychological Science, 6*(6), 574–588. Accessed at https://doi.org/10.1177/1745691611421204 on July 3, 2023.

Wachtel, T. (2016). Defining restorative. *International Institute for Restorative Practices.* Accessed at www.iirp.edu/images/pdf/Defining-Restorative_Nov-2016.pdf on June 30, 3023.

Wallace, D. F. (2005). *This is water.* Accessed at www.wsj.com/articles/SB122178211966454607 on August 31, 2023.

Walsh, J. (2019). *How to get your students to ask more questions.* Accessed at www.middleweb.com/40383/how-to-get-your-students-to-ask-more-questions on August 31, 2023.

Walsh, D. (2022). *How to boost curiosity in your company—and why.* Accessed at https://mitsloan.mit.edu/ideas-made-to-matter/how-to-boost-curiosity-your-company-and-why on June 22, 2023.

Walt Disney Pictures, Jerry Bruckheimer Films, & Yakin, B. (2000). *Remember the Titans* [Motion picture]. United States: Buena Vista Pictures.

Wamsley, L. (2021). A guide to gender identity terms. *National Public Radio.* Accessed at www.npr.org/2021/06/02/996319297/gender-identity-pronouns-expression-guide-lgbtq#cisgender on April 8, 2023.

Wamsley, L. (2022, March 10). *Even many decades later, redlined areas see higher level of air pollution.* Accessed at www.npr.org/2022/03/10/1085882933/redlining-pollution-racism on March 5, 2023.

Warren, C. (2020). Colleges must take a new approach to systemic racism. *Inside Higher Ed.* Accessed at www.insidehighered.com/views/2020/06/09/defeat-systemic-racism-institutions-must-fully-integrate-truly-diverse-subject on April 11, 2023.

Waters, S. (2021, June 9). *The power of positive self-talk (and how you can use it)* [Blog post]. Accessed at www.betterup.com/blog/self-talk on July 10, 2023.

Wegmann, K. M., & Smith, B. (2019). Examining racial/ethnic disparities in school discipline in the context of student-reported behavior infractions. *Children and Youth Services Review, 103*, 18–27. Accessed at https://doi.org/10.1016/j.childyouth.2019.05.027 on July 3, 2023.

Well, S. (1998). *Choosing the future: The power of strategic thinking.* Boston: Butterworth-Heinemann.

Wepfer, A. G., Allen, T. D., Brauchli, R., Jenny, G. J., & Bauer, G. F. (2018). Work-life boundaries and well-being: Does work-to-life integration impair well-being through lack of recovery? *Journal of Business and Psychology, 33*, 727–740. Accessed at https://doi.org/10.1007/s10869-017-9520-y on July 3, 2023.

White, K. (2022). *Student self-assessment: Data notebooks, portfolios, and other tools to advance learning.* Bloomington, IN: Solution Tree Press.

White, S. (2012). *Time to think: Using restorative questions.* Accessed at www.iirp.edu/news/time-to-think-using-restorative-questions on March 5, 2023.

Wicaksono, S. R. (2020). Joyful learning in elementary school. *International Journal of Theory and Application in Elementary and Secondary School Education*, *2*(2), 80–90. Accessed at https://doi.org/10.31098/ijtaese.v2i2.232 on July 3, 2023.

Widlund, A., Tuominen, H., Tapola, A., & Korhonen, J. (2019). *Gendered pathways from academic performance, motivational beliefs, and school burnout to adolescents' educational and occupational aspirations.* Accessed at www.sciencedirect.com/science/article/pii/S0959475219304682 on July 2, 2023.

Williams, K. (2022a). *Ruthless equity: Disrupt the status quo and ensure learning for all students.* Sharpsburg, GA: Wish in One Hand Press.

Williams, R. (2022b). Homophobic misinformation is making it harder to contain the spread of monkeypox. *MIT Technology Review.* Accessed at www.technologyreview.com/2022/06/17/1054408/homophobic-misinformation-spread-monkeypox-social-media on May 1, 2023.

Willis, J. (2020). *Teaching assertiveness in the early elementary grades.* Accessed at www.edutopia.org/article/teaching-assertiveness-early-elementary-grades on June 2, 2023.

Willis, J., & Willis, M. (2020). *Research-based strategies to ignite student learning: Insights from neuroscience and the classroom* (revised and expanded ed.). Alexandria, VA: ASCD.

Wilson, S. (2018). *Making deposits into your child's emotional bank account.* Accessed at www.edweek.org/teaching-learning/heres-how-to-give-feedback-that-students-will-actually-use/2023/04 on July 10, 2023.

Wiseman, L. (2017). *Multipliers, revised and updated: How the best leaders make everyone smarter.* New York: Harper Business.

Wolfe, P. (n.d.). *Interview with Dr. Patricia Wolfe: Author of Brain Matters* [Video]. Accessed at https://mybrainware.com/blog/interview-with-patricia-wolfe-author-brain-matters on November 4, 2023.

Wood, A. (2021, July 1). *Go beyond diversity: Inclusive leadership is vital for DEIB success* [Blog post]. Accessed at www.betterup.com/blog/inclusive-leadership-deib-efforts-succeed on July 10, 2023.

Woodyatt, L., Worthington, E. L., Wenzel, M., & Griffin, B. J. (2017). Orientation to the psychology of self-forgiveness. In L. Woodyatt, E. L. Worthington, M. Wenzel, & B. J. Griffin (Eds.). *Handbook of the psychology of self-forgiveness* (pp. 3–16). New York: Springer.

Workman, J., & Heyder, A. (2020). Gender achievement gaps: The role of social costs to trying hard in high school. *Social Psychology of Education, 23*, 1407–1427. Accessed at https://doi.org/10.1007/s11218-020-09588-6 on July 3, 2023.

Yang, D., Cai, Z., Wang, C., Zhang, C., Chen, P., & Huang, R. (2023). *Not all engaged students are alike: Patterns of engagement and burnout among elementary students using a person-centered approach.* Accessed at https://bmcpsychology.biomedcentral.com/articles/10.1186/s40359-023-01071-z on July 2, 2023.

York, J. (2021). *Why it's so hard for U.S. workers to ask for time off.* Accessed at www.bbc.com/worklife/article/20211209-why-its-so-hard-for-some-workers-to-ask-for-time-off on September 1, 2023.

Youth Participatory Action Research. (n.d.). *Youth Participatory Action Research hub.* Accessed at https://yparhub.berkeley.edu on August 5, 2023.

Zakrzewski, V. (2016). *How humility will make you the greatest person ever.* Accessed at https://greatergood.berkeley.edu/article/item/humility_will_make_you_greatest_person_ever on August 30, 2023.

Zeman, E. (2019, December 15). *How to check the facts* [Blog post]. Accessed at www.mindsoother.com/blog/how-to-check-the-facts on July 10, 2023.

Zolkoski, S. M. (2019). *The importance of teacher-student relationships for students with emotional and behavioral disorders.* Accessed at www.tandfonline.com/doi/abs/10.1080/1045988X.2019.1579165?journalCode=vpsf20 on May 3, 2023.

Index

A

B

C

L

M

N

O

P

S

The Language of Possibility

Michael Roberts

Language can help lift or limit students. Based on brain research and authentic classroom experience, this book will help you get back to the optimism of teaching by connecting with the possibilities and gifts each student has to offer.

BKG048

Raising Equity Through SEL

Jorge Valenzuela

Activate social-emotional learning effectively in your classroom with this trusted source for sound pedagogy that addresses the academic and SEL needs of diverse learners. Each strategy, tool, and template shared is meant to facilitate your practice by making SEL easier to implement.

BKG041

Teacher Leaders, Classroom Champions

Jeanetta Jones Miller

Gain a clear path to activate school improvement from within your classroom. This book shares a vision of teacher leadership not as teachers who lead other teachers but as those who take responsibility in supporting other teachers, students, and families in a variety of ways.

BKG110

The Landscape Model of Learning

Jennifer D. Klein and Kapono Ciotti

This essential guide offers the landscape model and its three elements: understanding what students bring to the ecosystem, defining the horizon, and charting the pathway. Access practical strategies for drawing on students' experiences and strengths to create a more meaningful and inclusive educational ecosystem.

BKG043